THE SPIRITUAL LEADER

a GUIDEBOOK *for* PASTORS
and CHRISTIAN LEADERS

PAUL W. CHAPPELL

First published in 2008 by Striving Together Publications, a ministry of Lancaster Baptist Church, Lancaster, CA 93535. Striving Together Publications is committed to providing tried, trusted, and proven books that will further equip local churches to carry out the Great Commission. Your comments and suggestions are valued.

Striving Together Publications
4020 E. Lancaster Blvd.
Lancaster, CA 93535
800.201.7748

Cover design by Andrew Jones
Layout by Craig Parker
Compiled and edited by Cary Schmidt
Special thanks to our proofreaders.
Thank you for investing into this project.

The contents of this book are the result of twenty-five years of spiritual growth in life and ministry. The author and publication team have given every effort to give proper credit to quotes and thoughts that are not original with the author. It is not our intent to claim originality with any quote or thought that could not readily be tied to an original source.

ISBN 978-1-59894-052-7

Printed in the United States of America

DEDICATION

To My Dear Wife and Children

Terrie, your example to me and our church family is amazing.
Thank you for your love, counsel, and friendship.

Danielle, your zeal for the Lord is contagious.
May God bless you and Peter as you serve Him.

Larry, your love for God and His people is a blessing.
May you and Ashley be greatly used for His glory.

Kristine, your spirit to serve is awesome!
May God bless you, your marriage and ministry.

Matthew, your spirit and influence is a gift from God.
May you use these gifts for His honor and glory.

ACKNOWLEDGEMENTS

I wish to express my sincere thanks to Cary Schmidt for his heartfelt passion to encourage me and labor with me in the production of this book. I also wish to thank our staff and church family at Lancaster Baptist Church for encouraging me and allowing me, as their pastor, to provide spiritual leadership in their lives and for joining me in the development of a new generation of spiritual leaders. A special thanks also to those pastor friends who provided insight during the final editing of this work.

TABLE OF CONTENTS

PART FOUR—THE SPIRITUAL LEADER'S TEAM

PART FIVE—THE SPIRITUAL LEADER'S TRIALS

PART SIX—THE SPIRITUAL LEADER'S TRIUMPHS

FOREWORD

Seldom is a book written that should not only be carefully read, but attentively reread until the scripted truths and principles found in its pages have made their entrance into the heart and life of the reader. *The Spiritual Leader* is one of those books!

Pastor Paul Chappell is a man who has been used of God in a treasured and magnificent way. His life has demonstrated a compassion for people, a fervency for serving others, and a dedication for serving God that is truly remarkable! His leadership in the work of God has not been birthed in the digests of what others have written, but his leadership is a result of the closeness of his walk with the Lord and the immersion of his mind and heart in God's Word.

The shelves of bookstores are crowded with writings on the subject of leadership, as well as the attendant skill sets that authors think are essential if you desire to lead. But *The Spiritual Leader* goes to the very core of what "leadership" in God's plan and purposed will is truly all about.

This wonderful book is written from the heart, the mind and the life of a man whom God has greatly used. Its insights will help every leader avoid some of the most serious mistakes that a leader can make, as well as give Scriptural guidance that will stand the test of review for all eternity.

Read and reread. For the test of leadership rests not on how our leadership will be judged by others as to its effectiveness during our length of days on this earth, but rather how the Lord God will eternally evaluate our spiritual leadership when we stand before Him.

Leadership is a sacred trust. What a wonderful and eternally helpful book!

Sincerely,
David C. Gibbs, Jr.

PREFACE

I can still remember the first time someone called me "Pastor." At that moment I felt the joy and the burden of spiritual leadership in a very unique way. Although the Lord had called me to ministry many years before, my spiritual leadership journey was now underway with earnest.

The word *pastor* has always been an endearing term to me and to those with whom I have fellowshipped throughout my life. I grew up in Baptist churches where the preacher or spiritual leader of the church was called "pastor," and I prayed when God called me to preach in 1975, that perhaps someday God would allow me the privilege of serving as a pastor.

Whether you are a pastor or you serve in another role of spiritual leadership, yours is a high and holy calling. I have served a small congregation—we had less than twenty members in 1986. I have also served a larger congregation—for the past thirteen years Lancaster Baptist has been what church growth experts call a "mega-church."

The Lord has given me the privilege and opportunity to travel across America and to several foreign countries to encourage and train pastors.

For twenty years we have conducted an annual Spiritual Leadership Conference for pastors and personal workers here in Lancaster, California. Each Friday I teach a pastoral theology class of over 250 pastoral students at West Coast Baptist College.

Simply stated, I love pastors and spiritual leaders. The book you hold in your hands is written from my heart to yours. The truths contained in this book are biblical principles that I am learning and endeavoring to practice in my own life and ministry. As spiritual leaders, we must seek God's wisdom and anointing as never before. The complexities of ministry in this hour require us to be totally yielded servants of our Lord. It is my prayer that these pages will give you insight and instruction for the next steps of your spiritual leadership journey.

Paul Chappell
April 2008

I thank the Lord for the privilege and opportunity that He has given me to preach His Word and to provide spiritual leadership in His local church for the past twenty-five years. I love to serve the Lord and His people. I love to preach His Word. And I am thrilled to see His changing grace at work in the lives of Christians. I never tire of seeing God save a soul, establish a young believer, bless a faithful Christian, and do a mighty work in His local church. These blessings are new every time I experience them. They delight my heart, flood my soul with joy, and remind me of the high calling of God in Christ Jesus. Truly, the privilege of spiritual leadership is a wonderful joy, a sacred delight, and a holy calling!

I pray that you've picked up this book because you have experienced God's call upon your life to spread the Gospel and to serve in a church. If you pillow your head at night thinking of the needs of people, if you live every day with the knowledge that Sunday is coming, if your heart burns with a vision of what God desires to do in and through your church, if you long to see souls saved and Christians established in their faith, if you crave private time in study to meet with God and to prepare your heart to preach; then you know what it is to be called to spiritual leadership!

Over the past twenty-five years of ministry, the Lord has led me on a wonderful journey of faith and blessing. At times the road led through deep valleys of trials and at others to high mountain peaks of victory—and sometimes both at once! Yet, through it all, the Lord has been faithful, and He has never failed to prove Himself and His promises true.

The life calling of a spiritual leader is both delightful, yet trying. It is wonderful, yet difficult. It is joyfully hard and blessedly strenuous. It is happily disappointing and stressfully glorious. It is filled with the most magnificent of victories often simultaneously accompanied by the most trying of discouragements. It is a journey near to the heart of God that will often lead you to the depths of despair. It is a faith life that tenderly bears the burdens of one lamb while simultaneously celebrating the victories of another.

The spiritual battles of Christian leadership are certainly not for the faint-hearted or those uncertain of their call. For truly, it is only the surety of your call that will keep you steadfast and faithful in ministry for the rest of your life. No paycheck, perks, possessions, or physical blessings could keep a man faithfully and fully engaged in such intense spiritual battle for very long. Only the rock-solid, unquestioned call of God can sustain a man of God.

In the coming pages we will explore this high calling. In short chapters and with a practical approach and a transparent heart, I will attempt to share the most important faith lessons that God has taught me over the past twenty-five years.

First, we will examine the spiritual leader's heart—studying the qualifications, lifestyle, motives, and strength of a spiritual leader. We will study daily life, weekly schedule, friends, and matters of personal testimony and daily dependence upon God.

Part two explores the spiritual leader's ministry—examining the responsibilities of oversight, principles of church growth, and ministry administration. We will be reminded of the many daily roles of a spiritual leader.

Part three will take us to the pulpit ministry of the spiritual leader—including biblical preaching, using music and technology, and leading a biblical church service.

In part four, we will study the spiritual leader's team—beginning with family. We will learn how to love, lead, and develop those around us. In this section our study will focus on how to build, train, and develop a staff to accomplish a great work for God.

Part five will show us the spiritual leader's trials. Culture has changed, and those changes have impacted the role of Christian leaders. This section will reveal the costs of church growth, the grace to respond rightly to criticism, and the way to stay the course through troubled waters.

Part six will conclude with a brief look at the spiritual leader's triumphs. We will be reminded of the promises of God, the victories of ministry, and the joy of finishing the course!

Welcome to the most spiritually intense and most wonderfully rewarding calling in life. Welcome to a lonely life filled with close, rewarding, wonderful relationships. Welcome to "the good fight of faith." Welcome to the sheepfold. Welcome to a vocation that is very near to the heart of the Great Shepherd.

God's people need you. Our nation and our world need you. And your ruthless enemy has already determined how he will take you out of this life-calling. His sights are set. His traps are laid. But the church of Jesus Christ is depending upon you. The flock of God awaits your firm but loving guidance. God's people await your biblical care and passionate leadership. If you will answer the call and depend upon God's power, many lives and many families will be changed forever.

I encourage you to read this entire book from cover to cover, but feel free to skip to the chapters where you are currently facing the greatest need. In the first few chapters we will lay a foundation by examining the heart of a spiritual leader. Upon that foundation, we will study many biblical and practical aspects of the life and ministry of a spiritual leader. These pages are the compilation of more than twenty-five years of ministry experiences and study. Throughout these chapters I have made every effort to give appropriate credit for quotes, illustrations, and concepts that were gleaned from other authors and leaders over the years. If I have forgotten a source or if we were unable to find it before this book went to press, it was not intentional.

Join me now as we take a wonderfully challenging look at the high calling of spiritual leadership!

1

THE SPIRITUAL LEADER'S HEART

All ministry begins with the heart. God desires that all public ministry would flow from a heart that loves Him fully and walks with Him privately. Your fruit and faithfulness in the ministry will only be as effective *for* the Lord as your heart is right *with* the Lord.

> *"And ye shall seek me, and find me, when ye shall search for me with all your heart."*—JEREMIAH 29:13

CHAPTER ONE

QUALIFICATIONS OF A SPIRITUAL LEADER

Every spiritual leader lives with a heart awareness that the ministry is a holy calling—it is a life separated and distinct, designed to be an example to believers and unbelievers. Yet, Satan is actively trying to hinder the cause of Christ, and one of his primary targets is the spiritual leader. If he can ruin the testimony of a man of God, he can negatively influence an entire church family, an entire city, and often many others.

Leadership is influence. When God entrusted you with the call to lead, He entrusted you with influence for Him. Along with that influence comes some very clear and vital qualifications—life attributes that are essential in encouraging God's people and accomplishing God's work. If you desire God's blessing upon your ministry, you must begin with His blueprint—His biblical mandate. You must align your life with biblical authority.

THE CALLING OF A SPIRITUAL LEADER

"And he gave some, apostles; and some, prophets; and some, evangelists; and some, pastors and teachers;"—EPHESIANS 4:11

"This is a true saying, If a man desire the office of a bishop, he desireth a good work."—1 TIMOTHY 3:1

The calling of a pastor is a *special* calling. It is not just another career or life option. It is the pre-ordained plan of God. It is a *specific* calling—one for a man who carefully fulfills God's prerequisites. It is a *spiritual* calling—one that must be purely motivated by spiritual values and God's agenda. A spiritual leader must be driven by an inward passion for God and must desire to *serve* in the work of God. Spiritual leadership is no place for selfish ambition for an office or title. This calling is a *serious* calling; God calls it an "office." Whether or not you serve as a pastor, God's qualifications for pastors set the standard for all who earnestly seek to lead spiritually.

Dr. Richard Clearwaters often taught these five Greek titles for the office of the pastor:

> **Episcopos**—a bishop or overseer (Titus 1:7, 1 Peter 2:25, Acts 20:28)
> **Presbuteros**—an elder or one who presides over a deliberative assembly (1 Timothy 5:17)
> **Poimen**—the shepherd of a flock (1 Peter 5:2)
> **Keruk**—a preacher to a congregation (1 Timothy 2:7, 2 Peter 2:5)
> **Didaskolos**—a teacher to a church school (1 Corinthians 12:28–29, Romans 2:20)

These are the responsibilities of a spiritual leader. You are the overseer of the church, the shepherd of the flock, the preacher of the Word, and the teacher of God's truth. What a high and holy calling. What an amazing job description!

Finally, this calling is a *sacrificial* calling. God calls it a "good work." Work implies sacrifice, labor, and personal cost. The work of the spiritual leader is never done and the burdens of leadership never really leave a leader's shoulders. The pastor cannot "clock out" at the end of a long work day. This life-calling is unlike any other.

Accept your call. Understand that it is unlike any other life vocation. Never doubt or second guess it—and most of all, don't be surprised by it. Cherish it! Determine now to embrace the call just as Jesus Christ embraced the Cross—"not my will but thine be done."

THE CHARACTER OF A SPIRITUAL LEADER

"This is a true saying, If a man desire the office of a bishop, he desireth a good work. A bishop then must be blameless, the husband of one wife, vigilant, sober, of good behaviour, given to hospitality, apt to teach; Not given to wine, no striker, not greedy of filthy lucre; but patient, not a brawler, not covetous; One that ruleth well his own house, having his children in subjection with all gravity; (For if a man know not how to rule his own house, how shall he take care of the church of God?) Not a novice, lest being lifted up with pride he fall into the condemnation of the devil. Moreover he must have a good report of them which are without; lest he fall into reproach and the snare of the devil."
—1 TIMOTHY 3:1–7

God's Word is powerful, clear, and convicting. Let's briefly examine each of God's qualifications regarding our character.

> *There is no softer pillow than a clear conscience.*

Blameless—This literally means "not able to be held." The spiritual leader is to be above reproach. This doesn't mean you won't be accused of wrong; it means there must not be any truth to the accusation or evidence of wrongdoing. Walk with such integrity that if slander ever comes your way (and it will), it would be unthinkable to those who truly know your character. It has been said, "There is no softer pillow than a clear conscience."

"Not because we have not power, but to make ourselves an ensample unto you to follow us."—2 THESSALONIANS 3:9

The Husband of One Wife—This challenge refers both to marital status and to moral practice. Simply put, a spiritual leader is to be a one-woman man! A godly leader must be characterized by moral purity and holiness. He must choose to guard his heart, his mind, and his testimony, keeping himself only for his wife and abstaining from all forms of moral impurity.

"But whoso committeth adultery with a woman lacketh understanding: he that doeth it destroyeth his own soul. A wound and dishonour shall he get; and his reproach shall not be wiped away."—PROVERBS 6:32–33

Vigilant—This word refers to one who thinks clearly and who exercises his mind to discernment and careful awareness. Vigilance will help a leader know when to study, when to rest, when to counsel, and when to pray. Vigilance causes a man of God to carry out a resolution long after the mood in which it was made is passed.

Sober—This refers to having a self-controlled, sound, and serious mind. This is a man who is well disciplined in life's priorities—one who understands that busyness doesn't always equal productivity. A leader must be purposed in his thinking and focused in his direction.

Of Good Behaviour—In other words, he is respectable and orderly in his lifestyle. Homer Kent in his commentary on the pastoral epistles says, "The ministry is no place for a man whose life is a continual confusion of unaccomplished plans and unorganized activities."

Hospitable—This literally means "fond of guests" and refers to a genuine love for strangers. A spiritual leader opens up both his heart and his home on a regular basis to Christians and to those he is trying to reach with the Gospel. Few things bond lives and open hearts like Christ-centered hospitality. I challenge you to make hospitality a centerpiece of your ministry. Have new Christians and church members to your home at least once a month.

Apt to Teach—This means "able to instruct," and it is the only qualification that refers to giftedness in function. A pastor must have the gift of teaching (Romans 12:7) and be ready to teach with a spirit of humility (2 Timothy 2:24–25) from a life of holiness (1 Timothy 4:7) and with a heart to study the Word consistently. One man said, "Never be afraid to state the obvious. It is what most people have forgotten."

Give your mornings to God. Be a student of His Word and prepare your heart to teach and feed His flock. Make your time in the Word a true priority in your life.

Not Given to Wine—Simply, this is a man who avoids alcohol. *"Wine is a mocker, strong drink is raging: and whosoever is deceived thereby is not wise"* (Proverbs 20:1). In a day when so many are excusing this sin, choose to be a man of God who avoids all appearances of evil and who refuses to put a stumbling block in the path of a weaker Christian (1 John 2:10).

I believe with all of my heart that Timothy practiced total abstinence from alcohol as a beverage. (Please refer to my minibook *Discerning Alcohol* from strivingtogether.com.)

No Striker—This is a man who is not a brawler—does not strike back quickly, either physically or verbally. This is a man who is patient and who doesn't react but rather responds—prayerfully and carefully. A spiritual leader refuses to place himself in situations where tempers could flare. He doesn't resort to physical violence or verbal abuse. He is not competitive in a selfish way.

Not Greedy of Filthy Lucre—This is a man who is not motivated by money. He does not love money or desire excess. He has learned to be content—to let God bless financially on *His* timetable and in *His* predetermined proportion. This is a man who refuses to compare himself with others—especially other leaders. *"I have coveted no man's silver, or gold, or apparel"* (Acts 20:33).

One That Ruleth Well His Own House—This means "to preside or to have authority over." This mandate refers both to the orderliness and lifestyle of our children as well as the handling of our household finances and possessions. God wants His undershepherds to have well-ordered and disciplined homes. Show your family the kind of love that is a delight to obey!

Not a Novice—The pastorate or a position of spiritual leadership is not for a new convert or a young Christian. This is for a man of spiritual maturity and proven experience. Immature leaders tend to seek significance from the esteem of others rather than from a growing relationship with Jesus Christ. Make sure you are well-grounded and growing spiritually.

Of a Good Report—This man must have a good reputation in the community. When this man's name comes up amongst others, there are good things to be said!

THE COMMISSION OF A SPIRITUAL LEADER

Every spiritual leader has a sacred commission from Scripture. It is a commission to serve, feed, lead, oversee, and be a living example to the flock of God.

Be a living example to the flock. *"Neither as being lords over God's heritage, but being ensamples to the flock"* (1 Peter 5:3). Motivational speaker, Dr. Alan Zimmerman said, "Some people dream of worthy accomplishments while others stay awake and do them." A biblical pastor is a living, vibrant, forward-moving man of action—living out his faith and pursuing his God for all to see. He does this in obedience to Christ, not for the applause of men.

Feed and give oversight to the flock. *"The elders which are among you I exhort, who am also an elder, and a witness of the sufferings of Christ, and also a partaker of the glory that shall be revealed: Feed the flock of God which is among you, taking the oversight thereof, not by constraint, but willingly; not for filthy lucre, but of a ready mind"* (1 Peter 5:1–2).

We have seen the call, the character, and the commission of the spiritual leader. These qualifications are not man's ideas; they are God's! Commit yourself to your call; align your life with these qualities. Anything less is beneath the office and diminishes God's work. God's people deserve this quality of leadership, and by God's grace, you can exemplify these qualities!

CHAPTER TWO

THE ATTRIBUTES OF A SPIRITUAL LEADER

Have you ever heard someone say, "He's a self-made man!"? When it comes to spiritual leadership, being self-made is an impossibility. Spiritual leaders are God-made in every sense, and their hearts and lifestyles must be the product of the filling and power of the Holy Spirit. The qualifications we studied in the last chapter must be embraced with willingness out of love for the Lord and not merely because of the "restraints" of the office. God's Word says we are to lead "willingly" and with a "ready mind"(1 Peter 5:2). That is to say that these attributes must be embraced with joyful readiness and availability, not with resentment or unwillingness. Exemplifying these attributes requires full heart devotion and glad surrender to "the Great Shepherd."

Has it ever occurred to you that many leaders in the Bible never had a desire to lead? Men like Moses, Joshua, Daniel, David, Paul, and John the Baptist were essentially "caught off guard" by God's anointed plan for their lives. They were not seeking position, prominence, or preeminence. They were simply servant-hearted men who humbled themselves before God, and God exalted them in due time (1 Peter 5:6). These were men who were given influence by the sovereign hand of God, and they rightly chose to use that influence for His glory. This attitude must be the heart of every spiritual leader.

In his book *Spiritual Leadership*, J. Oswald Sanders contrasts the attributes of a natural leader and a spiritual leader. Consider this contrast:

> The natural leader is *self-confident*, but a spiritual leader is *God-confident*. The natural leader *knows other men*, but the spiritual leader *knows God*. The natural leader makes his *own decisions*; the spiritual leader seeks *God's will*. The natural leader is *ambitious* but the spiritual leader is *self-effacing*. The natural leader originates his *own methods*; the spiritual leader finds and follows *God's methods*. The natural leader enjoys *commanding others*, but the spiritual leader delights to *obey God*. The natural leader is motivated by *personal considerations*; the spiritual leader is motivated by a *love for God and men*. The natural leader is *independent*; the spiritual leader is *God-dependent*.

What a contrast! Truly, the call to spiritual leadership is a paradox. It is a call to descend into greatness. It is a call to lead by serving. It is a call to expend one's self for the glory of God. This call begins on its knees in a genuine spirit of humility, transparency, and honesty before God. First Peter 5:5 says to spiritual leaders, *"...be clothed with humility: for God resisteth the proud, and giveth grace to the humble."*

Only disciples can make disciples!

I believe a ministry leader should be a servant leader. Our pattern is the Lord Jesus Christ, and our mission is to carry out His heart, to reflect His love through the influence that He has entrusted to us. That isn't to say our personalities and uniqueness have to be sacrificed, but rather that God will live the life of Christ through us and use our personalities and gifts to His glory. We must relinquish all rights to "be who we want to be" and lay ourselves on the altar to be all that Christ desires for us to be.

Consider with me twenty attributes that I believe characterize the life and leadership style of a biblical, Christ-like leader:

1. He is a follower of Jesus Christ.

In John 15 Jesus exhorts us to abide in Him. He extends a personal invitation to an intimate relationship. Before you can lead others into this relationship, you must experience it yourself—regularly. Only disciples can make disciples! This relationship requires a daily choice to walk personally and closely with Christ, and what a different life the ministry is when you are walking close to Him!

2. He is willing to deny himself.

In Luke 9:23–25 Jesus invites us to take up our cross, deny ourselves, and follow Him. Any position of spiritual leadership begins with the denial of personal pursuits. The godly leader will gladly expend himself for others and for the Lord. If you are trying to lead while holding on to personal dreams, your double heart will eventually catch up with you. Abandon self and fully embrace the call!

3. He is submissive to and filled with the Holy Spirit of God.

This attribute too is a daily choice. A godly leader will seek moment by moment to obey every impulse of the Holy Spirit of God (Ephesians 5:18). Do you know what His impulses feel like? Do you know that still small voice of God when it is speaking to you and leading you? Spiritual leaders practice the moment-by-moment presence of God and live constantly with a sense that every moment belongs to God. As God's ambassador, I am on His mission in even the smallest of details and circumstances, and I must listen to His guidance and obey His direction in the minutia of life as well as in the big picture.

4. He possesses and practices discipline in his life.

The word *discipline* could be defined as "controlled behavior that results from training." You must first bring your own life and habits into order before you can lead others to do the same. God is not the author of confusion, and He prefers that all things be done decently and in order (1 Corinthians 14:33, 40). This discipline begins with your personal life, your car, your closet, your home, your sleeping habits, your study habits, and your walk with God; and then it extends throughout your ministry (1 Thessalonians 2:10).

5.   He reads the Word of God and good books consistently.

You've heard the statement, "Leaders are readers!" This statement is never more true than for a spiritual leader. God instructs us to grow in grace and in knowledge (2 Peter 3:18). He tells us to be students of the Word (2 Timothy 2:15). He commands us to understand and teach the "meat" of the Word (1 Corinthians 3:1–2). Also, He challenges us to know well how to edify the church (1 Corinthians 14:12). Pastor, you must be a lifelong student of God's Word and a constant reader of good books.

6.   He seeks, asks for, and uses God's wisdom.

This is the ability to see life's circumstances and events through the eyes and understanding of God and His Word—and it is the knowledge of how to properly and spiritually respond (Hebrews 4:12). Again, this is a daily process of simply asking, believing, and receiving. God promises to give His wisdom liberally and without partiality to those who ask and believe that He will give it (James 1:5).

7.   He is sincere and deeply cares.

Theodore Roosevelt said, "Nobody cares how much you know until they know how much you care." The ministry is no place for cold-hearted, merciless, or authoritarian men. God's flock requires men *"likeminded, who will naturally care..."* (Philippians 2:20). Allow God to soften your heart and burn within you the desire to be sincere, without offense— truly a man of compassion and tender concern (1 Peter 3:8).

8.   He has godly friends and stays accountable.

We will talk more in another chapter about friends, but the spiritual leader should surround himself with "iron-sharpening-iron" relationships

(Proverbs 27:17). Your friends strongly influence you, and wrong friends will hinder your heart and hurt your church. Every godly leader must have a spirit of accountability and transparency with a few godly friends. Few priorities will better help you fight the good fight of faith and finish your course (2 Timothy 4:7)!

9. He knows how to forgive.

If you have not yet discovered this truth, you soon will. Pastors get hurt. They are unfairly criticized, wrongfully slandered, maliciously attacked, and often misunderstood! The ministry is sometimes a caustic environment. Hurting people hurt people, and often the pastor finds himself in the crosshairs—the object of scorn from the heart of a hurting person that he only tried to help.

And yet, the ministry has no place for resentment, bitterness, or anger. In fact, the quickest way to quench God's work in your church is for you to harbor your pain. Good leaders are good forgivers (Ephesians 4:32; 2 Timothy 4:16).

10. He finds his acceptance in Jesus.

Often the ministry is lonely, and just as David *"encouraged himself in the LORD"* (1 Samuel 30:6), a spiritual leader must find his daily strength and identity in his personal relationship with Christ. We often find our greatest insecurities through comparison. Not only are we warned in Scripture not to compare ourselves (2 Corinthians 10:12), but comparison leads down a dangerous road of discontentment and personal crisis.

It has been said, "Everybody has opportunity and everybody has ability. No two have the same opportunity and no two have the same ability." Friend, you are fully accepted at the feet of Jesus, and you will give an account to Him alone for what you did with the opportunities and abilities that He gave specifically to you. Song writer Gary Mathena wrote, "When you come to the place that He's all you have, you'll find He's all you need."

11. He prays for others.

I once heard Dr. John R. Rice say, "All of our failures are prayer failures." Prayer is the weapon of spiritual warfare, and the ministry is a call to live on the front lines of spiritual battle—for yourself, your family, and others. To win this battle you must become a man who keeps an open line of communication with your Heavenly Father, instantaneously lifting up others in prayer to Him as quickly as their names enter your mind (Colossians 1:3). Charles Spurgeon said, "The neglect of private prayer is the locust which devours the strength of the church."

12. He helps others succeed.

The call of the ministry is a call to give your life to the success, health, and growth of others (Ephesians 4:11–12). Your success is defined by the forward motion of others—not yourself. Give yourself to developing success in those within your influence, whether they be many or few. Success in ministry is not about numbers, size, or church growth. It is about how effectively you are influencing and developing those within your reach!

13. He knows the difference between ambition and vision.

Ambition is self-centered; vision is God given. Ambition feeds the ego; vision fulfills a call. Later in this book we will look more closely at vision, but you can expect some to criticize your God-given vision, as they will mistake it for personal ambition. Others will attempt to judge your heart, but when God places a holy and biblical vision upon your heart, you must pursue it in pure obedience to your Lord.

14. He is able to articulate vision.

A good leader shares the vision that God has placed upon his heart. He unashamedly enlists, trains, and inspires others to invest their lives and their resources into eternal endeavors. Everyone likes to be on a winning team, and when a leader casts God's vision before a church family or a team, and then leads them to realize that vision, this is the very essence of a holy, heavenly "winning team"!

15. He possesses a sense of urgency for God's work.

While a spiritual leader will not be dominated by urgency, he will view all of life and every responsibility and opportunity as a timely open door for ministry. You may have heard the statement, "Opportunity seldom knocks twice." A holy urgency for Christ will compel you to seize the day, capture the moment, and fulfill God's call now with passion (Ephesians 5:16)!

16. He stands on strong convictions.

We live in a day when leaders are capitulating to the whims of men and the winds of culture. A biblical leader stands upon the Word of God unapologetically and yet compassionately. It is possible to have a strong stand and a tender heart at the same time.

17. He is kind.

Many view the ministry, especially preaching, as an opportunity to blow off some steam and to "whip the flock into shape." This is not the heart or the practice of Christ. To be sure, Jesus had His predetermined moments of righteous indignation, but never with His flock—even when they reasonably deserved a harsh rebuke. Allow the Holy Spirit to develop a tender and kind spirit in your heart toward God's people, toward the lost, and toward fellow leaders and pastors. The ministry is no place for unkind or harsh-spirited men.

18. He has a growing love for Jesus Christ.

Right now, in your deepest thoughts, you know what you love. You know what motivates you, what drives you. Are you sincerely in love with Christ? Do you walk with Him and grow to love Him more each day? If so, this sincere love will flow into every part of ministry and be evident to everyone you influence.

19. He loves his family.

A spiritual leader recognizes that his family is his first ministry! This kind of love requires action—intention, planning, and deliberate care. If you lose your family, you lose the privilege to pastor. Take a look at your weekly schedule and ask yourself, "Does my family have some of my best time?" Ask yourself that question every week for the rest of your life. You'll never go more than a week without staying in balance and giving your family what they truly need.

20. He loves the local church.

Many spiritual leaders seek recognition outside the walls of their local church—through speaking or writing or traveling. I must remind you, ministry never gets any bigger than it is at home! Your greatest call, your best ministry, your most abundant fruit, and your Saviour's heart are closest to the local church for which He gave His life. Love your church! Immerse your whole heart, life, soul, and strength into ministering in your own pulpit to the flock that God has entrusted to you!

Twenty qualities of a biblical leader—these things may intimidate you. You may wonder how you could ever measure up. None of us truly can. Without Him we can do nothing, and no one is ever worthy of the high calling of God!

On your own, you cannot embody these qualities. Don't let this list discourage you, but let it direct you to the power of God. Surely, with God's calling comes God's enabling. If He has called you to lead, then His power can make you what you ought to be.

Take a moment right now, review these qualities, and ask God to make them a part of your heart and life.

CHAPTER THREE

SPIRIT-FILLED LEADERSHIP

C harles Spurgeon said, "Without the Spirit of God, we can do nothing. We are as ships without wind, or chariots without steeds. Like branches without sap, we are withered. Like coals without fire, we are useless."

God's Word contains five commands in the New Testament regarding the Holy Spirit:

1. Quench not the Spirit (1 Thessalonians 5:19).
2. Grieve not the Spirit (Ephesians 4:30).
3. Walk in the Spirit (Galatians 5:16, 25).
4. Pray in the Spirit (Jude 20).
5. Be filled with the Spirit (Ephesians 5:18).

The foundation of all significant ministry is the work of the Holy Spirit. A biblical leader cannot afford to go one day or one hour without the filling and guidance of the Holy Spirit of God. He—His power, His presence, His leading, and His anointing—is truly the essential component, the all-important ingredient of God's work.

All of our efforts, our best plans, our grandest ideas will come to nothing except for the touch of God's Spirit. We must long for His presence, seek His touch, and pursue His power first and foremost. All fruit and blessing in ministry hinges on this one fundamental absolute.

The filling of the Holy Spirit is a moment by moment, by-faith process of yielding control. It does not involve strange experiences or mystical events. It does not involve frantic emotion or sensationalism.

The Holy Spirit is easily quenched or grieved, but He is just as easily invited back—through immediate confession and acknowledgement of wrong. He assumes control the moment He is invited, and He steps aside the moment He is usurped. He desires to fill and permeate every thought, every decision, and every attitude, yet He is often ignored and disregarded through an entire day.

I challenge you to begin your day by asking the Holy Spirit to fill you and control you. Then remain sensitive throughout your day—moment by moment—to whether you have grieved Him or obeyed Him. When you have grieved Him, quickly repent and acknowledge the wrong; immediately invite Him back into the driver's seat of your life. Throughout your day, continually seek His presence and guidance.

What is the result of this kind of Spirit-sensitive living? What does the life and ministry of a Spirit-filled leader look like? What are the evidences? I would like to share ten indicators that reveal the Holy Spirit's filling in your life:

1. A Spirit-filled leader is personally yielded.

The key to effective *public* leadership is a genuine *private* walk with God. "Walking in the Spirit" involves both a private time with the Lord daily as well as the moment by moment sensitivity of yielding yourself to the Lord (Ephesians 5:18).

F.B. Meyer said, "How we live our lives is more important than how long we live our lives." The Holy Spirit is the presence of God in your moments. Do you habitually yield yourself to God? Do you live each moment in the context of a yielded life? Is the Holy Spirit truly the power and strength behind your daily ministry?

Bernard "Kip" Lagat is a world-class Olympic runner from Kenya. During the 2000 Summer Olympics, an interviewer asked him how his country was able to produce so many great distance runners. With clever wit, Lagat told of the African strategy for motivating success in running. He said, "It's the road signs that say, 'Beware of Lions.'"

May we be similarly motivated to avoid Satan's traps by yielding to the controlling power of the Holy Spirit. The Apostle Paul expressed it this way, *"Whereunto I also labour, striving according to his working, which worketh in me mightily"* (Colossians 1:29).

2. A Spirit-filled leader models godliness.

First Peter 5:3 commands us, *"Neither as being lords over God's heritage, but being ensamples to the flock."* Friend, your character is what makes you a leader worth following. It is what forms the trust that others place in you, the foundation upon which their following is built. God commands us to lead by example, to model the godliness that we preach. Dr. Howard Hendricks rightly stated, "You can impress people from a distance, but you only impact them up close."

The lifestyle of a spiritual leader is to be an open book—a living testimony—easily seen, clearly examined, and able to be emulated. Does this mean you will be constantly scrutinized? Yes. Will you "live in a glass house"? Yes. But what a privilege! What a joy to be entrusted with such transparent influence! Accept this responsibility with a grateful heart and a sober mind. You are the best Christian many people will ever see.

A Spirit-filled leader will not resent or begrudge this burden. Rather, he will see it as a wonderful, glorious opportunity to lift up Christ through his life for all to see.

3. A Spirit-filled leader leads others in sanctification.

Did you notice that God calls His Spirit "Holy"? This implies that being filled with the Spirit is a holy life—a separated, sanctified life unto the Lord Jesus Christ.

First, I believe a Spirit-filled leader will lead his family in sanctification. In Numbers 27:18 we read that Joshua was a man *"in whom is the spirit...."*

Later in Joshua 24:15 we read where this same man states, *"as for me and my house, we will serve the Lord."* The Spirit of God in Joshua caused him to lead his family in the right direction.

Are you leading your family in a separated walk and lifestyle? Is your home a holy place where the presence of God's Spirit is evident? As we will see later, God intends your home to be a center of hospitality and an open example of Spirit-filled family life.

Second, a Spirit-filled minister will lead his church family toward sanctification. It has been said, "When you have influence, people follow you. When you have respect, they keep following you." God intends that your leadership be deeply rooted in a respected, Holy Spirit-led lifestyle. He desires that you would lead your church by example, away from sin and into holiness.

Many spiritual leaders today have completely lost sight of this practical, day-to-day holiness—the avoidance of sin and worldliness and the embracing of sanctification and purity. In fact, it seems in this "grace gone wild" age, many have opened the front doors of the church to all the trends of the world merely to attract visitors. Quite literally, the world is evangelizing the church! When we attempt to please the world, we become just like the world. Yet when God's Spirit is in control of our lives and leadership, there will be a noticeable direction away from sin—both privately and publicly, at home and at church.

4. A Spirit-filled leader maintains spiritual priorities.

We will discuss priorities in depth later in this book, but the context here is that right priorities begin with the Holy Spirit! They are the product of God's leading. You can read all the time management books, attend all the seminars, and try every kind of gadget and planner; but without the Holy Spirit's guidance, you'll never truly zero in on God's priorities for your life. You'll pillow your head at night knowing you were busy but still frustrated that you really weren't "doing the right stuff."

5. A Spirit-filled leader leads others to Christ.

Acts 1:8 instructs us to be "witnesses." Simply put, the product of the Spirit at work in your life will be a soulwinner's heart. You will share the Gospel. You will recognize divine appointments when God intersects your life with a person who needs Christ. You will regularly share Christ and see others come to Him through your influence.

John Downey was a postal carrier in our city. He, his wife, and three daughters visited Lancaster Baptist Church because someone had left a gospel brochure at their door. What a joy it was to stop by John's home a few days later and to visit with his family. We talked about the children's programs and the ministries of the church, but most importantly, we opened the Scriptures together and shared the Gospel. John and his whole family trusted Christ that night and have faithfully served the Lord with us for more than two decades. Without a doubt, leading the Downey family to Christ is one of the great privileges and memories of our ministry in Lancaster!

Since we are commanded to lead by example, I challenge you to let others see you actively reaching others. Be present at the soulwinning meetings of your church (even if you're the only one there) and be strategic about your soulwinning, which we will explore more in another chapter. Consider taking a moment and looking through your church directory and asking this question: "How many of these members were adopted into the flock, and how many have I seen born into the flock?" Your church growth should represent a sizeable percentage of new Christians—not merely transfers from other churches. Jesus said in Matthew 4:19, "...*I will make you fishers of men*"—not "traders of fish"!

6. *A Spirit-filled leader maintains oversight.*

Another product of the filling of God's Spirit will be a greater awareness and intensity of oversight in ministry. He will give you a greater capacity to oversee and a greater burden to "know the state of your flock." How is your oversight? Is the Holy Spirit of God increasing your ability and your awareness? I love the little acronym M.B.W.A.—manage by walking around.

Spirit-led oversight will make you both observant and obedient. In other words, you will notice things you never noticed, and then the Holy Spirit will lead you to take action and to obey His impulses.

7. A Spirit-filled leader encourages orderliness.

Our God is a God of order. When His Holy Spirit is active and working, order will be the natural result. As the Holy Spirit leads, you will be prompted to bring order to both the business and the structure and ministry of the church. The Holy Spirit will prompt you to fix up the buildings, give careful account of the finances, create an orderly flow chart and job descriptions of the staff, and establish a careful strategy and operation of daily ministry. This "order" might be as simple as picking up a piece of trash or as complicated as restructuring your adult Sunday school.

The campus of Lancaster Baptist Church is in the desert, and God has blessed us with real, live tumbleweeds. I'm amazed that visitors from out of state often want to take pictures of tumbleweeds. On occasion when the wind blows, our campus becomes littered with tumbleweeds. I can't count the number of times I've walked the campus picking up and throwing away tumbleweeds!

You might wonder, "Does the Holy Spirit lead you to do that?" Indeed He does! Let God stir your heart and allow disorder to bother you as much as it does Him. While order is not the secret to God's blessing, it certainly creates an environment in which He is free to work in hearts.

Titus 1:5 teaches us that we are to *"set in order the things that are wanting."* Take a look around your church. Consider your ministry. What is "out of order"? What isn't working? What ministry is suffering? What is languishing in disarray? The Holy Spirit placed you there, and He means to lead you and guide you into establishing order for God's glory. (For more on "order," you might consider getting a copy of my book *Order in the Church* from strivingtogether.com.)

8. A Spirit-filled leader remains impartial.

The Holy Spirit will lead you to serve every member of your church with the same concern and intensity. He will not guide you to partiality or favorites. He will give patience, understanding, and caution where you might otherwise be reactionary or emotionally charged. A Spirit-filled leader uses the Bible as his guide and knows that the Lord is his supply.

In Acts 15 the Apostle Peter displayed this character trait so well when in verse 19 he encouraged Christians to *"trouble not them, which from among the Gentiles are turned to God."* In an emotionally charged and tense moment, Peter had patience and Spirit-led impartiality in his ministry position.

> *Apart from the Holy Spirit, we tend to "fall apart"!*

I've seen young leaders who accept gifts from well-meaning church members and eventually lose their ability to lead those members because they feel indebted to them. I've seen others who were intimidated by those they thought were big givers, and yet others who got involved in personal politics in ministry and became reactionary against critics or those they sided against. Recognize that the Holy Spirit will guide you to stay impartial and discerning in such situations.

9. A Spirit-filled leader is gracious in trials.

Hebrews 4:16 teaches us that we can *"come boldly unto the throne of grace, that we may obtain mercy, and find grace to help in time of need."* This ninth evidence of the Holy Spirit is simply a peaceful, gracious, and strong spirit through the most difficult of times. Surely this quality is supernatural. Apart from the Holy Spirit, we tend to "fall apart"!

When the Holy Spirit is in control, He makes it possible for you to forgive. Remember how Stephen forgave the very ones who stoned him in Acts 7? In just one chapter before, the Bible calls him *"a man full of faith and of the Holy Ghost"* (Acts 6:5).

When the Holy Spirit is in control, He allows you to be faithful. In Acts 14, we find the Apostle Paul stoned and left for dead. The very next day, Paul rose up, went to another city, and preached the Gospel again! What an amazing difference the filling power of the Holy Spirit makes in a man of God!

10. A Spirit-filled leader exercises spiritual authority.

Simply put, the way spiritual authority flows from a Spirit-led man is vastly different from that of a carnal man. Spiritual authority, when flowing from the Spirit's filling, always takes place in accordance with God's Word, in a spirit of submission to the Saviour and with longsuffering and doctrine (2 Timothy 4:2).

First Peter 5:3–4 reminds us, *"Neither as being lords over God's heritage, but being ensamples to the flock. And when the chief Shepherd shall appear, ye shall receive a crown of glory that fadeth not away."* Godly authority is not lorded or demanded; it is carried out in humility, with accountability to the "Chief Shepherd" in view. When a minister exercises spiritual authority, he must do so with a spirit of sincerity, humility, and with the knowledge that the Lord Jesus Christ is looking over his shoulder, taking record of how the undershepherd is treating His flock.

Spirit-filled authority will always avoid the following:

A demanding spirit—It doesn't respond with harshness when others disagree or resist.

A demeaning spirit—It doesn't condescend or act with arrogance or puffiness.

A divisive spirit—It doesn't sow discord, and it avoids those who relish discord.

Holy Spirit-led authority will lead authoritatively but kindly, and it will always seek to resolve discord rather than stir it up. This kind of authority responds kindly to those who disagree and still loves and gives from a deep heart of compassion and grace.

Since ministry is a public life—an ensample to the flock—it quickly becomes obvious to a church family and a community when a spiritual leader truly is filled with the Holy Spirit. This filling is not merely internal. It is a lifestyle that is abundantly different, joyfully unique, and wonderfully peculiar. It is clearly seen and evident to others. And it is beautifully attractive, both to Christians and unbelievers alike.

Are you Spirit-filled? If so, your leadership will be different; your life will display the Spirit's control; and your church and community will be forever changed because of the grace of God obviously flowing from your heart!

CHAPTER FOUR

THE SERVANT LEADER

J esus stated, "…*Ye know that they which are accounted to rule over the Gentiles exercise lordship over them; and their great ones exercise authority upon them. But so shall it not be among you: but whosoever will be great among you, shall be your minister: And whosoever of you will be the chiefest, shall be servant of all. For even the Son of man came not to be ministered unto, but to minister, and to give his life a ransom for many*" (Mark 10:42–45).

Servant leadership was Jesus' idea. The word *minister* literally means "to attend to or to wait upon." Jesus took on Himself the "*form of a servant*" (Philippians 2:7). No greater example of service could ever be seen than that of Jesus Christ. He is the ultimate display of servant leadership.

How do you view your role as a spiritual leader? What led you to desire this office, and how was it granted to you? Your perspective on this principle will play out in every facet of your day to day leadership—both in personal settings and from behind the pulpit. This concept is a deep heart-level trait rooted in how you perceive your position as a minister of Christ.

If we were to ask Jesus "how should we view this role," His simple answer would be "as servant of all." He taught us to minister—to give ourselves as He gave Himself. He exemplified a kind of leadership that is foreign to secular corporations or government hierarchies. He introduced a "towel and bowl" kind of leadership—the kind of leadership where the Creator of the universe stoops to wash the dirty feet of His creation. This is the kind of leadership where the God of all power and glory gives His life to save the souls of fallen men who have rejected Him—the kind of leadership that gains by giving, lives by dying, and rises by kneeling.

Some time ago I heard a well-meaning pastor use an analogy which compared the office of an Old Testament king to the local church office of the pastor. While I understand there can be some simple parallels made concerning God's anointing, God's call, and even a position of leadership and influence, I also feel that this analogy is dangerous because of the privileged and humanly elevated position that kings held. Let us remember that God never intended for Israel to have a king other than Himself. It was their disregard of God's will that led to kings.

The role of a pastor is much more closely associated with the Old Testament role of a prophet or a man of God, who was called to shepherd the people in spite of the carnal, self-absorbed, and often idolatrous leadership of kings. These men had an amazing blend of leather-lunged boldness to declare the truth of God, combined with tender-hearted compassion to shepherd His people. They had a fierce love for God and a fiery protection for the flock.

Second, Jesus never draws the same analogy, and never in the New Testament do we see the role of pastor compared to a king. In fact, the picture we see in Jesus is quite the opposite. In Him, we see a true King kneeling to wash His disciples' feet. We see the King of kings serving men, loving people, and living among those to whom He ministered.

In Jesus we do not see One with lavish appointments, extensive entourages, and a luxurious lifestyle. Even though He was worthy of that, He chose to live a serving life. He is called the King of kings, but He called Himself the Son of man. He is called the Lord of lords, but He never lorded over anyone. His greatness and power and love were exemplified and displayed through simple obedience to His Heavenly Father and through steadfast compassion upon all He touched.

This is servant leadership, and this is the call of God upon every pastor and spiritual leader. As undershepherds, we must assume the model and example of the Great Shepherd. As His children, we must humble ourselves in simple service and obedience. We must see ourselves not as kings but as shepherds—one of the most common and lowly of all first-century Jewish professions!

In this short chapter, I challenge you to have a biblical perspective of your calling. Your *office* is a high and holy call, but your *role* is one of lowliness and humility. Your *purpose* is the grand, eternal purpose of Almighty God, but your *function* is one of Christlike understatement. For, if you see yourself as a king, your heart will become lifted up, your spirit self-absorbed, and your God will become distant—actually resisting your "kingly" efforts "*...for God resisteth the proud, and giveth grace to the humble*" (1 Peter 5:5). Yet, if you see yourself as Christ saw Himself, you will live in humility, thereby freeing the mighty hand of God to bless your service and *"exalt you in due time"* (1 Peter 5:6).

THE MINISTRY OF A SERVANT LEADER

Yours is a call to minister—to serve. That ministry will involve labor and hard work. *"And we beseech you, brethren, to know them which labour among you..."* (1 Thessalonians 5:12). A servant leader is not afraid to get his hands dirty, work hard, or exhaust himself for his Master. A serving pastor will labor in prayer, preparation, oversight and in feeding, leading, and equipping the flock.

Consider the great kenosis passage where Jesus completely emptied Himself and became obedient to the will of His Father:

> *If there be therefore any consolation in Christ, if any comfort of love, if any fellowship of the Spirit, if any bowels and mercies, Fulfil ye my joy, that ye be likeminded, having the same love, being of one accord, of one mind. Let nothing be done through strife or vainglory; but in lowliness of mind let each esteem other*

better than themselves. Look not every man on his own things, but every man also on the things of others. Let this mind be in you, which was also in Christ Jesus: Who, being in the form of God, thought it not robbery to be equal with God: But made himself of no reputation, and took upon him the form of a servant, and was made in the likeness of men: And being found in fashion as a man, he humbled himself, and became obedient unto death, even the death of the cross.—PHILIPPIANS 2:1–8

THE MOTIVES OF A SERVANT

Spiritual servants do not seek status; they seek the mind of Christ. Success is a moving target, but leadership is a fixed goal. In spiritual leadership, Jesus—His glory, His pleasure, and His purpose—is the goal. A servant leader is motivated not by a personal agenda or self-gratification, but by the lifting up of Jesus Christ. John the Baptist said, "*He must increase, but I must decrease*" (John 3:30).

Paul exposed his motives clearly in 1 Thessalonians 2:3–6, "*For our exhortation was not of deceit, nor of uncleanness, nor in guile: But as we were allowed of God to be put in trust with the gospel, even so we speak; not as pleasing men, but God, which trieth our hearts. For neither at any time used we flattering words, as ye know, nor a cloke of covetousness; God is witness: Nor of men sought we glory, neither of you, nor yet of others, when we might have been burdensome, as the apostles of Christ.*"

The great preacher Jonathan Edwards said, "I go out to preach with two propositions in mind. First, every person ought to give his life to Christ. Second, whether or not anyone else gives Him his life, I will give Him mine."

Do you see the purity of motive in these words? This is the kind of leader that God entrusts with influence, and it is the kind of leader that God's people can follow with willing-hearted sincerity.

Not long after our family arrived in Lancaster, we experienced a particularly difficult week of financial need. We were literally wondering how we would buy groceries for the coming week. Our cupboards were bare, our checking account depleted, and our motives were being tested.

That Sunday evening, a couple of families in the church invited us to join them for a bite to eat at a local fast food, taco restaurant called Naugle's. The invitation was a blessing because we didn't have food at home that we could prepare.

That evening, we were the last ones to leave the church after locking up. As we drove to the restaurant, it occurred to me that our hosts were probably already eating which meant we would most likely need to pay for our own dinner. As we drove, I asked Terrie to give me some money. She said, "I don't have any money."

Now, usually when a wife says she doesn't have any money, she still has some! So I said, "I know you don't, but give me some money so I can pay for dinner."

My wife looked at me with big tears in her eyes and said, "Paul, not only do I not have any money, but we don't even have any food at home and I'm not sure what we're going to eat tomorrow."

> *Success is a moving target, but leadership is a fixed goal—Jesus is the goal.*

I cannot describe to you how I felt in that moment. While I knew we were following God to Lancaster, I felt that I had failed as a provider. Immediately, I turned to human solutions. I asked our five-year-old daughter Danielle to look under the seats for any spare change. A few moments later she had managed to find a grand total of seventy-two cents. With disappointment I decided this was enough to buy an iced tea for the whole family to share and we would tell our hosts that "we just weren't hungry."

It was about that time that Terrie looked at me and asked the obvious, "Why don't we pray about it?" A little embarrassed that I hadn't thought to, I swallowed my pride and began to explain our situation to the Lord and ask for His provision.

Moments later, we stepped into Naugle's and before we could even begin to order our iced tea, the cashier held up two large bags of food and said, "Sir, we just had a van full of teenagers come by the drive-through, order all this food, and then drive off. Would you like to eat it?"

Terrie and I looked at each other with tears in our eyes. We high-fived, hugged, and rejoiced in God's provision. We returned home with full stomachs to bare cupboards, but we had confidence that God would come through.

At 7:00 the next morning, there was a knock on our door. I was surprised to see a dear friend, Pastor Rick Houk and his wife standing at our door with their arms full of grocery bags. He said, "Pastor, the Lord put you and your family on our hearts last night. Our church took an offering; we went to a twenty-four hour grocery store, and we drove straight here through the night to deliver these groceries!"

We were reminded once again that truly our Heavenly Father is a faithful provider! This was only the first of many times over the years that God has wonderfully provided for our every need. When your heart and motives are pure as a spiritual leader, you can rest in the faithful provision of your gracious God!

THE METHODS OF A SERVANT LEADER

A servant leader will boldly and powerfully proclaim the truth of God, but he will do so with a spirit of sincere love and humility. There is no conflict between the boldness of preaching and the humility of a servant leader. In fact, bold preaching from a servant's heart is the kind of preaching that God will magnificently bless and use.

The Apostle Paul made two declarations in 1 Thessalonians 2. He said first that he was bold to speak the Gospel, and he then stated that he spoke without guile, only with Christ-centered, pure motives. What a wonderful blend of Holy Spirit boldness and a Christlike servant's heart.

THE MESSAGE OF A SERVANT LEADER

Again in 1 Thessalonians 2, Paul stated that he labored night and day to preach the Gospel. He said again in 1 Corinthians 1:17–18 that he did not use the wisdom of man's words, but rather preached the Gospel which is the power of God.

A servant leader confines the message of his entire life to the Gospel and the Word of God. His words, preaching, teaching, and living all speak of Christ, the Cross, and the Christian life. He understands that the power is not in the preacher's personality, delivery style, or cunning illustrations. The power is in the Word of God *"which effectually worketh also in you that believe"* (1 Thessalonians 2:13).

The role of a spiritual leader is one of servant leadership. We are not kings; we are shepherds. We are not self-made, self-appointed, or self-sustaining. We are Christ's servant-ambassadors—and He repudiates status-seeking. In a world where kings and governments lead people into bondage, we are called to guide them to spiritual freedom. In a world where men are climbing political and corporate ladders—where men seek to enthrone themselves by using the worship of others—we are called to humbly lead men to the worship of Christ.

Some men might argue, "If I take that kind of servant role, people will 'walk all over me.'" Yes. That's what they did to Jesus. It's called "being used"!

Take a moment now and humble yourself before the true King. Purge your heart of any impure motive, selfish agenda, or personal ego. Then take up your shepherd's staff and love His sheep.

CHAPTER FIVE

THE SPIRITUAL LEADER'S FRIENDS

L oneliness is a part of the ministry, but isolation will ruin your ministry. First Kings 19:4–5 gives us a glimpse into the loneliness of an Old Testament man of God, Elijah: *"But he himself went a day's journey into the wilderness, and came and sat down under a juniper tree: and he requested for himself that he might die; and said, It is enough; now, O LORD, take away my life; for I am not better than my fathers. And as he lay and slept under a juniper tree, behold, then an angel touched him, and said unto him, Arise and eat."* Elijah had just slain the prophets of Baal. God gave a great and miraculous answer to prayer, but Jezebel had announced a contract on Elijah's life. In distress, Elijah withdrew alone, sat down under a tree, and in despair, asked the Lord to let him die!

Have you ever been there? Have you been physically, spiritually, emotionally exhausted, lonely, and wondering what God is doing? Most likely you have already been there, and if not, you surely will be there sooner or later. This is a part of ministry.

Over the past decades, it has become clear to me that ministry and life are about relationships. I am a highly relational person; I live every day desiring to know that my relationships are right. I enjoy developing new relationships and strengthening old ones.

In this chapter we will examine those relationships that the spiritual leader calls "friends." We will see God's wonderful plan for strengthening His men, for filling some of the loneliness that accompanies the call, and for maintaining godly accountability and influences.

THE FOUNDATION OF ALL GODLY FRIENDSHIPS

The solution for all loneliness and the foundation for all friendships begins with God. The spiritual leader must be the friend of God—even as the Bible refers to Abraham in James 2:23. No earthly relationship can ever begin to meet the needs of the heart or fill the void within as a close relationship with the Lord does.

Throughout the Scriptures we see men of God depending upon Him—seeking His presence, coming before His throne, and encouraging their hearts in Him. This dependence must be every leader's first "friendship" priority.

A famous actor was once the guest of honor at a social gathering where he received many requests to recite excerpts from various literary works. An old preacher who happened to be there asked the actor to recite Psalm 23. The actor agreed on the condition that the preacher would also recite it. The actor's recitation was beautifully intoned with great dramatic emphasis for which he received a lengthy applause. The preacher's voice was rough and broken from many years of preaching, and his diction was anything but polished. But when he finished, there was not a dry eye in the room.

When someone asked the actor what made the difference, he replied, "I know the Psalm, but he knows the Shepherd." Draw close to the Shepherd. When you truly know Him, all other friendships will pale in comparison.

THE FORTIFICATION OF MARITAL FRIENDSHIP

Ephesians 5:25 tells us, *"Husbands, love your wives, even as Christ also loved the church, and gave himself for it."* Again we read in Ephesians 5:31, *"For this cause shall a man leave his father and mother, and shall be joined unto his wife, and they two shall be one flesh."*

Next to the Lord Jesus, every pastor's greatest friend must be his wife! I've never seen a leader in the ministry who didn't find it a challenge to balance marital time and ministry time. The work of the ministry is never done. The needs are never fully met, and the souls are never all reached. The preacher doesn't "clock out and go home"—ever. Sunday is always coming. The next appointment, the next message, the next event always looms just around the corner.

If you're not deliberate and predetermined, you will rob time from your marriage, and you will find yourself (and your wife) wrestling with more loneliness than God intended. Pastor, may I challenge you to give yourself to your wife as Christ gave Himself to the church? The church is not *your* bride; it is Christ's. He gave you a bride to love, cherish, know, and nurture. Are you loving *your* bride as He loves *His*? One simple way to find out would be to ask her; and then listen to her answer, receive it with an open heart, and determine to respond as Jesus would.

Like every relationship, a marriage will not grow to become a close friendship unless it is given time. And, the more time and energy you invest into your marriage, the more you will discover you really *like* each other. Give scheduled, predetermined time to your marriage. Schedule time on the calendar, plan it, and make it happen. Cleave to your wife physically, emotionally, spiritually, and relationally. Let her become your best friend and closest companion!

THE FRAMEWORK OF A GODLY FRIENDSHIP

I believe there are seven biblical qualities of a godly friendship—seven benefits to having the right kind of friends in the ministry. And I believe that God wants to provide these qualities in the life of every leader:

1. Godly friends sharpen each other.

Proverbs 27:17 teaches us that *"iron sharpeneth iron."* A godly friend will "sharpen" you, and you will "sharpen" him.

2. Godly friends assure each other through adversity.

Godly friends love each other. Proverbs 17:17 teaches that friends love at all times—especially in adversity. Do you have the kind of friendship that unashamedly could declare love? As a man of God, are you able to say you have friends for whom God has truly given you a love? The old saying is true, "Prosperity begets friendship; adversity reveals them."

3. Godly friends participate with each other.

Proverbs 18:24 teaches that friends show themselves friendly. I believe this is a picture of action. Godly friends are eager to cooperate, encourage, and help each other.

4. Godly friends rejoice for one another.

A Swedish proverb states, "Friendship doubles our joy and divides our grief." Godly friends rejoice in the blessings of a friend. This kind of relationship is no place for jealousy, comparison, or envy.

5. Godly friends forgive one another.

Friends will eventually hurt each other—and usually unintentionally. Yet, where the Spirit of the Lord is, there is peace. Godly friends resolve tension and quickly forgive.

6. Godly friends do not share or harbor anger.

Proverbs 22:24 teaches that we should avoid friendship with an angry or furious man. Yes, there are some men the Bible simply teaches us to avoid or break from. A godly friendship will not be characterized by shared anger or bitterness. Amazingly, even amongst spiritual leaders, often the very thing that draws two men together is a common grievance or hurt against another brother. Some men even go so far as to create issues—straw men, if you will—just to divide others and build a personal quorum! Will the gospel ministry of Jesus Christ be reduced to such childish behavior in your life?

7. Godly friends spark the truth in each other.

Proverbs 27:6 says, *"Faithful are the wounds of a friend...."* Godly friends are not afraid to lovingly and appropriately speak the truth to one another. In fact, they long to hear the truth from each other. They recognize that everybody has "blind spots" and they rejoice that God has given them "another set of spiritual eyes" to help guide, guard, and protect.

Beyond that, godly friends rejoice in truth. They discover truth together. They talk about truth. They encourage each other in it and through it. Truth is the common bond of their hearts—a love for God's Word and a love for communicating His truth to people. God desires to give you this kind of friend, and if you will allow Him, you will be most blessed!

THE FIGHT AGAINST GODLY FRIENDSHIPS

Satan fights a spiritual leader on every level, and this area is no different. You can expect your enemy to try to destroy your healthy, spiritual relationships with godly friends. He does not want you to be strengthened by your brethren. He does not want you to experience those "iron sharpening iron" relationships with other godly men who would help you in the ministry. He hates it when your heart is encouraged in the faith by a friend. I believe he fights these friendships in three critical ways:

Satan fights friendships with jealousy.

Jealousy is truly a cancer among leaders, and it is rooted in comparison. If Satan can get you to compare yourself or your ministry, you will always come up short somehow. It's a trick to prevent you from enjoying a healthy relationship with another man of God.

We are tempted to compare our preaching with guests and others; we are tempted to compare our attendance with other churches around town; we are tempted to see only the negative in our lives and only the blessings in others. Yet, the Sovereign Giver of gifts to His church is also the Sovereign Planter of men in His vineyard. Choose to bloom where you are planted. Take your eyes off those who are compromising and appear to be blessed. Take your eyes off those who appear to "have it all," and cast your gaze back upon the Lord.

> *Jealousy will destroy your walk with Christ, your joy in the ministry, and your perspective on your own church.*

F. B. Meyer held meetings in Northfield, Massachusetts, and large crowds thronged to hear him. Then the great British Bible teacher G. Campbell Morgan came to Northfield and people were soon flocking to hear his brilliant expositions of Scripture. Meyer confessed at first he was envious. He said, "The only way I can conquer my feelings is to pray for Morgan daily, which I do."

Decide now that you will not fall into the trap of jealousy and envy—no spiritual ministry can be sustained with this spirit. Jealousy will destroy your walk with Christ, your joy in the ministry, and your perspective on your own church.

Satan fights friendships with a critical spirit.

Have you ever met somebody who always sees the bad in everything—in a critical way, not a constructive way? These people are gifted to judge, criticize, and "arm-chair quarterback" everyone else's ministries and motives, even from great distances. Every church has members with critical spirits. Every denomination and fellowship has a group of members who are dominated by this spirit.

Are we so arrogant as to think that God accepts some of us on the basis of merit and others only by grace? Friend, we all fall short, and we all came to the Lord and into ministry the same way—through the blood of Christ. Truly, the ground is level at the Cross. One spiritual leader being critical of another is like one speck of dirt criticizing another speck of dirt for being dirt!

Criticism is a part of the ministry, and constructive, loving insight is even helpful. But a critical spirit does not have to corrupt your spirit or your friendships. I decided a long time ago that I would not criticize other men of God. I will use my words, my pen, and my life to encourage, equip, and edify those men for God's glory. I challenge you to avoid a man with a critical spirit at all costs.

Satan fights friendships with an isolation complex.

Like Elijah, Satan wants you to withdraw and to isolate yourself. He wants you to think you stand alone—that all others have compromised. This is always a lie and it's always an attempt to prevent you from developing a godly friendship with a brother.

If isolation is plaguing you, I challenge you to come out of the shadows. Get on the playing field with like-minded men; be sharpened, encouraged, and blessed.

THE FREEDOM EXPERIENCED IN A GODLY FRIENDSHIP

In closing this chapter, I believe that a godly friendship brings two very important freedoms into a man's life:

Godly friends give each other the freedom to fail.

I'm not referring to covering sin or ignoring major moral or doctrinal failures. I'm simply saying that right friendships extend to us a great degree of understanding. A godly friend will see you at your best and at your worst, and love you just the same.

Godly friends give each other the freedom to have other friends.

If I am a true friend, I will not bind my friends to me. When you are secure in your acceptance with Christ, you will rejoice that your good friends have other good friends!

In these last days, men of God need each other more than ever. Most likely, very close to you, either geographically or doctrinally, is someone with whom God would delight to knit your heart. You, your church, and the cause of Christ could benefit from this relationship, yet perhaps something stands in the way. What is it? Perhaps a phone call or a lunch meeting is all it would take to remove the splinter and begin the knitting process. Reach out to a like-minded spiritual leader and let God give you another godly friend today.

CHAPTER SIX

THE SPIRITUAL LEADER'S PRIORITIES

Burn-out might be a real possibility in ministry life, but I must confess, I do not see it as an impending threat to most spiritual leaders, because many were never fired-up in the first place. I see two extremes when it comes to ministry priorities. The most common is the leader who does not have a grasp of what the priorities should be; therefore, he struggles with finding purpose, living passionately, and filling the week with meaningful ministry. This man is not so much in danger of burn-out as dry-rot.

The second is the leader who knows the priorities, has a solid work ethic coupled with a burning passion for Christ, but doesn't have the structure to manage the priorities of his life. This man works diligently all day long and never catches up. This man is consumed by a mode of urgency and finds his life both out of control and chaotic. *Everything* seems important *right now*. This cycle surely will lead to frustration, depletion, and possibly burn-out.

Before we look at our ministry priorities, let us learn from our Saviour the real challenges we face in accomplishing those priorities.

BE REALISTIC ABOUT MINISTRY

Hebrews 4:15 teaches us that our High Priest, Jesus, faced every infirmity and temptation that we face. He knows our struggles and He understands our pressures. Before you can set the right priorities, you must be realistic about the ministry life to which God has called you. The ministry brings a man into an ongoing *lifestyle* of unusual pressures in every realm. Unless we take a realistic look at ministry life, we will forever struggle to understand what "balance" in the ministry even looks like!

Yet, Jesus knows these pressures well. In Matthew 14, we read about one of the most pressure-filled days in Jesus' ministry. John the Baptist, His personal friend and forerunner, was executed. At the same moment, religious and political leaders were plotting against Christ and planning to put Him to death, while crowds were pressing Him for time, teaching and healing. On top of this, Jesus was trying to prepare a band of uneducated fishermen to change the world. Talk about pressure! Personal time and rest was nonexistent for Christ. Let's break these pressures down. Think about what Jesus faced in one day of ministry:

Jesus faced the pressure of personal loss.
So will you. The ministry brings with it the loss of friends, the rejection of people you love and tried to help, and the scorn of a lost world.

Jesus faced the pressure of personal threat.
Those who speak the truth will always be threatened by those who reject truth. If you preach God's Word, not everyone will thank you. You can expect the wicked one to assault you and men to threaten you.

Jesus faced the pressure for private time.
After receiving the news of John the Baptist, Jesus tried to get some private time, but the crowds followed and Jesus continued to expend Himself, even in the midst of personal pain. In the same way, your ministry will sometimes crowd out the private time and rest that you desperately need.

Jesus faced the pressure of preparing His disciples.

When Jesus finally had a moment to pray and be alone, He found that His disciples were in trouble, and He went to them, walking on the water in the midst of a storm. Ministry training was immediately back in session as He helped His team grow in faith. The pressure never stopped for Jesus, and it will most likely never stop for you.

Years ago, when my oldest son Larry was small, we were playing basketball in our back yard. I was teaching Larry how to shoot the ball, but his little arms just weren't strong enough to get the ball up to the ten-foot rim. Every so often I would make a shot and say something like, "See, Larry—like that." Finally with boyish exasperation, Larry looked at me and said, "Yeah, it's easy for you up there! You don't know how it is for me down here!"

Thank God, we can never say that to Jesus! As the hymn writer said, "Jesus knows all about our struggles. He will guide 'til the day is done. There's not a friend like the lowly Jesus, no not one!"

Yes, the ministry is fraught with very real, unpredictable, and random pressures. These pressures cannot be prioritized or controlled. They can

> *Opinions are what we hold. Convictions are what hold us!*

only be responded to biblically. Scheduling your priorities becomes a completely different process in this light, and the spiritual leader's life is different from any other kind of "work life." The spiritual unpredictability will require a great degree of spiritual flexibility. So where do you begin? Let's start with identifying and recommitting ourselves to the central priorities of a minister's life.

BE COMMITTED TO YOUR PRIORITIES

It has been said, "Opinions are what we hold. Convictions are what hold us!" Every spiritual leader must establish some personal convictions about priorities. These cannot merely be preferences or opinions; they must be what "hold you"—the very pillars of your daily life.

First, you are a man of God.

Your walk with God and your heart for Him must be strong and consistent.

Second, you are a husband.

Your love for your wife and your time with her must be consistent and must meet her deepest needs, as well as yours.

Third, you are a father.

Your time with your children must be both quality and quantity, and you must fulfill your first ministry to pastor your home!

Fourth, you are a pastor and preacher.

God has given you the responsibility to feed and oversee a flock—to live out His heart in caring for His people.

Fifth, you are a friend.

God will give you relationships of renewal, encouragement, and strengthening that must stay strong and healthy.

Let these things become the pillars of your choices and decision making. Opportunity does not equal obligation—and your life will be filled with endless opportunities that God did not send your way. Stephen Covey in his book, *First Things First* wrote, "It's easy to say 'no' when there's a deeper 'yes' burning inside." Burning these priorities into your heart and engraving them upon the door-posts of your life will give you clarity week to week and moment to moment. These foundational priorities will help you to quickly say "no" to things that do not resonate with your primary, God-given roles.

See these priorities as walls of protection around the limited resource we call *time* or *life*. Choose gladly to live within those boundaries and do not feel a moment's regret saying "no" to something or someone that does not fit within those boundaries. Commit with pit-bull determination to these priorities and never let anything uproot that commitment.

BE PROACTIVE IN YOUR PERSONAL SCHEDULING

A realistic perspective of unique ministry pressures and a firm grasp on personal, God-given priorities lead us to a starting point in actually creating a plan for life. If you miss the first two points of this chapter, point three will be an exercise in futility. You will be building a stick to beat yourself with. Yet, in the light of what we've already seen, let's examine how to put a balanced weekly schedule into place.

Step One: Start each week by balancing your roles.

This is the simple process of taking 15–30 minutes each week to review the roles that God has given to you, looking at your upcoming week and placing those roles onto your schedule in some way. I recommend you do this at the same time and place each week. This involves looking back at last week and asking "how did I do?" And it involves looking at the coming week and setting a deliberate, Spirit-led plan.

What gets scheduled gets done! And if something doesn't show up in your schedule, then I guarantee you, it is *not* a priority, no matter how "warm and fuzzy" you feel about it.

Step Two: Identify your top weekly priorities.

As you balance your roles, the Holy Spirit of God will lead you to identify a couple of very important priorities in each role each week. If they do not come to your mind quickly, just ask Him. These are priorities *within* the bigger priorities, if you will. These are the actions that you will perform in each role to strengthen and fulfill that role or relationship for God's glory. Write out those priorities.

Step Three: Create your week at a glance.

This implies that you must live by some system other than your memory. If your memory is your weekly organizer, you are severely limiting your ministry and frustrating your life at the same time (not to mention irritating your wife and others with your forgetfulness!). There are plenty of tools, time management seminars, binder systems, and gadgets to help you streamline your information and schedule. Find the one that works the best for you and learn how to use it.

Decide that you will live by a reliable system that resides *outside* of your head. Be able to look at the entire week in one glance and see where all of your time commitments reside. Place every priority into the coming week during a Spirit-led moment of obedience.

Step Four: Work your God-given plan.

From this planning session, you will have a balanced schedule for at least the next seven days, as well as a solid grasp of the top priorities in each God-given role. Now it is time to work the plan. Live with integrity. Honor your commitments; keep your appointments, and stay focused on what God has given you to do. Without an action plan, you become the prisoner of events. With an action plan, events have a purpose.

Step Five: Set margins in your schedule.

A spiritual leader's schedule must have margins. Crises cannot be scheduled. The needs of the flock cannot be completely fit into a time-management system. The Holy Spirit will lead your schedule in a direction you did not anticipate—and don't forget, your life and your time are not your own. Thus, when you plan your week, give yourself enough flex time and advance planning so that you can bend where God leads you.

Step Six: Know when to disengage.

God commands this in Exodus 20:10. There are times when a leader must "come apart," just as Jesus did. The Gospels are clear that Jesus had times when He separated Himself from the crowds and from the busyness so that He could commune with His Father and find physical rest. Vance Havner once said, "If we don't 'come apart,' we will 'come apart.'"

You must know your limits. You are a finite resource; your time, your energy, your emotions, and your spiritual strength are not bottomless wells. They are like gas tanks. They become depleted regularly and must be re-filled. Only you and God can determine whether your pace is sustainable and for how long. Only with the guidance of the Holy Spirit can you read the gauges of your heart to know when you are running on empty.

If you're weary, frustrated, edgy, short with people, tired of people, frazzled, and visionless, that's a pretty good sign you're on empty! No need to panic or leave the ministry—just disengage and renew.

Step Seven: Make wise moment-by-moment choices.
As you live out your weekly plan, you will have daily opportunities that require quick discernment. Is this a Holy Spirit given detour, or is it a distraction from my God-given direction? Every day, you will have to make conscience calls that require integrity, wisdom, clarity, and honesty. Don't be afraid to make these calls, but do be afraid to make them *incorrectly*.

To make these calls correctly, you must set aside *insecurity* and have a clear conscience that you are maintaining God-directed balance. You must set aside *comparison* of your schedule with others. You must have the inner assurance that you are living the life and schedule that God has led you to live, not the life that comparison has forced upon you.

In this chapter we've seen three foundational habits—be realistic about your pressure, commit to your priorities, and be proactive in planning your week. These habits will establish within you a correct pattern of thinking and a right process of prayerful decision-making in your schedule. With these habits in place, you only need to sense the leading of God and obey Him moment by moment. Easier said than done, but by His grace, you can live a productive and ordered life for His glory.

James 4:14 reminds us, "*Whereas ye know not what shall be on the morrow. For what is your life? It is even a vapour, that appeareth for a little time, and then vanisheth away.*"

CHAPTER SEVEN

THE SPIRITUAL LEADER'S WEEKLY SCHEDULE

The weekly schedule is different for every spiritual leader, and there is not a one-size-fits-all solution or model. There are, however, some principles that God has blessed in my life, and I believe that transparency among God's men can often have that "iron sharpening iron" impact in our hearts that we visited earlier.

In this chapter I'd like to open my weekly planner to you. I've already said, "don't compare" so please know this is not to establish a standard or define a model. I'm sure comparison will cause us both to fall short in some way, beside the fact that rarely are two weeks of my life ever the same. It is merely to say transparently, this is what God has led to work in my life and maybe in seeing it you can glean some thoughts or ideas that might work in yours.

Ephesians 5:16 admonishes us to redeem or buy back our time—to attach value to that which was at one time lost. Thank God that because of Christ, our time and our lives can have eternal significance. It can be redeemed and be valuable to the work of the Lord. Our daily passion should be to use the time the Lord gives us as a stewardship unto Him—to invest and expend our resources in accordance with His purpose and plan.

May I suggest to you that "time management" is a myth? We cannot manage time any more than we can manage the wind. Not far from our valley is a mountain area filled with windmills that generate electricity for a largely populated area. Just as we can harness the power of wind, even so we can harness the power of time and manage our lives within it!

This chapter is about managing yourself on a weekly basis to be as effective as you can be for the Lord. Management expert, Peter Drucker wrote, "Executives who do not manage themselves for effectiveness cannot possibly expect to manage their associates and subordinates." Let me encourage you with three principles and some practical insight to developing an effective weekly schedule.

DEVELOP YOUR CALENDAR AND SCHEDULE

The foundation of a solid, balanced, and productive weekly schedule is a crystal-clear, long-term vision. So, before we even begin talking about this week, let's start with the next 365 days and work back incrementally.

Develop an annual calendar.

In another chapter we will look more closely at an annual ministry plan. Suffice it to say that your weekly schedule must flow from a pre-determined annual calendar—for you and for the church. If you do not have a one-year calendar in place, begin now to create next year's. My personal calendar as well as our church calendar for the next year is always in progress, but is usually complete by early November. In addition to this, our secretaries begin developing future calendars three to five years ahead of time.

There are events on my *personal* annual calendar that address all of my major priorities—my walk with God, my marriage, my children, my preaching, my leading, and my equipping.

Develop a monthly plan.

For many years, I have used a month-at-a-glance view of our calendar. I always have the present year in my binder and it goes with me everywhere. Many times each week I consult that calendar and plan ahead.

Develop a weekly schedule.

Personally, my weekly schedule is kept in Microsoft Outlook and is networked among myself, my wife, and my secretary. Every priority, appointment, and time commitment is entered into this weekly schedule.

Develop a daily list.

Each day, someone in my office prints out my "daily list" from Outlook, places it in my binder and into a plastic frame on my desk, creating a constant reference point throughout the day.

You might say this process of working from one-year-out to one-day-at-a-time gives multiple perspectives and helps keep the big picture connected to the daily details.

DISCIPLINE YOUR WEEKLY SCHEDULE

I've told our church family for many years that a "growing church is always in transition." The same applies with a growing leader—and I don't mean physically! As you and your ministry grow in God's grace, you will find that your life structure will go through a predictable and ongoing state of transition. Regularly you will need to make assessments and rework your organizational plan. What worked for you last year will not necessarily work for you this year.

In other words, if you're in search of the perfect balance, forget it. Balance is a moving target that changes with the dynamics of ministry and life. So get used to change and be willing to hit the pause button of life long enough to identify what isn't working anymore, then restructure and move forward.

Also, in a spiritual leader's life, rarely will two weeks ever be the same or even be predictable. Nevertheless, the list below is my "target" for what I would call a balanced and effective weekly schedule. Sometimes I nail it and wish every week could be as perfect as this one, and other times God just tears the schedule up and rewrites the whole week. When that happens, just go with God, smile, and enjoy the journey. In case you're wondering, His agenda always takes top priority!

I begin every day and end every day with personal time with the Lord. This time is not reflected on the list below because it is my *personal* Bible reading, prayer, and journaling. Occasionally I include some writing or planning in this time.

Monday

I begin the week by reading my texts and meditating for next Sunday's messages. (By the way, these texts are usually chosen four to six months ahead during times of long range, seasonal planning. Also, during the months preceding, I keep folders for upcoming sermons in which my staff or I place articles, news, and illustrations for upcoming sermon series. Sermons in progress are kept on my computer.)

Monday is also the time I review all of Sunday's church statistics and from that review create action notes for the upcoming leadership meeting. Monday morning I meet with my office staff, review all notes and correspondence from Sunday, and set the agenda for the week. During these hours I respond to as many requests as I can—scheduling appointments, making phone calls, writing letters, and reviewing membership needs.

> *A growing church is always in transition*

After lunch, which is often brief on this particular day, I conduct a 1:00 PM leadership team meeting. This meeting includes all of the pastoral staff and ministry leaders on our team and covers a wide variety of items both from me and each member of the team. We always review the calendar, ask questions, and share a time of prayer.

Tuesday

Tuesday mornings are blocked off for study. Later in the morning I try to go soulwinning or to have appointments. Lunch will usually be an appointment, and the afternoon is also for appointments. Afterwards is our evening church soulwinning time. Occasionally I'm traveling during these two days, which usually means our leadership meeting moves to Wednesday, and my study time and correspondence moves to late Tuesday night. When I am home, I attend Tuesday evening soulwinning. Also, once a month, our deacons' meeting is held on Tuesday evening.

Wednesday

Wednesday morning is also a study morning. My Bible study outline for Wednesday night is given to the secretary and the media team around noon. Then it is proofread, laid out for a handout, and processed to be used for our screens. Often on Wednesday morning, I will preach for college or high school chapel. Usually on Wednesday I have another lunch appointment followed by afternoon appointments or meetings. Later in the day, I try to carve out a little more study time before going home to eat dinner and to prepare to preach.

Wednesday evening is our midweek service during which I usually teach or preach. Often it is followed by hosting guests for fellowship in our home.

Thursday

This has traditionally been our staff's day off. (For teachers it is Saturday.) I've already expressed the great degree of flexibility that a spiritual leader's schedule must have, so quite often, Thursday ends up being a work day, and another time has to be used for rest. On a day off I generally like to spend time with my wife, my children, and maybe even get out of the house and get away. Usually this day is about restoring and resting in a multitude of ways.

Many pastors take Monday off, which works well for some. I like working Monday, although I'm tired, because I feel the people's needs from Sunday are worthy of a quick response. I like to get a jump on the week. I like taking Thursday off because it's a good time to catch my breath before a busy weekend build up.

Friday

Friday morning is usually more time in the study because I must deliver my outlines to the staff for preparation for the weekend. After lunch I schedule appointments and prepare for our 3:30 PM all-staff training. This meeting is required for all church, college, and school staff and is my one time each week to communicate my heart to the entire ministry team.

After staff meeting I often meet with smaller groups or individual staff members with needs. This is also the time when I might interview someone for our staff.

When there is a church event, I might run home, freshen up, eat some dinner, and then return. When there isn't, Friday evening becomes a family night, and I spend time at home with my wife.

Saturday

Saturday begins for me again in the study, early. It's quiet on campus and it's a great time to prepare my heart for Sunday. All-church soulwinning begins at 9:30 and usually goes until about noon. I usually spend all afternoon in the study and may conduct a couple of meetings with smaller groups of staff for special reasons.

At 4:30 PM, I usually lead our men's prayer meeting when the men of our church gather, share requests, and pray for the Sunday services. I really believe that this meeting is one of the primary explanations for God's blessings upon our church.

After this meeting, I go home to have dinner with my family and to go over my messages one more time in the quiet of the evening in our family room.

Sunday

Sunday begins with an 8:00 AM pastoral prayer meeting in my office. Our first service is at 8:30 and our second is at 11:00 AM. We usually have lunch as a family or often with guests—either at our home or at a nearby restaurant.

By about 3:00 PM, I meet back at the office with my assistant and plan the next week. Over the next two and a half hours I may have a few other brief meetings, depending on whether I'm going out of town. I also spend time finalizing and reviewing the evening message.

Our evening service runs from 5:30 to about 7:15, and afterwards we host a group of church members in our home for fellowship and encouragement. (We will talk about hospitality in another chapter.)

Again, rarely are two weeks the same, and many other events cause this schedule to shift as needed. It is often interrupted, yet this schedule is my goal, and I believe it pleases the Lord and addresses the right priorities in my life.

DEAL WISELY WITH INTERRUPTIONS

One final thought. What do you do with the interruptions? I encourage you to remember these three simple steps:

1.   Assess the situation.

Is this a need God is bringing to me and leading me to meet? Ask these questions: What needs my immediate attention? What can be delegated to another? What can be scheduled for later?

2.   Respond to the needs.

Allow God to break you out of your plan to do what needs to be done. It has been said, "As important as decision making is for a leader, making the decision is only half of the process. Living with the decision is the other half!"

3.   Return to your God-given priorities.

After the interruption, get back on point and press forward. You will often abandon things that you postpone for too long. Don't ever abandon a God-given plan. Obey the *instructions* and God will take care of the *obstructions*!

The three principles are: to develop a long range calendar that reflects God's vision; discipline your weekly schedule; and deal wisely with interruptions. May God grant you the moment by moment wisdom and courage to do what He desires for you to accomplish this week.

2

PART TWO

THE SPIRITUAL LEADER'S MINISTRY

From the foundation of a pure and right heart, a spiritual leader's responsibility extends into many different kinds of labor for the perfecting of the saints to the glory of God.

"For ye remember, brethren, our labour and travail: for labouring night and day, because we would not be chargeable unto any of you, we preached unto you the gospel of God."—1 THESSALONIANS 2:9

"Night and day praying exceedingly that we might see your face, and might perfect that which is lacking in your faith?"—1 THESSALONIANS 3:10

CHAPTER EIGHT

THE SOULWINNING LEADER

Spiritual leadership begins with *who we are* not *what we do* or *what we say*. Outside of the preaching the Word of God, I believe the first ministry of every Christian leader is to personally reach souls for the Lord Jesus Christ. This is the call of God for every Christian, and we cannot lead others to do what we are not personally doing.

Like every Christian, spiritual leaders must work to maintain an intensity in this area. This is one responsibility your enemy will fight you constantly to prevent you from fulfilling. In this short chapter I would like to share with you five thoughts regarding your personal soulwinning.

MAINTAIN A BURDEN FOR SOULS

We usually equate a burden with emotion. In other words, we're burdened if we "feel" a certain way. I submit to you that a burden is bigger than emotion, and it can remain even though the *feelings* of a burden may come and go. If you are waiting to *feel* a burden before you go soulwinning, you are misunderstanding what a burden is all about.

A burden begins with *obedience*. In other words, just as we teach our church members to obey God in faith and that the feelings will follow that faith, so it is with our soulwinning. A burden for lost souls begins with obedience to the Saviour. I must confess, I do not always *feel* an intense burden before I go soulwinning, but I know my Saviour is burdened for souls because I see it in His Word; thus I choose to obey Him regardless of how I feel—which always increases my burden!

Amazingly, within a few moments of knocking on doors or talking with people, the *feelings* of a burden return and I sense again that this is the heart of God. Choose to have a burden *by faith*. Study His Word and you will see His heart. Obey His commands and you will have His heart (Matthew 28:19–20).

You must make a choice to maintain your burden for the lost. This should not be dependent upon your feelings, but upon your belief. Then as you see God's heart in His Word and obey Him by sharing Christ, your burden will be very much alive and well.

BE DISCIPLINED IN YOUR SOULWINNING

I believe that every Christian has a desire to lead others to Christ. From the moment of our salvation, this desire is wired into us—it is the fruit of the indwelling Holy Spirit. Yet how to live out this desire is often missed. We know we should be leading others to Christ, but we struggle with how and when. And you can be sure that if *you* are struggling with this, then your *whole church* will.

> *Spiritual leadership begins with who we are not what we do or what we say.*

I realize that our soulwinning efforts should not be restricted to a brief weekly time or public setting. We should be soulwinners 24/7, always ready to give an answer for the hope that is within us. But I also believe that a spiritual leader should be disciplined and predetermined in his personal soulwinning. Put a plan into place for how and when you will obey this command of Christ. Here are a few suggestions on disciplining your soulwinning efforts:

Have specific soulwinning times.

Since the day I entered the ministry, I have personally planned several times a week when I will invite a partner, prepare my heart, and labor in God's harvest field. We have done this with our staff and with our entire church family for over twenty years. If you don't know *when* you will go, you probably won't go.

Have a specific soulwinning plan.

Decide *where* you will go or *to whom* you will go long before you get into your car. Get a map of your city and work systematically through neighborhoods. Be creative in finding prospects and planning your soulwinning time. Without this method, you may waste much of your soulwinning time just deciding what to do.

Have an active prospect list.

Maintain a prayer list of names that includes anyone you have met in town, and any visitors you are following up on. Live with this list. Put it in the front of your planner and pray over it every day. Write, call, or visit your prospects every week. Add names constantly and ask the Lord to give you fruit that remains. Nothing will spark your church to win souls more than when the members see the people you've won coming down the aisle for baptism and church membership.

For several years I had a friend named Bill on my prospect list. Bill's company had done some landscaping work on our campus over the years and I had tried to share Christ with him on several occasions.

One day not long ago he came by to speak with me about some landscaping needs on our campus, and the Lord opened a very special door to once again share the Gospel. This time Bill's heart was soft and receptive due to some health trials his wife had been experiencing. After a few moments in my office, he prayed and trusted Christ as his personal Saviour. The next day, he showed up again at the church—this time with his wife. He told me he wanted her to hear what I had shared with him.

It was a wonderful delight to sit down in my office with Bill's wife and share the message of Christ. A short time later, she prayed to receive

Christ. The following day, I was surprised to see Bill and his wife again. They had brought their twin sons to hear the Gospel. After hearing the plan of salvation, they too accepted Christ as Saviour.

As of this writing, Bill and his family are consistently growing in their new faith and God is wonderfully at work in their lives! One reason Bill came to Christ was that his name never left my prospect prayer list. I believe God honored those years of prayer and outreach.

Soulwinning still works, and God blesses discipline. If you believe in faith that God will bless your disciplined soulwinning efforts, He will. He has done it for me for over twenty-five years.

STAY FOCUSED ON SOULWINNING

I challenge you to make soulwinning a focus of your whole life and ministry. Many pastors attempt to win souls or lead the church in outreach for a brief time. Few actually live their entire lives in ministry focused on reaching the lost. Winning souls ought not to be some passing fad or an unusual season of evangelistic fervor. It must be the very essence of ongoing ministry from day one until the day we see our Saviour. A passion for souls must be the *norm* for every biblical pastor, spiritual leader, and local church.

Staying focused on souls takes predetermined commitment. It takes constant attention. Satan will try to divert you, overburden you, and fill your time with other good things. He will try to distract your church in other matters. He will try to make you turn inward. You must constantly fight a natural drift away from soulwinning. There are six ways that spiritual leaders (and hence their ministries) lose this focus and six simple solutions. Let me share them with you.

Six ways leaders lose focus in soulwinning:

1. **Rationalization**—The cure for this is to stop rationalizing and repent before God. Ask His forgiveness and covenant again to win the lost.

2. **Improper response to past hurts**—We often turn inward because we are nursing some wound. Forgive those who hurt you and look again to the fields that are white unto harvest (John 4:35).

3. **Overly interested in sports or hobbies**—Often men of God spend more time watching SportsCenter than reaching the lost. There's nothing wrong with leisure time, but make sure you limit it and stay focused on your call.

4. **Overly involved in a pastor's fellowship**—I'm not against fellowship with other like-minded leaders, but I do think we can become so involved in some fellowships that the mission of our hearts and our local church weakens. Remember your calling—to reach the lost.

5. **Apathy and comfort zone in ministry**—If the church is doing well, the retirement fund is strong, and people are happy, we can become complacent—which ultimately is disobedience. The best way to kick yourself out of complacency is to start a new soulwinning ministry or program and personally lead it. Few things will ignite your heart and your church's heart like fresh vision!

6. **Administration is choking your time**—If your church has grown and you haven't hired or structured properly, you can find that your soulwinning time is choked out by a multitude of important needs. It's time to delegate. Hire someone, enlist a volunteer, train and equip him, and then give away some of your responsibility to free up that priority soulwinning time once again.

MAINTAIN A SOULWINNER'S HEART

Few things will keep your heart tender for the Lord and for people as soulwinning. Be willing to go to any home and be willing to speak to any person. Seek to follow every impulse of the Holy Spirit and keep an obedient heart to God's Word.

Have a heart to train others in soulwinning. Be an equipping leader—practice 2 Timothy 2:2, *"And the things that thou hast heard of me among many witnesses, the same commit thou to faithful men, who shall be able to teach others also."* Every time you go soulwinning, take someone with you whom you can mentor and train along the way. I've done this with many men in our church as well as with our staff. Mentoring is where soulwinning ministry truly begins to multiply!

ENJOY THE BLESSINGS OF A SOULWINNER

Finally, I want to remind you that there are some wonderful blessings to the leader who will make soulwinning a priority. I think of three blessings that I can never "get over"! First, soulwinners have *joy.* There's nothing quite like sharing the wonderful Gospel of Christ with a lost soul. Second, soulwinners have *fruit.* Seeing a soul come to Christ and begin to grow is what the ministry is all about. Third, soulwinners have a *clear conscience.* One of the best ways to stay real in the ministry is to stay after souls!

Just a few days prior to writing this, the Lord interrupted the plan of my day with a visit from a dear Korean family. They had been teaching at a University in New York and were flying through Los Angeles on their way back to Korea. They scheduled some extra time in the Los Angeles area for the express purpose of visiting our ministry. As they visited my office with their teenage daughter, they began to share their story and their burden. They wanted their daughter to be sure of her salvation.

I knew immediately that God was working in the heart of this girl. It was a great privilege to open God's Word and to take the next thirty minutes to share the story of Christ with her. A few moments later, with tears of rejoicing streaming down her parents' faces, she bowed her head and trusted Christ as her Saviour. This was the highlight of my day! I never want to get over the simple delight of leading someone to the Lord Jesus Christ.

May God help you to savor these three blessings every week as you strive to win souls to the Saviour!

CHAPTER NINE

LEADING A SOULWINNING CHURCH

What begins in the pastor's heart will be contagious if it is communicated and structured biblically. This is God's design. He works through spiritual leaders to mobilize His people and accomplish His purpose. This has been true from the time of the book of Genesis to today in your church. If your church is not a soulwinning church, it is either because you are not a soulwinner, or because you are not communicating and managing your soulwinning passion properly. What God does in *your* life, He desires to spill over into the entire church's life if you will allow Him!

In this chapter I'd like to briefly explore how you can develop a climate of soulwinning and a local church philosophy of soulwinning. A soulwinning church will grow, but growth is not the goal. I challenge you to make God your goal, not growth. The reason you should desire to lead your church in soulwinning is obedience, not growth. For many years, God has allowed the Lancaster Baptist Church to grow every single year, yet if the church did not grow next year, we would not change the foundation of soulwinning.

There is a kind of church leader in modern Christendom that constantly has to reinvent or re-engineer the church. Many leaders are experimenting with new methodology and uprooting biblical principles for the sake of "relevance" and church growth. If you study this movement closely, you will find it is rooted in discontent, faithlessness, and disobedience; and you will find it is failing over decades. The same writers who, two decades ago, were inventing the seeker-friendly, contemporary church, are now writing that this model does not work, and they are trying yet another model.

We would do well to find our security in Christ and to leave the growing of His church up to Him, as we return to simple, faith-filled obedience to His Word and to His basic instructions. Soulwinning is a basic part of the mandate of Jesus Christ to every Christian given in Matthew 28:19–20—the Great Commission.

Acts 20:20–21 teaches us, *"And how I kept back nothing that was profitable unto you, but have shewed you, and have taught you publickly, and from house to house, Testifying both to the Jews, and also to the Greeks, repentance toward God, and faith toward our Lord Jesus Christ."*

Let's examine four thoughts regarding leading a church that wins souls.

ESTABLISH SOULWINNING LEADERSHIP

Soulwinning is better caught than taught. God's Word clearly teaches that we should perfect the saints for the work of the ministry (Ephesians 4:12). Paul commissioned Timothy in 2 Timothy 2:2, *"And the things that thou hast heard of me among many witnesses, the same commit thou to faithful men, who shall be able to teach others also."*

The best way for your church to become a soulwinning church is to see you and the leaders in the church winning souls.

Model soulwinning.

People do what people see, and they will respond to your soulwinning example. Be sure that you are present at public soulwinning meetings, maintain your own soulwinning prospect list, and introduce your church visitors and new converts to your church members. Often we will host new Christians and faithful members at our home at the same time for fellowship. The faithful members greatly benefit from hearing the salvation testimonies of new Christians.

Mentor soulwinners.

The most valuable gift you can give another person is a good example. Establish a pattern in your life and in the church of having experienced soulwinners take new soulwinners as partners. Every few months, trained men and women in our church enlist new partners for soulwinning for the express purpose of mentoring.

Motivate soulwinners.

The climate of soulwinning flows both from your example as well as your pulpit. Strong Bible messages explaining God's mandates and the blessings of reaching others is the best way to motivate Christians to win souls. Are you preaching about souls? Are you sharing the heart of Christ from your pulpit?

Beyond this, there are several other things you should do to encourage soulwinning. Write regular letters of encouragement to those who display a heart for souls. Consider having soulwinning testimonies in your church services, and sing soulwinning songs in church.

Require soulwinning from all church leaders.

I realize that soulwinning should never have to be a *requirement*, but long ago we determined that the leaders of our church would be faithfully involved in soulwinning. We wait until someone is a faithful soulwinner before we even enlist them into leadership, but when accepting their leadership position, they also commit to remain a faithful soulwinner.

All of our teachers, deacons, and ministry staff are involved in soulwinning with our church family at least once a week, and each one fills out a weekly report of his ministry efforts. If the leadership is not involved in soulwinning, why should the church family be involved?

Quite simply, you will not motivate the church family to do what those in leadership are not doing.

ESTABLISH A SOULWINNING PHILOSOPHY

Nineteenth century preacher, James Freeman Clarke said, "Strong convictions precede great actions." A great soulwinning church is a product of a strong soulwinning conviction. You will never go wrong emphasizing your purpose and your mission to your church family. The more effort you put into crystallizing, understanding, and articulating the mission of Christ to your church, the more your church will embrace it and live it.

As you labor to establish this conviction of soulwinning, first you must uplift the mandate of Jesus Christ. Upon the authority of God's Word, stand and declare the Great Commission. We win souls because our Saviour commanded us to be witnesses for Him (Acts 1:8).

Second, you must emphasize the power of the Holy Spirit. The Holy Spirit *connects* to the listener, *conveys* truth to the listener, and *convicts* the listener all at the same time (John 16:7–8). Teach and remind your church family that we have a very present help in the person and power of the Holy Spirit.

Third, establish a soulwinning conviction that is based upon the entire Great Commission. We are commanded to win souls, baptize them, and disciple them. This process doesn't just *add* disciples, it *multiplies* disciples. Make baptism and discipleship as much a part of your soulwinning program as sharing the Gospel with the lost, for this is the command of Christ!

ESTABLISH AN EFFECTIVE PROGRAM

With the leadership of the church involved in soulwinning, and the conviction of the church established, having a practical program for living out the conviction is the next priority. Now the conviction must become action. How will you and your leaders actually involve the entire membership in the effort of reaching the lost? What system, what program, what training materials, and what details must be put into place? Let me share a few things that have consistently worked well for our church.

Have an annual soulwinning kickoff.

Twice each year we enlist and re-enlist our church family into weekly soulwinning. We often have a big service, decorations, special handouts, and some fresh training ideas. This is a big event on our annual church calendar.

Provide multiple soulwinning opportunities.

The more scheduled soulwinning opportunities you have in the week, the more people you will involve. We have three primary church soulwinning times—Tuesday morning, Tuesday evening, and Saturday morning. Each of these meetings, conducted by a pastoral staff member, includes an exciting time of encouragement, and offers a printed lesson followed by a time of soulwinning.

Cultivate the field of souls.

Many modern efforts of "church marketing" are meant to replace door-to-door soulwinning. I challenge you to view your media efforts differently than the modern-day "church architects." View all of your media and mailing efforts the same way you would view a farmer plowing a field. These efforts prepare the soil for the seed. Every time we have a billboard or TV commercial campaign, our soulwinners are more warmly received at the front door. These media outlets do not replace soulwinning; they prepare the way for it!

Vary your approach in soulwinning.

For many years, we have knocked on every door in our valley at least four times each year. This required us, long ago, to come up with creative variations so that we're not merely annoying people. Our church family still goes door-to-door soulwinning, but now we go with new-move-in welcome packets, with tickets or brochures about special events, or with some other seasonal gift. Also, a couple of times a year we simply canvass large areas, leaving brochures or materials on doors. Other times of the year we focus on follow-up from special outreach events.

Establish a strategic system of tracking contacts.

Do you know who visited your church last month, who followed up on them, and what happened? Do you know if anyone is continuing the

Soulwinning is better caught than taught.

follow up? Every week the visitors of your church should fill out a card which must become the very first priority of your soulwinning ministry. These cards must be entered into a system, printed into visitation cards, and carefully assigned and tracked every week. You must review these cards and visits every week in the form of a weekly report sheet.

(For more information about the soulwinning program and the detailed organization, please refer to *Order in the Church* available from strivingtogether.com.)

REIGNITE SOULWINNING FERVOR

Perhaps as you've been reading this, you are thinking, "this would be great if I were starting over, but what do I do with a church that long ago lost its soulwinning fervor?" The best remedy for a sick church is to put it on a soulwinning diet! Let me close this chapter with a few suggestions of how you can lead a revival of soulwinning in your church:

Assess the involvement of the church.

Do a thorough review and ask some very important questions. What is the purpose of our church, and do the people know what it is? When are our soulwinning times, and are they organized and well prepared? Who is involved in soulwinning in the church and who is not? Are your expectations for leaders and others clear? From this assessment, you are going to have a lengthy list of Spirit-led conclusions that must be addressed.

Adjust the program as needed.
From your review, you will need to begin planning and adjusting the program of the church. Maybe you will add an outreach opportunity or an outreach event. Maybe you will cultivate the field better through mailing and media. Maybe you will clearly define your leadership requirements and have a training banquet when you re-introduce them.

Announce the program through preaching.
Use the pulpit that God has given you. Share your heart, share His Word, and challenge your church to rise to the call in obedience to the commission of Christ. Nothing is as vital as the preached Word when it comes to challenging God's people for soulwinning.

Ask the membership to enlist for training.
Many Christians do not go soulwinning simply because they are fearful and don't know what to say. They've never been trained, and many actually desire training. In planning your kick-off, encourage your church family to sign up for training. Place sign-up tables in your lobby, place cards in the bulletin, and hand out the cards in your Sunday school classes. Rally the whole church family in learning how to win souls to Christ.

Assign soulwinning partners.
Be strategic about soulwinning partners—carefully place people together. Place experienced Christians with inexperienced. Encourage partners to keep each other accountable for several months and to go soulwinning together every week. You've heard the proverb, "Tell me and I'll forget. Show me and I'll remember. Involve me and I'll understand." Strategic soulwinning partners make "understanding ministry" a reality.

Prepare the soulwinning calls.

Help your partnered teams have a plan. Give them a map, some visits, or some new move-ins. Don't merely have a rally. Have a focal point for the distribution of strategic information. Give your teams a place to go and a reason to be there. This plan will require some secretarial or volunteer support in preparing the visitation cards and maps, but it will be well worth it. Finally, consider organizing these calls and visits through your Sunday school. Doing so will give every class a reason to attend the soulwinning meetings and give you a way to accurately follow up on prospects for each class.

Analyze the soulwinning results.

Look at the soulwinning results every week for two reasons. First, as the leader, you must have the pulse of how all the follow up went. You need to know if souls were saved, if they were followed up for baptism and church membership, etc. Second, you want to look at the results of the soulwinners. Do they need encouragement? Do they need training?

Propagate soulwinning through discipleship.

Make soulwinning a part of your regular discipleship program in training new Christians. From the moment people begin to grow in your church, they should be learning and hearing about soulwinning.

Soulwinning is not only mandated by Jesus Christ, but soulwinning is still effective. The pages of this book would not permit me to share all the incredible stories of changed lives that have unfolded through the soulwinning ministry of Lancaster Baptist Church. Going from house to house, door to door in the Spirit of Christ still makes a difference.

I'm reminded of a story I once read about the great NFL receiver Jerry Rice. He was once asked in an interview why he had attended such a small and obscure college as Mississippi Valley State University. It was obvious that his talent could have taken him just about anywhere he wanted to go. Rice replied, "Out of all the big-time schools (such as UCLA) that were trying to recruit me, MVSU was the only school to actually come to my house personally." The big schools sent cards, letters, and advertisements, but just one school gave him a personal invitation.

More and more, in a high-tech society, people still crave the personal attention of someone who truly cares about them. Dr. David Gibbs says, "Hi-touch can get lost in hi-tech!" The Lord Jesus Christ blesses and uses soulwinning churches to change their communities.

We've seen in this chapter that, while soulwinning is the responsibility of every Christian, the responsibility of leading by example and holding the soulwinning banner high rests squarely on the leader's shoulders. May God bless your passion to lead your church to become a dynamic soulwinning family.

CHAPTER TEN

THE OVERSEEING LEADER

M any men who are "called to preach" would not readily say they are called to *administrate*. Yet, when God calls a man to lead in a local church, He is calling him to assume several roles, and one of them is an *overseer*. You may not feel gifted to administrate or oversee; you may not enjoy this part of ministry, but your oversight is as much a part of your calling as your preaching. In this chapter and the next, let us consider the spiritual leader's responsibility to *oversee* the work of God.

First Peter 5:2–4 admonishes spiritual leaders: *"Feed the flock of God which is among you, taking the oversight thereof, not by constraint, but willingly; not for filthy lucre, but of a ready mind; Neither as being lords over God's heritage, but being ensamples to the flock. And when the chief Shepherd shall appear, ye shall receive a crown of glory that fadeth not away."*

This passage gives us a wonderful portrait of the kind of oversight that pleases the Lord Jesus Christ, the kind of administration that will allow a minister of Christ to hear "well done!" when the Chief Shepherd appears. Every leader's heart must beat with the passion to please the

Lord Jesus Christ—to manifest His heart and to lead according to His good pleasure.

The Apostle Peter gives us a very detailed portrait of a godly overseer in these verses. Look at what this apostle and first-century pastor had to say about our responsibility to *oversee*:

Recognize Christ's divine ownership.

This is the *"flock of God."* Peter unequivocally states that this flock belongs to God. Jesus is the purchaser of the church (Acts 20:28), the Head of the church (Ephesians 5:23), and the Chief Shepherd of the church (1 Peter 5:4). The pastor is the undershepherd. Don't ever lose sight of your true role. You are not the Lord of the church—Christ is. This is His body; these are His people; and you are appointed for a brief time to nurture their lives toward Him.

Feed the flock.

Peter's first admonition is to *"Feed the flock of God...."* We will study more closely this primary role of the pastor in part three of this book. This same command is used in conjunction with our command to be overseers in Acts 20:28.

This command is first a command to *study*—to prepare strong meals that will strengthen, nourish, and edify God's flock. Second, it is a command to preach and teach the truth. Outside of prayer, nothing you do in the pastorate is as vital and important as preparing and delivering the truth of God's Word from your pulpit.

Know the state of the flock.

Peter says that we're to take the *"oversight thereof...."* This means we are to assume spiritual responsibility for the direction, the growth, and the care of God's local church. We're to know the state of the flock, to be active in understanding and meeting its needs through the Word of God.

Knowing the state of the flock includes understanding the spiritual terrain—that is both the state of the culture in which the "sheep" live as well as an understanding of the spiritual health of individual church members. Proverbs 27:23 says, *"Be thou diligent to know the state of thy flocks, and look well to thy herds."*

A wise shepherd will know the sheep. Someone wisely said, "Shepherds smell like sheep." Nothing can replace the time you spend with your church family—loving them, teaching them, fellowshipping with them, and praying with them. Immerse yourself in their lives and know what they are going through.

Willingly accept responsibility.

Peter instructs us to take the oversight of God's flock *"not by constraint, but willingly…."* There could be the temptation to enter into this part of our office begrudgingly. Frankly, this overseeing role is where we get our hands dirty. Oversight requires time, sacrifice, and spiritual warfare. Oversight involves ministering and leading *outside* the pulpit; it is accepting responsibility for the direction of the church and the condition of the sheep.

> *Outside of prayer, nothing you do in the pastorate is as vital and important as preparing and delivering the truth of God's Word from your pulpit.*

This kind of oversight requires courage. It takes courage to face brutal facts, to require accountability, and to deal with the messy problems of ministry. It takes spiritual insight and dependence upon God to deal wisely and decisively with a failing employee or a struggling Christian.

When it comes to courageously taking oversight, I'm afraid many spiritual leaders feel like the character Linus in one of Charles Shultz's famous Charlie Brown comics. In a particular moment of transparency, Linus said to Charlie Brown, "No problem is so big or so complicated that it can't be run away from!" Often, we run from confrontation or from conflict. Yet, a loving shepherd (not an hireling) willingly enters into this type of brutal and often hostile kind of care-giving.

This kind of oversight also requires faith. I recently read this simple proverb, "Fear knocked, faith answered, and no one was there!" When we enter into fearful confrontations or step into a realm of ministry that we feel unprepared for—like a building project or a business meeting—we must step into this role with faith in Almighty God. He who called you will enable you! *"Faithful is he that calleth you, who also will do it"* (1 Thessalonians 5:24).

This kind of oversight requires action. Passionate leaders have a bias for action that is centered around shared goals. They don't sit around in endless meetings. They quickly identify what needs to be done to move the vision forward, and then they get to it.

This kind of oversight also requires the ability to strategize. As the flock grows, you will find the church needs a plan to care more effectively for the people that God adds to your sheepfold. The plan will need an effective strategy, a purposeful team, and a method to activate the plan. Just as a shepherd rotates pastures and plans ahead to protect and watch over the sheep, so a spiritual leader must think ahead, develop a plan, and lead that plan to execution.

Accomplishing this kind of oversight will involve carving out time to develop a strategy and a structure for adult classes, youth ministry, children's Sunday school, care groups, deacons training, visiting widows, and many other responsibilities of the local church body.

Serve with pure motives and servant-hearted readiness.

Peter says, *"not for filthy lucre, but of a ready mind...."* This challenge is to serve the church family with willing-hearted readiness—to be gladly available. Impure motives run "by the clock," but a shepherd-hearted spiritual leader never really goes off the clock! One who serves with the mind of Christ delights to be available for spiritual needs.

I'm not saying that a spiritual leader can never have personal or family time, but simply that a shepherd is available and glad to help when he is needed. The phrase *"a ready mind"* implies a sincere servant's heart. This is a joyful, happy kind of servant leader. One preacher said, "I have never met a contentious servant."

Live a life of integrity and humility.

Benjamin Franklin said, "A good conscience is a continual Christmas." As we have already seen, our oversight must flow from a life of truth—a godly example.

See again what Peter says in this passage: *"Neither as being lords over God's heritage, but being ensamples to the flock."* He goes on to say later in chapter 5 that we should be *"clothed with humility"* and that we should humble ourselves under the mighty hand of God. Again, God's Word challenges us in Acts 20:28 that we are first to *"take heed"* unto ourselves. Remember, leadership begins with *who we are*, not *what we do*.

The first challenge is in the area of humility—to not "lord over" God's flock. This phrase refers to being a ruler who wants to subjugate, control, or dominate, to demand his authority, or emphasize it frequently; and this trait is usually born out of both pride and insecurity because he feels a need to have control for reasons of ego or personal gratification. Power can be intoxicating, and we must remember that all power belongs to Jesus Christ. If you find yourself grasping for authority or having to repeatedly tell others who you are and how they should respond to you, check the root—something is awry in your approach to spiritual authority. God says we are not to lord over His flock or exercise dominion over it.

Integrity comes from the same word that we derive our English word *integrated*. It refers to the fact that your life should be one whole truth—not double or divided in any way. Our hearts and inner man should match up with what we say and how we behave. One preacher said, "Preach the gospel…and if necessary, use words."

A man of God must lead from a personal platform of moral, financial, and doctrinal integrity. Men fail in ministry primarily because of moral, financial, or doctrinal problems. If you want to finish your course with joy, commit to maintaining a life of integrity—a life integrated with the biblical principles of moral fidelity, financial propriety, and doctrinal purity!

Paul said in 2 Timothy 3:10, *"But thou hast fully known my doctrine, manner of life, purpose, faith, longsuffering, charity, patience."* His life was gladly an open book; it was cheerfully accountable and joyfully inspected by all (Acts 23:1).

The word *humility* also means *modest,* and the word-picture is that we are to be *"clothed"*—completely covered and totally wrapped in a spirit that lifts up Christ and decreases the emphasis on self. Charles H. Spurgeon said, "Humility is to make a right estimate of one's self."

We need leaders who rightly view themselves as unworthy, but called; humanly incapable, but spiritually empowered; undeserving, but desiring to serve. F.B. Meyer wrote, "The branch that bears the most fruit bows lowest to the ground."

Acts 20:28 states, *"Take heed therefore unto yourselves, and to all the flock, over the which the Holy Ghost hath made you overseers, to feed the church of God, which he hath purchased with his own blood."*

If God called you to lead, then He called you to *oversee.* Remember, God doesn't call the qualified, but He does qualify the called! Assume your role by God's grace, but do it with the right spirit and stay within bounds.

In review, Peter gives us three ways *not* to oversee followed by three ways to *rightly* oversee. Here are the boundaries for an overseeing leader:

Not out of constraint, but willingly—not because you must but because it is your delight.

Not for filthy lucre but with a ready mind—not for what you can get out of it, whether pay or personal pleasure, but with a delighted availability, ready to serve and give of yourself.

Not lording over God's heritage but being an ensample to the flock—not relishing or abusing your authority with a dominating spirit, but rather leading a life of integrity and humility. Let your authority be emphasized through your life more than through your words!

This undershepherd will be eternally rewarded when the Chief Shepherd appears: *"And when the chief Shepherd shall appear, ye shall receive a crown of glory that fadeth not away"* (1 Peter 5:4).

CHAPTER ELEVEN

THE ADMINISTRATIVE LEADER

In his book *Less is More Leadership*, Pastor Dale Burke wrote, "The pastor must spend time doing his best stuff, not just stuff." The *best stuff* you can do, as a spiritual leader, is to study the Word of God, pray, and prepare biblical messages for your church family. Nothing will help the church more than the time you spend in study and prayer.

The leader's role as an administrator is about enlisting, training, delegating, and working with a team of people who will carry out a multitude of details in ministry so that the spiritual leader can remain focused on the "best stuff"!

Any growing ministry will repeatedly come against a ceiling. In other words, the administrative structure will only grow to what it can handle. At that point, growth either stops, or the leader restructures and administrates to handle more growth.

Don't misunderstand, better administration won't *create* growth, only God can do that. Yet, effective administration *clears the way* for growth. It makes growth possible. Essentially, good administration helps us "get out of God's way." Consider this. If we're not effectively meeting the needs of the congregation God has already given to us, why would we expect Him to make it larger?

We will discuss church growth in a coming chapter, but effective administration is essential. God placed us into the ministry to *"set in order the things that are wanting…"* (Titus 1:5), and He is glorified and does greater things when we bring order from confusion. First Corinthians 14:33 says it this way, *"For God is not the author of confusion, but of peace, as in all churches of the saints."*

There are several aspects to ministry administration that I would like to highlight.

THE FIVE-FOLD PURPOSE OF ADMINISTRATION

The first question is *why* do we administrate? For what reason do we bring order to our responsibility of oversight? I believe there are five reasons that should be kept in mind.

1.   To glorify God

First Corinthians 10:31 tells us to do all to the glory of God. When you bring order from confusion in God's local church, you are giving Him glory; you are making Him look better before all men. Be sure that His preeminence is your highest goal in overseeing His church.

2.   To allow the pastor study time

Burke goes on in his book to give four kinds of time that pastors must have—rest time, results time, response time, and refocus time. Rest time focuses on physical, spiritual, and family renewal time. Results time occurs when a leader focuses on his primary responsibilities—including study and prayer. Response time occurs when a leader deals with all the other things that ministry requires—meetings, appointments, correspondence, and any other responses to the needs of people. Refocus time occurs when a leader reviews life and ministry and then makes any necessary adjustments.

In addition to glorifying God, the second greatest purpose of the pastor's administrative duties is to give him more time to study and pray.

A large percentage of every pastor's time must be allotted for prayer and study. That time is the best gift you could give your church. Nothing else will make your church family stronger and healthier. It is the Word of God that produces growth, and it is your study time that prepares for the delivery of that truth.

I believe you could trace nearly every major decision a Christian makes, to an altar where he responds to a message. And you can trace that message back to the study where a pastor met personally with God! When you are studying, you are doing that which most directly and most powerfully affects the hearts of people. Don't ever lose sight of that, and don't ever apologize for making this kind of time your first ministry commitment.

3. To allow the pastor leadership time

There is a difference between *leadership time* and *management time*. It is imperative that the spiritual leader appoint others to some of the management of the ministry so that he can focus on the leadership of ministry.

Dale Burke shares these principles in *Less is More Leadership*: Leaders focus on vision, but managers focus on organization. Leaders focus on what could be, but managers focus on what is. Leaders focus on aligning people, but managers focus on assigning people. Leaders focus on motivating people, but managers focus on controlling people. Every spiritual leader needs time to chart the course, time to crystallize the vision and to think through God's direction for the future. If you are burdened down with daily operational details, it's time to find someone else you can trust with those details. Delegate those things, and let God enlarge your heart toward a greater vision.

4. To meet the needs of the congregation

Acts 6:1–4 documents the first time in church history when administration was greatly needed. The needs of people were falling through the cracks. Widows were being neglected, and people were frustrated. The apostles held a meeting to determine what to do. Their solution was simple—

appoint some other godly men to "this business" so that they could remain focused on the ministry of the Word and of prayer.

Here is a perfect example of when and how the spiritual leader serves as an administrator. He oversees, appoints, trains, and then finally delegates some of the ministry to the congregation so that he can stay focused on "the main things"! There's no doubt about it, effective administration will result in the needs of your congregation being met more effectively.

5. To reach lost souls

Good local church administration allows everyone in leadership to have an appropriate amount of time to commit to soulwinning and reaching the lost.

THE PATTERN OF EFFECTIVE ADMINISTRATORS

What do good administrators do? What does this part of our job description look like? There are two primary functions of a good administrator. The first is to clearly see needs, and the second is to appoint the right people to meet those needs. That's a very simple way of saying it, but these really are the two key functions. The challenge is seeing the needs properly. Sometimes our blind spots hide the needs or we fail to see them for a variety of reasons—from willful neglect to distraction to a lack of discernment or spiritual insight. (Not to mention that our enemy is doing his best to hide them from us!)

Then, determining by God's grace the best approach to meeting those needs can be equally as daunting since it involves finding the right people, training them, delegating responsibilities to them, and then instituting the processes and structures in which they can function effectively. That makes "seeing the needs and meeting those needs" seem a bit more complex. Let's study more about these two functions.

Clearly see the needs.

This statement means that it is your responsibility to identify the needs and vulnerabilities in ministry as early as possible. It is often said, but so true, blind-sighted leaders are often blind-sided. You must ask the Lord for spiritual perception to detect vulnerability in its earliest stages.

The approach of many spiritual leaders is to ignore needs—to bury their heads in the sand for as long as possible, hoping that problems will simply disappear, or self-absorb. This just doesn't happen. Problems require solutions, and the sooner you see the problem, the sooner you can solve it.

Time doesn't make problems go away; it makes them grow bigger. You can either solve the problem now while it's manageable, or wait a long time and try to solve it later when it has grown. Neglect does not solve problems, it just makes them worse. Spirit-filled administrators discern the problems and resolve them while they are still hatching!

Appoint the right people to meet those needs.

Here is where a spiritual leader begins to involve co-laborers in the work of the ministry (not because of the size of the church). The heart of the leader yearns to reproduce leaders. A church of *any* size needs administration. Every ministry leader could use help visiting shut-ins, ministering to the sick, and handling the daily needs of people. Don't wait until you have a paid staff to develop an administrator's mentality. Start when your church is small or young.

> *Problems require solutions, and the sooner you see the problem, the sooner you can solve it.*

Begin right away looking for godly, servant-hearted people who can join you in the work. This will give others a chance to invest their lives into eternal efforts, and it will give you a chance to get more ministry done while you stay focused on study and prayer. Our first staff meetings during the early days of ministry were with volunteer secretaries. Today, some of these dear ladies still serve faithfully on our staff.

I encourage you to consider these simple points with regard to involving people.

First, start by giving someone a short term project. This could be helping with an event or a time-sensitive need. It will give you a chance to work with them and see how they respond.

Second, assign jobs without titles. Give someone a job long before you give him a title. Let the title be a product of the success of that person in that role; let it be earned not assumed.

Third, take him soulwinning with you. Doing so will give you a chance to see if this person has a heart for souls. It will also give you some bonding and mentoring time in sharing your heart for ministry. Use this time to train and equip.

Fourth, appoint him to responsibility. Write out a clear job description of what is required and what is expected. Give this co-laborer a clear picture of what success in this area looks like.

Fifth, empower him to lead. At this point, be willing to step aside and let this person take leadership. Let others see him leading and let others know that you trust his leadership. Allow great freedom within set boundaries. Don't ever completely separate yourself from oversight, but stay in touch behind the scenes through meetings, weekly reports, predetermined checkpoints, and clearly established boundaries.

Finally, train the young converts of the church to get involved. Keep a heart to involve new members and new Christians. Over time, your local church teams can become cliques—the same people doing the same things for many years. In many respects this faithfulness is a great thing, but it can also make it difficult for a new member to get involved. New members need to find it easy to get involved and they need to know they are needed. If they don't sense a need in your church, they will find a church where they are needed. Keep looking for ways to involve new members and new Christians and continually partner them with the mature Christians who already serve in ministry. Don't let your church ever become a place where it is difficult to find a place to serve God.

The sign of a great leader is finding the right place for people. Placing the right people into the right positions equals the multiplication of ministry.

I warn you, as you begin this process, a large part of your administrative job will be about helping to strengthen relationships on your teams. Take responsibility for making relationships work and become good at resolving inter-relational problems between good people. Help them to continually see the big picture of what we can accomplish for God if we continue loving each other and serving with pure hearts.

A good word for this kind of administration is *mobilization* which simply means "to prepare and organize troops for active service." The key to leading and still "having a life" is mobilization.

Nineteenth century businessman and steel magnate, Andrew Carnegie, wrote his own epitaph. It reads, "Here lies a man who knew how to enlist in his service better men than himself."

DELEGATION IN ADMINISTRATION

Many spiritual leaders struggle with delegation. It's not that we love performing the details of the work, but rather that we do not want to give away something we love. We love to visit the shut-ins. We truly care about the widows. We long to be in every class, be at every function, and be a part of every person's life. This is the natural heart of a minister. Beyond this, some leaders struggle with giving away responsibility for more carnal reasons. I believe there are four reasons worthy of our consideration and heart inspection. You see, failure to delegate ultimately hurts the ministry. If you do not grow in administration, your church will only grow as far as you alone can take it.

Four reasons we fail to delegate even when it hurts the success of the ministry:

1. **Ego**—No one can do it better than I can. Ken Blanchard said, "Feedback is the breakfast of champions, but some people's ego can't handle it."

2. **Insecurity**—If someone does it better than I do it, I will look bad. Can you handle someone doing something better than you? We should hope our delegation results in improvement. Be willing to enlist people who can take a part of ministry farther than you can.

3. **Naivete**—This attitude says, "I don't need anyone else." This is very short-sighted and indicative of a man who really does not have a very large vision for ministry.

4. **Temperament**—Working with others is too complicated. Ministry just has no place for this temperament—for in truth, ministry is people work!

If you sense a failure to delegate due to one of these factors, ask the Lord to grow you and mature your leadership style. Delegation is the responsibility of the leader; it is part of your job description!

The characteristics of the right co-laborer

What kind of person should you look for as you are appointing men to God's business? Here are the qualities I believe God blesses:

Integrity—a pure, godly life of maturity. This should be someone who obviously has the filling of the Holy Spirit (Acts 6).

Intelligence—at least the basic competence to know or to learn the ministry functions you are delegating. I like what one leader said, "The only job security you have today is your commitment to continuous personal improvement."

Intensity—a willingness to bear a burden, to work hard, to intervene, and to get into action. In his book *The Heart of a Leader*, Ken Blanchard wrote, "There is a difference between interest and commitment. When you are interested in something, you do it only when it is convenient. When you are committed to something, you accept no excuses. Do not equip people who are merely interested; equip those who are committed. The Kamikaze pilot who was able to fly fifty missions was involved but never committed."

A person with intensity will truly be committed and will care about the work. Ken Blanchard put a lack of intensity this way, "*Trying* is just a noisy way of not doing something."

Intuition—an instinctive understanding of the heart. Paul wrote of this in reference to young Timothy in Philippians 2:19–21. Sadly, when Paul looked for a man who shared his heart for God's people, he could only find one at the time—Timothy. *"For I have no man likeminded, who will naturally care for your state. For all seek their own, not the things which are Jesus Christ's"* (Philippians 2:20–21).

Your co-laborers must be men who understand your vision and are willing to express your heart in ministry. There should be no room on your team for a renegade or someone with his own personal agenda.

A SUGGESTED PROCESS OF WEEKLY ADMINISTRATION

In closing this chapter, allow me to give you a three-step process that you should exercise every week in your administrative role:

1. Take oversight.

Set aside some time every week to review your entire ministry. Have good peripheral vision, and write down reminders constantly. Those reminders and notes become the agendas of team meetings or memos. Allow the Holy Spirit to place the details on your heart and follow through on these details tenaciously.

Create report forms for each area of ministry and ask your team leaders—both paid and volunteer—to fill out these forms each week. Include these in your weekly ministry review. Remember, you *get* from people what you *expect* from people—and you must *inspect* what you *expect*. Establish Christian service reports for all of your paid and volunteer staff and for your deacons, and then review these reports personally.

2. Prioritize the work.

During your weekly oversight review, you should gather all of the notes you've taken, all of the needs you've been made aware of, all of the reports, and all of the impending events and projects. Then follow this formula.

Accumulation—I learn to stop all unnecessary tasks before they even enter into my work stream.

Admission—I learn how to admit legitimate tasks and to reject what is unnecessary.

Action—I take action on those things I admitted as necessary by priority.

Assessment—I determine what areas or projects need follow-up.

This review will help you get control of every pertinent item that needs follow-up. Now you are ready to enter into meetings with your team members.

3. Meet with leaders.

Do you have a regular staff meeting, either with paid or volunteer staff or both? Once you have appointed people to the Lord's work, it is vital that you meet with them for ongoing training, encouragement, celebration, and edification. In these meetings you communicate vision, share requests, solve problems, and rejoice in blessings. It is vital that you have regular meetings for encouragement and accountability. A good leader is always preparing for his next staff meeting. Below is a short formula for a successful team meeting:

- Meet weekly.
- Talk informally.
- Share burdens and prayer requests.
- Pray.
- Talk through your prepared agenda.
- Allow others to raise questions or issues.
- Close in prayer.

Remember, effective administration should primarily accomplish two things. It should give the pastor more time for study and prayer, and it should meet the needs of the church family more effectively. These two results will ultimately clear the way for growth, both spiritual and numerical.

God delights to work in a church where things are "set in order." He will not find glory in confusion or chaos. Take a moment, review this chapter, and ask the Lord to make you an effective administrator.

CHAPTER TWELVE

PREPARING THE CHURCH FOR GROWTH

When the Lord led my family to Lancaster in 1986, it was to take the pastorate of a very small church. In fact, there were twelve voting members the night the church called us. Though the church had been in existence prior to our arrival, the membership had dwindled, the church building was in foreclosure, and the future was bleak. For all intents and purposes, we were starting over. The Lord had held together a small remnant of faithful, mature Christians, and within just a few months of taking the pastorate, the Lord began to greatly bless our soulwinning and discipleship efforts. You might say Lancaster Baptist Church became a new church.

My wife and I completely immersed ourselves, for all practical purposes, in planting and establishing a New Testament church. There was no staff, no paycheck, no beautiful campus, and no welcoming committee when we pulled into town. There were simply a few God-loving people, a run down building, and a dream that God would do something great. And He has!

When I look back on those years I recall the sacrifice, the long hours, the loneliness, and the trials. It seemed Satan unleashed his entire arsenal on us within just the first few days—the church was broken into, our new sign destroyed, and it seemed every bank and business were enemies of our church because it had a bad credit history. The first few weeks we lived in a very small apartment in a run down part of town. Regularly there were gun shots, drug deals, and vagrants. One lady literally came into our front doorway and had a seizure in front of my wife. It was clear to both of us that the powers of darkness were not happy that a new pastor had moved to town.

Through all the trials, God gave His grace and guidance for this young pastor and his family. We had invested our life savings into the move and into fixing up the church as best we could. We knew no one, we had nothing, and we were utterly dependent upon the provision and power of God. While our entire ministry journey has been of faith, those early faith experiences have never left me. I believe those experiences are the reason God has given me a love for pastors, church planters, and young families who are launching out in faith.

In retrospect, I clearly see that God blessed our proper priorities. The result was church growth. We could not do all that we wanted. Our dreams were certainly bigger than our resources. We longed to see God do a great work, and little did we know the ways He planned to exceed all of our expectations. In these few pages, I would like to share with you what I believe positioned our church for God's blessings.

Believe it or not, though our church has grown by an average of two hundred per year for twenty-two years, we have never had a growth goal. Growth is not our goal—God is our goal. We have not emphasized growth; we have emphasized obedience. We've never set an attendance goal; we've set "work goals." We've always left the results up to God.

If you desire to prepare your church for growth, you must also prepare yourself for the cost of growth. You must be willing to pay the price—to accept the burdens as well as the blessings. And you must prepare your church. You must put right priorities in place, and God will do the rest. The following are the priorities that allowed God to grow our church. I believe He will bless them in yours as well.

PRIORITY 1—A PURE HEART IN MINISTRY

Matthew 5:8 teaches us that the key to *"seeing God"* is having a pure heart. In essence, a pure heart leads to clear vision and a sincere church. A pure heart sees God's leading and follows it. It is not distracted by impure motives, personal agenda, pride, or ego. It is not blinded by hidden sin, past hurts, or unresolved offenses. Seek to have a pure heart personally and in ministry, and lead your church to have a pure heart. Having a pure heart is one of the only ways your church family will ever share your vision—they must also *"see God."*

PRIORITY 2—A TEACHABLE SPIRIT IN LEADERSHIP

Determine that you will have a teachable spirit, and lead your church to have one also. In many ways your church family will capture all of these qualities as they see them in you. If you try to "be somebody" your insecurity will be obvious, and it will greatly limit your ministry. Jesus repudiates status-seeking. A teachable spirit requires a sincere transparency. Have a spirit that admits you do not know it all, but you are willing to learn.

Your church family will not expect you to know everything, and they will readily connect with and be drawn to a transparency that is willing to express itself in humble sincerity. People like to follow a transparent leader—someone who can identify with their struggles and burdens. (Remember that Jesus was touched with the feeling of our infirmities [Hebrews 4:15].)

From the earliest days of ministry, to the present day I have taught our church that "a growing church is always in transition." Our church family understands that we are growing and going forward together. We are learning God's will day by day and striving together for the faith.

This spirit should also cause you to stay connected to those from whom you can learn. Develop healthy mentoring relationships with those who can sharpen and help you. Don't be too proud to ask for help, get counsel, and be developed by others. No matter how long you lead, don't ever lose that spirit!

PRIORITY 3—A CLEAR PURPOSE AS A CHURCH

During the early years of our church, the Lord led me to write a purpose statement and to share it with the church. I wrote about it in detail in *Order in the Church.* I urge you to get alone with God, articulate a purpose that reflects God's mandate for your church, and then begin to live it and teach it to your church family. Our purpose statement has developed to be more specific over the years, but it has been put consistently before our church family, and they have truly accepted ownership of it. Every ministry and every event flows somehow from this purpose. Remember, it is much more than an outline, it is an all-encompassing philosophy of ministry.

The purpose of Lancaster Baptist Church is summed up in five words—inspire, include, instruct, involve, impact. Our purpose statement reads: *The purpose of Lancaster Baptist Church is to inspire people to develop a heart for God* (beginning with salvation and then continuing through preaching, music, and worship), *to include them into a loving church family* (involving baptism, membership, new members brunches, and every other effort to assimilate new Christians into our family), *to instruct people from the Word of God* (involving preaching and teaching and discipleship in many different settings for all ages), *to involve them in ministry* (enlisting, training, and empowering our church family to serve the Lord), *and to impact the Antelope Valley and the regions beyond with the Gospel of Christ* (including every soulwinning and outreach opportunity, as well as missions efforts).

The sooner you can articulate and teach a purpose, the sooner your church will unite and mobilize around it—*"striving together for the faith of the gospel"* (Philippians 1:27).

PRIORITY 4—A MENTORING, SERVING ENVIRONMENT

Pastor, you are always teaching, and you are always an example. Nothing you do goes unnoticed. Nothing you say falls on unhearing ears. You are always influencing and training. For this reason, you must always be the example and never the exception! Some spiritual leaders are caught up in their mystique—their persona or image. They seem to be aloof, untouchable, and unapproachable. I'd like to shout, "WRONG!" This is not a shepherd's heart. Be real, be accessible, and be a godly influence in personal and direct ways. Warren Wiersbe said, "Some preachers are invisible all week and incomprehensible on Sunday!"

Establish the habit of mentoring new Christian men in prayer, in Bible study, in leading their families, in soulwinning, and in serving the Lord. Nothing you do will build the core of your church family more surely, and you will find that this process is an ongoing one.

For example, I often invite new men to join me for men's prayer each Saturday evening. This meeting provides a good mentoring opportunity. Get into the trenches of mentoring and discipleship. Disciples are made, not born, and mentoring happens because of availability, hospitality, and approachability. May God help you to start this habit now, and may you never stop!

PRIORITY 5—A DISTINCTIVE POSITION ESTABLISHED

Convictions are the spark plugs that fire the engine of the local church. Many spiritual leaders struggle to take a loving, distinctive stand in fear of losing people. I believe far more people leave the church *in search of* convictions than leave *because of* them! You may have people who threaten you or try to get you to compromise, but most Christians are expecting you to stand for something. Do not be afraid to define a distinctive position, but do it with a loving spirit and a compassionate heart. Articulate it, teach it, explain it, and support it biblically. Even those who disagree will at least respect your kind heart and clear biblical direction.

Make sure your church understands your doctrinal, musical, and biblical distinctiveness. With younger Christians you will have to teach these things biblically, repeat them frequently, and then patiently nurture people along. In time young believers will come to your convictions if they are drawn there with compassion.

PRIORITY 6—A RELEVANT, UNDERSTANDABLE APPROACH WITH PEOPLE

Relevance speaks of one's ability to understand. In other words, you want to be understood by those to whom you preach and minister. This word scares some Christians because it has been so closely connected to compromise, but let me challenge your thinking for a moment.

When you teach five-year-olds, do you teach or preach differently than you would to mature adults? Of course you teach the same truth, but deliver it differently. Second question: If you were a missionary, would you learn the language of the people you were trying to reach? Of course! Same truth, different language. This is relevance!

Understandable ministry is vitally needed. Relevance does not mean capitulating to culture; Christ is supreme over culture. The principles of *distinctiveness* and *relevance* do not compete. Relevance simply involves having an approach that allows people to grow to your distinctive position—understanding that *connection* precedes *conviction*!

Relevance simply acknowledges that the people I'm reaching may not speak the same cultural, social, and relational language I do! They may not understand biblical truth. Relevance does not compromise truth; it merely makes it understandable and applicable to a different mind set! For the record, the only alternative to *relevant* ministry is *irrelevant* ministry—and the Gospel is always relevant!

PRIORITY 7—A COMMITMENT TO QUALITY MINISTRY

I've talked and prayed with more than a few leaders who bemoan what they cannot do, what they do not have, and where they cannot go regarding a quality of ministry. Quality isn't necessarily having high-tech equipment, new buildings, the best fixtures, and the newest communication tools. Quality is doing the very best with what you have, with whatever resources and opportunities that God has given you. I've seen some ministries with much polish that still do not have quality. I've also seen some ministries with very little—not much more than a pulpit and a pastor—who have very high quality ministry! Choose to steward God's resources and opportunities with the highest of standards because you desire quality ministry.

Are you expending more emotion on what you cannot do, or on doing the very best with what you have? When we arrived in Lancaster, we had very little, but we did the best we could by God's grace. We established a goal for quality and a standard of excellence toward which we continue to strive. When we had to settle for second, third, or fourth best, we smiled and thanked God for His provision, and we proceeded to do it the very best we could.

Focus on developing quality first in your verbal communication, then in written communication, and finally in all non-verbal communication including the buildings, grounds, and environments. Mediocrity breeds indifference, but quality attracts!

PRIORITY 8—AN EQUIPPING MIND-SET

Early in the life of our church, we began holding volunteer staff meetings, weekly workers meetings, and regular training times. These were exciting and designed specifically to equip God's people for God's service. We began immediately training people how to win souls, how to teach classes, how to usher, and how to welcome visitors.

Every Sunday night for many years, twenty-five minutes prior to the evening service, I held a meeting called "Visit with the Pastor." This was open for the whole church family, and most attended (if only to get a good seat for the evening service). During this time I trained our church family on everything from how to treat an usher to how to sing in church to how to respect guest pastors and missionaries when they visited. The topics covered a wide range of church life and helped establish the behavior, the spirit, and the environment that still exists today.

> *Mediocrity breeds indifference, but quality attracts!*

In all you do, think of how to reproduce leadership and how to develop others to lead in God's work. Help people discover their spiritual gifts and then use those gifts for God's glory. There is a unique synergy that comes with an appreciation and development of each person's unique gifts. Your church family will appreciate being equipped, and your church will begin to thrive with a serving spirit!

PRIORITY 9—A PROBLEM-SOLVING SPIRIT

All churches experience problems. From a distance, we tend to look at another's ministry and think it's problem-free. I just want to encourage you—there is no such ministry anywhere on the planet! Ministries have problems, and so God gives us spiritual leaders to set in order the things that are wanting. You might say one of your titles is "problem solver." You might as well accept the fact that problems come and that God commissions you to deal with them.

Problems should be approached prayerfully and in a timely manner, and they must be handled scripturally. Be careful to not overreact. But at the same time, be careful not to ignore problems. No one enjoys confrontation, but everyone benefits from the courageous leader who spiritually will confront for the purpose of resolution. Remember, your mission is to resolve, not merely to police or pass judgment on others. People never like to be confronted, but afterward many are grateful for reconciliation.

Problem solving involves compassionate confrontation from a shepherd's heart. We will talk about this further in another chapter, but I believe that *structuring ministry* and *confronting problems* are two of the greatest weaknesses of spiritual leaders in ministry today. If you can learn these skills early in the life of your church, you will grow a healthier church!

PRIORITY 10—A FOCUSED HEART AND LIFE

There is a great cost to leading a growing church. Are you willing to pay that price? Preparing the church for growth will mean that you are willing to take risks, lose friends, get out of your comfort zone, and sacrifice. You must be willing to face harsh criticism. Vision always attracts critics. You must be willing to be chastened, molded, stretched, and burdened. Are you sure you want this life? If you do, then you must endure, and you must fix your eyes and heart upon your Saviour.

Hebrews 12 admonishes us to keep our eyes fixed on the Lord. From your first day in ministry to your last, your enemy will relentlessly try to distract you, discourage you, and destroy you. Focus your vision steadfastly upon your Lord, your family, and your calling—and never look back.

You will often wonder what the Lord is doing, where He is leading, and whether He remembers who you are. You will be tempted to look to other places. You'll compare yourself and your church to other churches and pastors. You could become discontented, or sidetracked by politics and by persons who are irrelevant to your local church. Satan will do everything he can to keep your church from growing and to keep you from leading well.

Keep your focus clear and your heart faithful. God will greatly bless your steadfastness.

What impact did these priorities have upon our church? They positioned us to grow! They helped us "get out of God's way." They put in place the heart, the structure, and the spirit that God blessed with new Christians and new members. He is still blessing this structure today.

I pray that these priorities become real in your church. As of this writing, they have been in place in our church for twenty-two years, and God has greatly blessed them. I believe they are what makes our church a very special, God-honoring place—a place that is growing for His glory!

CHAPTER THIRTEEN

LEADING THROUGH DIFFERENT STAGES OF GROWTH

Two little boys were playing with their pet turtles when one accidentally cut the head off of his. The headless turtle was still moving around, so they asked a neighbor boy if it was dead. The boy replied, "Oh, he's dead; he just don't know it yet!"

Sadly, that story reminds me of a lot of churches. They've lost their first love, and they're dead without even knowing it. Every statistic that can be found about church growth seems to indicate that churches are in a great decline in our culture. Very few churches experience growth, and even fewer experience healthy growth—actual growth from reaching lost souls for Christ.

If you get nothing else from this book, get this. God wants to bless, grow, and use your local church! He is still building His church. The local church is still His blood-bought institution for His work in the world of men. He still changes lives and impacts the world through the local, New Testament Church. In the last chapter we talked about preparing for growth, and in this chapter we will discuss leading through growth.

One preacher said, "Anything done in our own strength will fail miserably, or succeed even more miserably." God desires to work in spite of us! He blesses His plan. He blesses obedience to His Word. When He blesses your church with growth, your leadership responsibilities will greatly change and increase. You will be stretched, and you will have to employ careful strategy and understanding.

Christian pollster, George Barna, has recently written that the local church doesn't work and has encouraged a "revolution" of Christians to leave the church for home-based Bible study. I vehemently disagree with his assessment because I believe he's studying the wrong kinds of churches. While I do not endorse his present philosophy, some years ago he wrote a book on church ministry entitled, *A Fish Out of Water*. In that book he described six phases of organizational growth. These phase designations helped me at a very critical season of growth. I believe it is helpful for spiritual leaders to understand how to lead through these phases. Let's look at them briefly. I will use Barna's terms for phase development and then share some personal thoughts for navigating through these times of organizational growth.

PHASE 1—CONCEPTION

Conception is when a pastor is planting or re-establishing a church. During this phase the pastor is wearing multiple hats—grasping a vision, preaching the Word, and juggling every part of ministry. He's sort of a "jack of all trades."

He is laboring to turn energy and ideas into tangible ministry, but is often up against a wall for lack of resources. Vision is plenteous, but the resources to realize the vision are few! This task can be frustrating and distressing. Can you identify with having bigger dreams than you could possibly accomplish at the present time?

What is needed during this phase? First, clear priorities and great patience and persistence. You must stay focused on the priorities we studied in the last chapter and remain persistent in the work and patient for God's timing. Giving birth to a church takes great effort and involves great pains as well as blessings.

PHASE 2—INFANCY

Infants require sustenance and physical production. They sleep much of the day because their bodies are busy reproducing cells and structure. In the same way, during the infancy of a new church, there is much emphasis on production and sustenance. You will sense the need to reach people and to teach them simply so the church can become self-sustaining. During these days you hope the church will someday be able to afford to pay you, hire a staff, and expand ministry—but you'll be happy just to pay the light bill!

This phase involves an enormous level of personal sacrifice as your dreaming shifts to laboring. Your team will be skeletal as the church will not be able to afford a large staff yet. You might lose sight of your vision because of the size of the burden.

During this phase the pastor and his small team are more conscious of productivity than policies, roles, or systems. In fact, there is very little in the way of systems or structure, and very little in the way of evaluation. All of the focus is on the future and getting there as quickly as possible.

PHASE 3—EXPANSION

By this time, the church has grown to sustain the pastor and a staff. Focus shifts from attendance growth to quality ministry. In other words, you worry less if anyone will show up on Sunday, and you start to consider more seriously what they receive when they do!

At this point the church will start responding to opportunities rather than creating them. In other words, in the early days, you tried to think up things to place on the calendar, but during this time you start having to remove them just to catch your breath.

Also during this time the church leadership will be used to its utmost capacity, and the pastor will need to delegate some authority and responsibility. The pastor becomes more of a team leader/builder and the church starts to need more operational leadership—leaders who can help standardize policies, procedures, systems, and structure.

The key at this point is to find, recruit, and mentor co-laborers, both paid and volunteer. The pastor and other leaders will be under more pressure than ever and will sense the need to grow in leadership ability. The team of church leaders will also grow, but not all of them will be prepared for the pressure involved. They too will be required to grow personally and experience discomfort for the sake of the ministry. Your co-laborers must be willing to pay the price at this point.

PHASE 4—BALANCE

Balance is where every church should desire to grow and remain. In this phase, growth continues at a reasonable pace, and the systems put in place earlier now help and support the vision effectively. During this time, productivity and performance are above average for the entire church family and staff. The church has embraced the vision and the values, and the people are laboring together with unity, purpose, and balance. Each team member understands his role and appreciates the rest of the team.

In this phase, new ministry leaders (often younger) are in continual training. Assessments and evaluations are constantly made. Leaders spend time responding to current trends as well as anticipating future needs.

Anything done in our own strength will fail miserably, or succeed even more miserably.

One side note: As the ministry grows during this time some key players may no longer feel needed. Change tends to threaten our security. As job functions transition, some people will lose heart. Unfortunately you will not be able to take everyone to the next level with you. You should want to and try to, but some will choose not to make the journey.

During this time, the vision and purpose are central to all that is happening, and the systems and structure facilitate consistency and stability throughout the ministry.

PHASE 5—STAGNATION

This is when a ministry becomes comfortable, complacent, fat, lazy, and loses vision. The vision is still real, but the passion is lacking. The pastor and church stop taking risks. They stop building, dreaming, and pressing forward with intensity. The church leaders become caretakers, and the most listened-to individuals are the accountants and operation-minded leaders. At this point, the pastor and leaders have become defensive of turf and have started trying to protect what exists rather than claiming new ground by God's grace.

Churches in this phase need a fresh vision and strategy from a strong hearted pastor who can bring people together. They need to see beyond the petty power struggles and to be revived by the Spirit of God.

PHASE 6—DISABILITY

At this point, the original vision is a distant memory. Often the founding pastor is gone as well. The organization is all but dead and has lost its purpose and focus.

A church at this point needs a strategic, energetic pastor to cast new vision, give birth to new life, and essentially return the church to the expansion and balance phases.

A growing church will pass through most of these phases. The first four are healthy and normal. The last two are dangerous and must be avoided. Where is your church?

Ask God to help you grow steadily and healthily through the first four, and then ask Him to give you wisdom in avoiding the last two. If you lead in a church that is already in one of the last two phases, then seek the heart of God for fresh vision, renewed energy, and a passion to start over for His glory!

CHAPTER FOURTEEN

LEADING THE CHURCH IN BIBLICAL STEWARDSHIP

A southern preacher was passionately preaching to his church with great fervor about moving forward. At one point in his message, he began to build his intensity, trying to share his passion and heart for God's vision. With a southern drawl, in long emphasized tones, he declared, "I believe the Lord wants this church to walk!"

With that, a man on the front row nodded in agreement and loudly replied, "Yes, Lord, let it walk...let it *walk*!"

With greater volume the preacher continued, "I believe the Lord wants this church to *run*!"

Again the man on the front row responded with strong agreement, "Yes, Lord, let it run...let it run!"

Building yet again in excitement, the preacher shouted, "I believe the Lord wants this church to *fly*!"

And yet again with strong emotion the man on the front row shouted, "Yes, Lord, let it fly...let it fly!"

At this point, the preacher strengthened his tone and stated, "Now, it's going to take money to let this church fly!"

Suddenly the man on the front row softly responded, "Let it walk, Preacher...let it walk...."

This comical example reminds us that giving and stewardship are the most sensitive topics a spiritual leader can address with his congregation. In fact, one of the most difficult responsibilities you will face is helping people understand God's plan for financial stewardship.

A good shepherd doesn't *drive* sheep; he *leads* them. In the same way, a godly spiritual leader doesn't *drive* God's people into obedience; he *leads* them there. Never is this more true than when it comes to financial stewardship.

I am placing this chapter in this book for a few simple reasons. First, helping Christians grow in this area is as much a part of the ministry as anything else. Second, you will not be an effective leader if you do not help your church grow in faith regarding giving. Third, I believe there is a right way and a wrong way to address this subject. In these pages I would like to share some biblical perspective on a sensitive responsibility.

God says, *"But this I say, He which soweth sparingly shall reap also sparingly; and he which soweth bountifully shall reap also bountifully. Every man according as he purposeth in his heart, so let him give; not grudgingly, or of necessity: for God loveth a cheerful giver"* (2 Corinthians 9:6–7).

Leading your church in financial stewardship must be approached with a pure heart, sincere motives, and holy determination. Consider four aspects of leading your church in biblical stewardship.

UNDERSTAND THE BIBLICAL PURPOSE FOR TEACHING ON GIVING

The first question is "why should we lead our church in stewardship?" For what purpose do we broach the money issue? Consider these purposes:

1. Obedience to Scripture

There is no better reason to teach on stewardship! This is not only a major theme of the Bible, it was also a major theme of Jesus' earthly ministry. If for no other reason, we should approach this subject with courage because it is biblical. Never apologize for preaching or teaching the Bible!

In addition, obeying God in this matter positions us for His blessing. God honors faithful obedience, and challenging people to obey in this area ultimately helps *them*.

2.   Spiritual maturity for believers

Christians remain immature in their faith until they learn to trust God with their finances. *"For where your treasure is, there will your heart be also"* (Matthew 6:21). If you desire to help Christians mature, then teach about giving.

3.   Salvation of lost souls

Ministry that reaches the lost requires financial sustenance. When we teach and preach about stewardship, we are directly impacting the church's ability to reach the lost.

4.   Glory to the Lord Jesus

When Christians trust the Lord financially and churches give sacrificially, God is glorified.

5.   Fulfillment of godly vision

Someone said, "Dream no small dreams, for they stir not the hearts of men!" When you lead your church in this area, you are pressing forward to accomplish God's vision. Vision often attracts critics, but it attracts visionary Christians as well.

Look at these purposes again. What a high call. Woe be to the spiritual leader who avoids such powerful, faith-building preaching and teaching.

It was a great day in my ministry when I accepted the truth that preaching about giving was actually of help to people. How can a leader go wrong aligning the flock in obedience to the Shepherd? When Christians obey God in this area they position themselves for His best. I would never want to withhold that kind of joy from our church family.

EMPLOY A BIBLICAL PHILOSOPHY FOR CHALLENGING GOD'S PEOPLE

I believe the single most important factor about your church stewardship is that it be biblical. People may take issue with your personality, your delivery style, or your "tactics," but they cannot take issue with God's Word. His Word is so clear on this subject and so powerful that it truly does change hearts when presented as it is!

God's Word gives us essentially five core motivations—five heart-based reasons we should honor God through giving. As you lead your church and motivate people, focus on motivating them biblically from the heart.

Motivate by the love of God.

Second Corinthians 8:8 challenges to *"prove the sincerity of your love"* through giving. Make sure you are compelling God's people to express their sincere love to Him.

Motivate by the grace of God.

In reference to giving, 2 Corinthians 8:7 teaches that we should *"abound in this grace also."* In other words, God's grace should motivate us, move us to action, and enable us to give; and we should give in response to God's grace in our hearts. God's grace creates a joyful disposition toward the privilege of giving to our Lord.

Motivate by the Word of God.

God's Word is replete with examples of grace-giving, and His Word works in hearts. Don't use guilt, pressure, or manipulation; simply share God's Word with power and sincerity. There is no greater authority from which to speak. Romans 10:17 says, *"So then faith cometh by hearing, and hearing by the word of God."*

Motivate through the people of God.

"Moreover, brethren, we do you to wit of the grace of God bestowed on the churches of Macedonia; How that in a great trial of affliction the abundance

of their joy and their deep poverty abounded unto the riches of their liberality" (2 Corinthians 8:1–2). Do you see what the apostle was doing in this passage? He was using one church's example to motivate another. He was encouraging one group with the testimony of another.

As you motivate your church, use the stories, testimonies, and the faithful lives of other godly Christians. Let new Christians see that God really *does* bless and provide for those who are obedient. Personal testimonies can be powerful when we need to encourage others to give.

Motivate toward personal involvement.

"And this they did, not as we hoped, but first gave their own selves to the Lord, and unto us by the will of God" (2 Corinthians 8:5). Help your church family understand that all financial stewardship flows first from a heart surrendered to the Lord. This is an individual heart condition with God that overflows into the offering plate. Help people see that they are not giving "to the church." They are investing into eternal values, giving to the Lord *through* the church!

ESTABLISH EFFECTIVE COMMUNICATION

One of the greatest tools for involving people in giving is *effective communication*. The better you are at communicating the needs, the principles, and the vision, the more God's people will rise to the challenge.

Over the years we have labored diligently to communicate wisely and strategically to our church family in these matters. Here are a few thoughts.

Communicate godly vision.

Lead the church in giving to well-defined causes. Explain where the church is headed, what the outcome will be, and how you believe God will bless. Make sure the church family understands what they are giving to and why. Explain the project, show pictures, and share your heart.

Communicate in printed form.

Use giving envelopes with easily understood offering types; give positive news through quarterly reports or letters; and use seasonal brochures to communicate special needs or projects.

Communicate life transformation.

Use video, testimonies, and personal stories to help your church see the lives that are being changed through their faithful offerings. Highlight ministries that people wouldn't normally see. Share positive news frequently. People love to give to a winning cause and they need to see the eternal fruit of their investment!

Communicate integrity and approachability.

Put in place careful financial procedures, annual reviews from outside firms, and a high level of accountability. Then tell the church family about it. Make sure everybody knows that God's money is carefully and strategically stewarded. Many years ago we created a seven-point written financial policy and it is delivered to every new member in a welcome packet. We want every church member to know that their offerings are handled with the highest integrity.

The Lancaster Baptist Church Financial Policy

(As adopted from Scripture)

1. *We acknowledge that all that we have, God owns.* We believe that everything that is good on the earth is from God and that we are merely the stewards of God's possessions (James 1:17).

2. *We will trust God knowing that He will supply all of our needs.* We acknowledge that God leads us and provides all that we need to achieve His objectives (Matthew 6:31–33).

3. *We will teach and model scriptural giving, knowing that God will multiply* (Malachi 3:5–12).

4. *We will obey God's command to send missionaries throughout the world.* We will not allow missions giving to be decreased in order to support other ongoing ministries at home (Acts 1:8).

5. *We will be good managers, believing that God is the owner and that He will reward our faithfulness* (Matthew 25:14–30). Faithfulness in managing worldly wealth brings a spiritual reward (Luke 16:11).

    • We will keep clear and accurate financial records of all ministries which will be maintained daily by our accounting staff, reviewed monthly by our deacons and audited or reviewed annually by a competent, independent, certified public accountant.

    • We will provide an annual church report to our members and welcome questions throughout the year.

    • We will only purchase goods and services when we know we can pay the bills within the agreed upon terms.

    • We will only borrow money when the means to pay is certain (either through analysis of regular giving or pledged collateral, or both).

6. *We will endeavor to learn contentment as this is God's will for us.* We believe the Scriptures tell us to be content with little or much and to give God thanks in all things (Philippians 4:11–15).

7. *We will in all things seek to glorify Christ in His church* (Colossians 1:15–19).

PLAN SEASONS OF GIVING AND AVOID URGENCY

Don't forget that we are to preach and teach the whole counsel of God. *"For I have not shunned to declare unto you all the counsel of God"* (Acts 20:27).

I would caution you not to teach or preach in reaction to a situation, but be prayerful and predetermined. Often spiritual leaders become urgency-driven in their approach to giving—speaking of it too often, preaching on it spontaneously as financial needs arise, or even resorting to frequent, manipulative, or negative pressure. People will respond temporarily to emotional pleas and urgent needs, but eventually they will lose respect for the leader who delivers them too frequently. When people give out of guilt or pressure, they are not giving from biblical hearts.

I urge you not to fall into this trap. When every bill and every offering is an emergency, you are broadcasting a failure of leadership on your part, not a failure of generosity on the church's part. This approach will ultimately stifle people's motivation to give, because they will eventually see through it and stop responding to unbiblical leadership or manipulative, emotional tactics. This approach causes your church family to feel that you are not being a good steward as the leader!

We have not created an environment of "crisis giving," but rather "grace giving"!

For this reason, I encourage you to set aside specific times to teach or preach a series about giving. Let your church family know what is ahead, announce it with a positive spirit of anticipation, and then move on to other topics after the series is done. For many years I have taken several weeks each February and early March to teach about tithing and special offerings, and to motivate our church in the ways we have described. Then in October we host an annual Missions and Stewardship Conference when our guest speakers challenge us toward faith-promise giving, tithing, and the work of world-wide evangelization.

That is not to say that there haven't been times when an urgent need is brought to the church. Emergencies happen, and our church has responded. But in twenty-two years of ministry, they've been brought to the church family only a few times. I have made it a habit to take these emergency needs to the Lord, to plan ahead, to make sure we are managing our day-to-day finances with wisdom, and then to bring these needs to the church as rarely as possible. We have not created an environment of "crisis giving," but rather "grace giving"!

Be seasonal and predetermined in your leadership in giving. Be biblical, be positive, and avoid crisis and urgency. Avoid being reaction-based. Don't poor mouth the financial picture or your financial burden—again, this is manipulative and ultimately exposes a leadership weakness.

People will respond generously to a loving leader with biblical motives. They will respect wise financial management and a positive spirit of faith. They will thank you for biblically leading them in this area. Lead your church into biblical stewardship. When you do, you are truly leading them into God's blessings. They will one day thank you for being so courageous!

CHAPTER FIFTEEN

OVERCOMING BARRIERS IN MINISTRY

The church is a living organism—God designed it for growth. Just as an acorn was created to become an oak tree, so the church was established by Christ to expand with life and health. Even as an oak tree may grow faster in some seasons than in others, the growth of a church is dynamic; therefore, our focus should be on the health of the tree, not the growth of it. The question is not "is my church *growing*?" The question is, "is my church *healthy*?"

Often times, a lack of *growth* in a church is due to poor *health*. There are far more factors that *prevent* a church from growing than those things which cause it to grow. A wise spiritual leader will learn to recognize growth killers such as health problems in the structure or life of the church that are preventing it from becoming what God desires. You might call these things *barriers*.

During the past two decades our church has hit many barriers. All churches do. Recognizing them and addressing them are critical to moving forward. If you fail to remove the barriers, your church will plateau indefinitely, and perhaps even decline.

Addressing these barriers requires patience, courage, wisdom, honesty, and strategy. And because anything that moves forward experiences resistance, expect some opposition when you try to break through barriers. Let's examine six barriers that most churches run into, and how to lead through them.

1. THE BARRIER OF INDIFFERENCE

Indifference is a lack of interest. This is a difficult barrier to detect early, but it's deadly. Just as every Christian battles spiritual indifference and needs regular revival, so does a church. As you lead in soulwinning and spiritual service, you will find that your church family can become complacent. This often happens when the "newness" of a program or project has worn off. The vision may still be a passion in the leader's heart, but the flock's indifferences will kill the possibilities.

You must address indifference—and the sooner the better. Here are three ways I believe God leads us to deal with indifference:

Detect the decline.
This requires a spiritual sensitivity in your *own* heart. You must be able to read the complacency in the lives of the people you lead.

Pray for wisdom.
"If any of you lack wisdom, let him ask of God, that giveth to all men liberally, and upbraideth not; and it shall be given him" (James 1:5). God promises to give you wisdom if you will ask, believing that He will give it. Wisdom will help you both to discern the decline and to respond to it. During these times of prayer be sure to inspect your own heart. Change usually begins with the leader, and it is possible that the spiritual indifference began "at the top."

Confront the decline.
At some point God will lead you to confront the indifference. Again, many leaders avoid confrontation at all costs, but compassionate confrontation

yields great fruit. God may lead you to preach or teach a series addressing the problem. Perhaps you will confront it in your staff through a training time. Maybe the church needs a revival meeting, a special preaching event, or a prolonged focus on prayer. Get on your knees and ask God to lead you in confronting the spiritual apathy.

Think of this confrontation, first personally then corporately. In other words, there may be key leaders or influential people with whom you set personal appointments to address indifference before you address it in the church.

2. THE BARRIER OF UNFRUITFULNESS

Have you ever looked at your church program and ministry and seen much activity but not much fruit? This barrier is, quite simply, a lack of fruit that *remains*—and it is hardest to see in a very fervent ministry. We feel good when we are busy, when our calendars and schedules are full of ministry activity. But how long has it been since you really analyzed what all the "activity" is producing?

Is your church producing saved souls? New disciples? Mature Christians? A visionary church family? A revival of godliness and distinctive Christian living? Or is it merely a lot of busyness to fill time? These are tough questions, but worthy of careful and prayerful consideration. If you evaluate your church ministry and come up with little fruit, you've hit the barrier of unfruitfulness.

Jesus said, *"Herein is my Father glorified, that ye bear much fruit; so shall ye be my disciples"* (John 15:8). God desires for you to bear fruit. You may be doing the *wrong* things, or you may be doing the *right* things the *wrong* way.

Our church has hit this barrier more times than I can count, and every time we step back, re-evaluate, restructure, and re-engage. It's almost like getting your tire stuck in the mud—the engine is revving; the tire is spinning; all the motion is in place; but the vehicle isn't moving. What do you do? You step out, evaluate the situation, and figure out a way to get some traction so you can move forward.

Here are five ways to make sure all the activity of your church is finding some traction and taking the church toward fruitfulness.

Clearly identify ministry classifications.

Structure is important. Often a church is spinning its wheels because of a lack of clarity—either in purpose or in ministry function. A lack of clarity could be true of the whole church or of one ministry within the church. Step back from the situation and ask, "What is this ministry trying to accomplish? Does the team understand the function and purpose? Is the structure in place for it to function fruitfully?"

Clearly identify accountability mechanisms.

Define what you expect and then hold up those expectations. As a leader, you are the overseer of the ministry and you must *inspect* what you *expect*. Something that is not productive may be lacking in basic accountability. Dr. David Gibbs once told me, "Your standard is not what you write down on paper. Your standard is what you allow in reality." Sometimes ministries cannot get traction simply because they established something for which they are not accounting.

For instance, if a staff engages in soulwinning, they will bear fruit. If they are not bearing fruit, it may be that they are not faithfully going, with the right heart and the right equipping. The only way you could identify these problems and help to regain traction is through a system of accountability when you regularly review your staff's Christian service involvement.

Institute annual evaluations.

I realize this sounds "corporate," but it is biblical and healthy. Have you ever had an evaluation with the individuals on your staff? Have you ever conducted a thorough personal review of every ministry in your church? Have you ever just walked around on Sunday morning to watch teachers teach, nursery workers serve, and greeters welcome people? If not, it's time. Establish a system of reviewing your ministry—both your staff and your program.

We conduct annual reviews for our staff in January. This is a formal time when each staff member meets with his team leader or with the pastor. In this meeting we talk transparently and openly about strengths and weaknesses. It is a non-threatening, growth-oriented time of personal review and challenge. The feedback goes two ways in this meeting, and while there is some nervousness building up to it, everyone appreciates the meeting in the end. These reviews help us to stay productive as a team and to not take our responsibilities lightly or for granted. You might say it helps us find traction when we're spinning our wheels!

Realign responsibility flow.

Sometimes your ministry review will lead you to the basic conclusion that there needs to be some restructuring. Maybe some responsibility needs to be transferred, or a ministry needs to be realigned with new leaders. These are sensitive changes involving the emotions and insecurities of people, and so they need to be addressed wisely and compassionately.

Most sincere people appreciate a leader who senses barriers and strategizes through them. There is often a sense of relief that needed changes are taking place. The key is communication. When the leader communicates to his team clearly and positively, a true team will rise to the prospect of accomplishing more together for Christ. Help your team set aside personal insecurities and "personal turf" so that the whole church can become more fruitful for the Lord.

Add new staff.

In a growing church, often the realignment of responsibility involves hiring for a new position. Finding the right people, training them, and then giving them the right responsibility is one of the most labor-intensive responsibilities a spiritual leader can have.

3. THE BARRIER OF SPIRITUAL LETHARGY

While indifference is a lack of interest, lethargy is a lack of *energy* or *enthusiasm*. Spiritual lethargy is a lack of the Holy Spirit's power and anointing. It is the lack of the power of God within the work. Of all the barriers, I believe this one is the easiest to see. Lethargy is experienced when you are doing everything you can do, but it is being done in your own power, not God's. What should you do?

Seek a new anointing for ministry and preaching.

Get alone with God, make your heart and life right with Him, confess any known sin, and ask Him to anoint your ministry once again. I'm not referring to some emotional experience. I'm referring to the filling of God's Holy Spirit. Ask God to once again fill you and your church with His power. Ephesians 5:18 reminds us, *"And be not drunk with wine, wherein is excess; but be filled with the Spirit."*

Quite honestly, this barrier usually rests with the leader. Ask yourself some tough questions before the Lord: Is my calling sure? Is my vision clear? Am I developing my gifts? Is my character submitted to Christ? Is pride subdued? Am I overcoming fear? Is my pace sustainable? Is my love for God and people increasing?

Seek God's will for a project of faith.

God's empowerment is always for a purpose. Every great Bible leader was moving toward a goal which required great faith. God always calls His people forward—to press toward the mark and strive together for the faith. When you reach a point of spiritual lethargy, it may be time to pray, "Lord what faith journey do you desire to lead us into next? In which direction do I step out of my comfort zone?"

I have asked the Lord such questions many times and He has never failed to answer. His answer is sometimes frightening, but it always leads over the barrier of lethargy!

One word of caution: there is a difference between a work of *faith* and a work of *driven-ness*. Driven people are caught in an uncontrolled pursuit of expansion. They feel like things *must* get bigger. They are abnormally busy and often bemoan their responsibility. They are frequently trying to prove something subconsciously to a father figure who was angry, absent or abusive. Don't get caught in the trap of driven-ness.

4. THE BARRIER OF STAGNATION

Stagnation means "to cease to flow or move" and relates to the flow of ministry, especially as it pertains to winning and discipling new Christians into the body of Christ—helping them to assimilate into a class, connect with people, and begin growing in their faith. Stagnation may relate to the fact that your church has reached its present seating capacity and that you need to begin a new service or change your service schedule to allow for more Sunday school classes.

> *Your standard is not what you write down on paper. Your standard is what you allow in reality.*

I am not for creating change just for the sake of change, but sometimes fresh vision brings change that "increases the circulation of the body." It gets something that was stagnant moving once again. Just as exercise causes your body to increase circulation, grow in health, and be safe from sickness, so the exercise of faith and forward motion causes a church family to break through the barrier of stagnation.

5. THE BARRIER OF LIMITED STRUCTURE

The barrier of limited structure may often seem outside of your control, but it is certainly not outside of your scope of faith or leadership. Every growing church runs into the barrier of physical or financial limitations. These could involve limited auditorium seating, limited educational space, limited parking, or limited land restrictions. Like a plant in a small pot, you will sometimes feel that your church has great potential "if only…," and the "if only" will somehow relate to a physical or financial need. Often this barrier is a limited staff—after all, the pastor and existing staff can only do so much. What do you do with limitations?

First, you do the best you can with what you have. You steward the existing staff, the land, the structure, and God's physical provisions to the best of your ability. Second, you begin to pray for God's provision and direction. Third, you prepare your heart for some new step of faith and prepare your church family for it as well. The solutions to these limitations will involve taking risks and following God into realms that appear to be impossible. It will involve financial and personal sacrifice that will ultimately lead to blessing and greater provision.

For instance, every time we have added a new staff member it involved a measure of faith in God to provide the resources to support the staff. Every time, God has provided the means and blessed the church.

Don't see your "if only…" as merely a limitation. See it as an opportunity for faith in which God can do something great in spite of your limitations. Isn't it in the face of impossible limitation that God does His best work? (A certain Red Sea crossing comes to mind!)

6. THE BARRIER OF TIME LIMITATION

You probably haven't closely associated your personal time struggles with the health of your church, but you should. This barrier is more personal and hits the spiritual leader very close to home, and yet it is also very public because your time allocation is also your example to the flock and greatly impacts your ability to lead.

Your schedule is your choice, and no one else can be held accountable for it at the Judgment Seat of Christ. If there are unhealthy extremes in your time allocation, you must make the choice to change. I've met some leaders who are far too busy (this is the way I tend to lean), and I've met other leaders who are far too consumed with leisure and personal interests. If you are passionate about serving God, you probably lean toward being too busy.

I encourage you to deal with this limitation by trusting God's sovereignty. He is the one who gave you a twenty-four-hour day, and He expects you to sleep a good number of them, eat, spend time with Him, nurture your family, and lead His church. You do not need more time in a day; you need more balance and deliberate decision-making regarding the time you have.

Also, *your schedule is your example*—it is what you lift up outwardly to display what is godly and right. Others will follow your example. If you never take a day off, rarely spend time with your family, and live with unhealthy extremes, others around you will too. They will assume that this schedule is the expected norm. This is not only a bad example, it is unhealthy for you and for everyone who is following you.

Spend time each week balancing your roles, and give the right amount of time to each one. Make courageous choices in the light of God's will. Don't get stuck in the rut of only making urgent decisions in the moment.

We've seen six barriers to local church ministry—*indifference, unfruitfulness, lethargy, stagnation, limited structure, and limited time.* Every growing church and spiritual leader faces these barriers. They are more than barriers; they are opportunities to press forward in faith and see God do something great. Embrace your barriers, and trust God to help you break through them in faith!

CHAPTER SIXTEEN

DEVELOPING AN ANNUAL PLAN

It is *possible* to be drowned in ministry, but it is not *necessary*. Drowning happens when we fail to plan and steward our time—when we fail to make wise choices about the future. Benjamin Franklin said, "Dost thou love life, then do not squander time, for that's the stuff life is made of." Ephesians 5:16 reminds us to *"redeem the time."*

In all of life and ministry, our most precious commodity is time. It is a gift from God. Time is life, and when we waste time, we waste life. Time can *never* be retrieved or replaced and it is *always* being spent. God holds us accountable for our time—for every minute of every day. Many spiritual leaders have been destroyed because of an unstructured use of time. A lack of discipline in our weekly schedule invites Satan's invasion and prevents our church from being all that God would have it to be.

In addition, well-planned time is essential in accomplishing any project or task. At the end of your life, your ministry will be the summation of what you did with the time that God gave you. Failing to plan is planning to fail!

Following the thought from the last chapter, I'd like to close this section of the book by developing a broader understanding of planning. The key to making the most of your time *today* is to discipline yourself in long-range planning. I challenge you to begin constantly and deliberately thinking six to twelve months in advance.

Don't misunderstand; I certainly believe in following the moment-by-moment leading of the Holy Spirit. I understand that much of ministry cannot be planned. I have experienced those days of crisis when "the plan" is irrelevant to the needs of the moment. Yet, there's something very biblical and wise about redeeming the time—thinking ahead and articulating a direction that honors the Lord.

God's voice can most clearly be heard in times of quiet solitude and prayer. It is during these times that His Holy Spirit causes you to lift up your eyes, look further down the road, and sense His direction for the longer term. If you live your ministry life only in the *now*, you will miss these special times of divine leadership. You will not hear God's voice regarding a theme for your new year, a new ministry, or a long term vision which may take many years to accomplish.

> *It's very difficult to lead with joy and passion when you're not one-hundred-percent sure where to go!*

I could write many pages on the long-range vision that God has placed upon my heart during quiet seasons of planning—the stories are numerous and the blessings bountiful. It is in prayerfully looking ahead that God directs the heart of the leader toward loftier goals and higher levels of ministry.

To put it simply, you *must* have a season every year when you get alone with God and ask, "Lord, where do you want us to go next year?" I call this an annual plan, but it's far more than just a plan. It's a spiritual moment with God that gives way to much spiritual growth in the church. It's a time when God works mightily in me before He begins His mighty work in His church. It's a time when I quiet the busyness of my life simply to hear God's voice regarding the coming twelve months. It always refreshes my spirit, strengthens my heart, ignites my vision, and helps me step back into leadership with clarity and direction. It's very difficult to lead with joy and passion when you're not one-hundred-percent sure where to go!

This time of planning lifts the fog and gives true clarity. And few things excite a church family more than fresh direction and a God-confident spiritual leader!

Why should you set aside time to create an annual plan? First, I believe it is wise stewardship. *"Moreover it is required in stewards, that a man be found faithful"* (1 Corinthians 4:2). Second, it will energize your spirit for ministry. Third, it will energize your church family to follow your vision. Fourth, it will help you accomplish much more for the cause of Christ. As the saying goes, "He who aims at nothing hits it every time!"

What I'm sharing with you is more than an exercise. It is a perspective of ministry that always thinks ahead and lays out a clear direction that the church can understand, own, and follow. This must become a part of the way you think and function. Let's consider some guidelines for the time spent creating this annual plan.

RECONNECT WITH YOUR PURPOSE

We covered the importance of purpose in an earlier chapter, but your annual planning is a time when you should review your purpose with a deliberate heart-check. This is when you reconnect with that purpose and realign anything in ministry that doesn't line up properly with it. This is the time when you ask the Lord to help you purge things that don't function toward the purpose and envision new things that would further that purpose.

CHOOSE A BIBLICAL ANNUAL THEME

One of the biggest aspects of our annual plan is our annual theme. Each year the Lord impresses upon my heart a biblical, scriptural theme on which to focus the church family. I begin praying and thinking about this theme six months ahead of time, and it always begins with a work of God in my own heart. It flows from what He is teaching me personally.

This annual theme flows into every aspect of our church life for the coming twelve months. It gives everything we do a biblical context. Our revival, our giving, our campus development, our conferences—all of ministry—somehow aligns with this theme. For instance, one of our recent themes was "For the Faith" from Philippians 1:27. This theme gave a powerful platform from which to preach and provided a strong context for every event and program in the year. The answer to every "why" in ministry—why preach, why sing, why give, why win souls—was "for the faith"!

Over the years, these themes have become spiritual signposts of our church's faith journey. Every member can connect his own growth to the memory of these themes. Some of the more memorable ones include: "A Heart for God," "Growing in Grace," "Consider Christ," "Together with God," "He is Greater," "He is Able," and "Streams in the Desert." Just repeating these themes to our church family spurs memories of decisions and victories that were won in each of these years.

This theme is always introduced to our staff during our late summer staff orientation and training retreat, and then it is introduced to our church family on "Vision Night"—either New Year's Eve or the first Sunday night of the new year.

CREATE AN ANNUAL CALENDAR WITH YOUR TEAM

If your church is smaller, this calendar might be created between you and your wife. If you have a staff, I would encourage some team effort in putting together a church calendar that reflects the theme. If you have a larger staff, it is imperative that your team work together to create a calendar that doesn't conflict between events and ministries.

We require our staff to submit any new calendar events in the early fall. My office keeps the calendar, and my secretary begins to finalize it in early November. By this time, several versions have been reviewed by all of our staff and changes have been submitted.

Along with the church calendar, my wife and I work on our personal calendar. We talk, pray, discuss, and make tough decisions about various seasons of our life. We schedule time together, we review busy seasons, and we agree together that the Lord has given us balance.

The completed church calendar becomes the foundation for all ministry for the coming twelve months. From it, every department and ministry begins to take serious steps toward planning, budgeting, and projecting the new year.

PRAYERFULLY REVIEW YOUR CALENDAR

Before the annual plan is complete, I spend some time reviewing the year ahead and asking the Lord if it aligns with His will. Our leadership team and others spend time reviewing the plan for conflicts and possible oversights. We look for areas of vulnerability—times when events fall too close or are too burdensome for the church family. We look for times when the church may have a conflicting focus of attention. For instance, we wouldn't try to have a Missions Conference directly next to a major outreach effort. When we see these vulnerabilities, we adjust. Sometimes we must postpone something; other times, we adjust the timing of events to avoid conflict.

This final review process is very valuable. It helps you step back and see the big picture, and it gives the Lord a chance to lead your heart from that perspective.

ALLOCATE RESOURCES ACCORDING TO THE CALENDAR

Allocating resources is the final step in the annual planning process, and one of the most important. With your year in view, outline how you will allocate the church resources to accomplish the plan. This involves allocating the following areas:

- **Ministry budget**—for each ministry
- **Employees**—payroll and benefits
- **Operations**—daily office expenses
- **Ministry related**—weekly ministry needs
- **Vehicles**—church-owned vehicles
- **Property**—buildings, grounds, and maintenance
- **Missions**—supporting missionaries and projects

Presently, our church leadership team helps with the budget by creating budget worksheets for each ministry during November and early December in preparation for the new year.

ASSESS YOUR PLAN WEEKLY AND MONTHLY

When the new year begins, you will find the dynamic of ministry does not always perfectly follow your annual plan. Needs will arise, and you will be forced to re-assess your plan. I suggest that you have a monthly and a weekly process of personally reviewing your roles, the budget, and your ministry schedule and priorities.

Be willing to make mid-course adjustments or corrections as the Lord leads you. Navigating your annual plan through the year will be like keeping a car on the road—continual attention and correction is vital.

If you're too busy to plan, you're too busy! Planning is what puts added value into tomorrow. Redeeming the time is about looking ahead and allocating purpose and priorities before it's too late.

One of the most valuable gifts you can give your staff or church family is clear direction and a well-defined plan. You can only *give* this if you first *receive* it from the Lord. Your team will embrace this direction with anticipation; God will delight to bless your faith; and your new year will exceed your expectations! Spencer Johnson wrote in *The Present*, "Once you have prepared for the future, you can enjoy the present."

Right now would be a great time to start working on next year's annual plan!

(For more information about the annual church calendar, please refer to Order in the Church, *strivingtogether.com.)*

3

PART THREE

THE SPIRITUAL
LEADER'S PULPIT

The highest responsibility of a man of God is to declare the truth of God—to preach the Word. The pulpit is central to the pastorate, and it is truly the foundation of all other ministry.

> *"Preach the word; be instant in season, out of season; reprove, rebuke, exhort with all longsuffering and doctrine."*—2 TIMOTHY 4:2

THE SPIRITUAL LEADER'S PREACHING

Much of a pastor's time finds him preparing for next Sunday's messages. No pastor ever escapes this deadline; it is always approaching. What a high calling and wonderful privilege it is to be a preacher of the Word of God. What a sacred honor and blessed delight to be immersed into the eternal truth of God, to prepare a biblical message, and then to stand before God's people every Sunday and declare the Words of life!

For over two decades, I have preached more than three times a week. I never tire of preaching God's Word, and I would rather preach in the pulpit of my own church than anywhere else in the world.

Your pulpit is the centerpiece of your biblical ministry. Paul wrote to Timothy, *"Preach the word; be instant in season, out of season; reprove, rebuke, exhort with all longsuffering and doctrine"* (2 Timothy 4:2). Isaiah spoke of the call to preach in these terms, *"The Spirit of the Lord GOD is upon me; because the LORD hath anointed me to preach good tidings unto the meek; he hath sent me to bind up the brokenhearted, to proclaim liberty to the captives, and the opening of the prison to them that are bound"* (Isaiah 61:1).

There is not a chapter in this book that I approach with more reverence and respect than this one. For as your preaching goes, so goes your entire ministry. First Corinthians 1:18 teaches us that the preaching of the Cross is the power of God, and 1 Corinthians 1:21 states, *"...it pleased God by the foolishness of preaching to save them that believe."* You have no greater responsibility and no higher duty than to deliver the mysteries of God to the hearts of men. It is a sacred responsibility with eternal implications.

Bill Bennet wrote in *Thirty Minutes to Raise the Dead*, "A preacher has thirty to forty minutes to awake men and women from the stupefaction of worldliness to realize the importance of spiritual things." Obviously we cannot thoroughly cover all the needed materials for biblical sermon preparation in this one chapter, but I want to share some basic principles I believe are vital in the pulpit ministry. May God use these thoughts to stir and equip you to become the preacher that He called you to be.

UNDERSTAND YOUR CALL TO PREACH AND TEACH

"And daily in the temple, and in every house, they ceased not to teach and preach Jesus Christ" (Acts 5:42). The Greek word that references the role of the preacher is *Keruk,* and it literally means "to herald or to publish." Our primary responsibility is to herald forth and publish God's truth. One preacher put it this way, "The business of the prophet is to fill the pulpit, not the pews."

Every pastor is called to preach. This is a call to speak God's truth with courage and passion. It is not a call to performance or showmanship. It is not a call to self-glorification or authoritarianism. It is a sacred mission to speak truth.

Every pastor is also called to teach. *"And the servant of the Lord must not strive; but be gentle unto all men, apt to teach, patient"* (2 Timothy 2:24). Teaching is a call to instruct God's people from His Word. Never be ashamed to be a *preacher* and a *teacher* of God's precious truths. His Word must be declared with passion, and it must be taught with clarity.

In *Lectures to My Students*, Charles Spurgeon wrote, "Sermons should have real teaching in them, and their doctrine should be solid, substantial, and abundant. We do not enter the pulpit to talk for talk's sake; we have instructions to convey important to the last degree, and we cannot afford to utter pretty nothings."

Spurgeon went on to write, "Whatever else may be present, the absence of edifying, instructive truth, like the absence of flour from bread, will be fatal." Many churches and many malnourished Christians are suffering today from a great hunger for solid, biblical preaching filled with practical truth and the power of God. We live in a day when many pastors are more concerned with cultural preference than with preaching the truth. Messages are reduced to little more than a few anecdotes, some jokes, a few movie clips, and some pop-psychology. This does not fulfill Jesus' command to *"Feed my sheep"* (John 21:16), nor the Apostle Paul's charge to *"Preach the word"* (2 Timothy 4:2).

Many pastors have mastered homiletical technique, but their messages lack power. Pastor, the Word of God is alive—it is *"quick, and powerful, and sharper than any twoedged sword"*—and it must be delivered to your church family. It has the power to discern the thoughts and intents of the heart (Hebrews 4:12). God's Word alone has the power to change hearts and effectually work in lives; so embrace your biblical call to preach and to teach God's Word.

EMBRACE THE POWER OF BIBLICAL PREACHING

The centerpiece of preaching must be the Bible, and yet how often it is not! I recall attending a preaching conference years ago during which one of the speakers stood to preach. A room full of preachers with hungry hearts were waiting for a feast on the Word of God.

As he started his message he held up the Bible and shouted in a long drawn tone, "Preachin'!" With a pause he did it again, and again, and yet again. For the entire message this supposed preacher stood behind a pulpit and shouted one single word—"preachin'!" over and over again. He never opened the Bible; he never talked about God's truth. He talked a lot about preaching, but he surely didn't do any! I left that service hungry and sorrowful that a man of God had wasted a precious opportunity to preach God's Word to hungry hearts.

Preaching isn't preaching until the Bible is opened, God's Word is read, and His truth is expounded within its appropriate context. Preaching is not biblical unless it flows directly from a text. Preaching is not powerful or life-changing unless it is thoroughly filled with the Word of God.

In his book *Homiletics from the Heart,* Dr. John Goetsch wrote, "Expository preaching is more a philosophy than a method. A man who rightly divides the Word of truth has a biblical philosophy of preaching." Expository preaching is biblical preaching and God blesses it. It declares God's Word the way God intended. It declares the whole counsel of God. It builds lives, precept upon precept, chapter by chapter.

> *Preaching is not powerful or life-changing unless it is thoroughly filled with the Word of God.*

Pastors have often asked me about the blessings of God at Lancaster Baptist Church. With all of my heart I believe that expository preaching is one of the foundational pillars of the strength and spiritual maturity of our church. For two decades I have labored to preach through entire books of the Bible—line by line, verse by verse. We have studied many books, some of them twice. It is my life's goal to preach through the entire Bible in this fashion.

At times the text wasn't what I would have chosen, but it was always what we needed. At times the text required great labor and study, but God always revealed Himself and blessed His Word.

Preaching verse by verse has kept me from choosing my favorite themes or passages. It has prevented me from being issue-oriented or from avoiding difficult topics or tough passages. It has placed the reigns of the spiritual development of God's people in God's hands.

Through this verse-by-verse approach to preaching, I have been astounded more than a few times at how the Scripture text fell directly in line with the obvious season or needs of the church. It's a wonderful experience to choose a book of the Bible to preach through, not knowing exactly where it will lead, only to discover that God foreordained a great season of specific application and spiritual growth for His people.

Expository preaching not only helps you to know what your next week's text is, it also helps you to preach the whole counsel of God. (I cannot emphasize enough the power of the pure Word of God.) How often pastors take verses out of context, manipulate Scripture to fit pet ideas, or simply use a text to introduce a thought, never to return to it for the rest of the message. These things ought not to occur in Bible-believing churches.

Paul talked about this kind of deceitfulness in 2 Corinthians 4:2, *"But have renounced the hidden things of dishonesty, not walking in craftiness, nor handling the word of God deceitfully; but by manifestation of the truth commending ourselves to every man's conscience in the sight of God."*

I challenge you, even when you are preaching a topical series of messages, to handle God's Word very carefully, going verse by verse through a passage which is carefully cross-referenced and true to the context. If you desire for God to bless your preaching—to change hearts through your pulpit ministry—do not look for new truth or new application. Don't try to be a pulpit sensationalist. Just stick with God's truth as He gave it to us. Preach the pure Word of God and let Him have the glory!

PREPARE THE PREACHER BEFORE THE MESSAGE

It has been said, "The preacher *is* the sermon. You cannot separate the character and conduct of the preacher from the message." The preparation of the preacher himself is the most important work a preacher can do. We are not great men, but we preach great matters; and before we begin, we must humbly beg God that all He wants done in the hearers' lives will first be done in our lives.

Charles Spurgeon said, "The preacher is always on the brink of abyss. Preaching sways the preacher's emotions, making great demands upon his nerves, and often producing physical and emotional exhaustion." Entering into the spiritual battle of preaching makes pastors susceptible to a variety of temptations from the enemy. The right preparation will protect you from spiritual vulnerability.

Before you step into your pulpit each week, I urge you to take these biblical precautions to prepare your own heart for your task:

1. The preacher must prepare through prayer.

Pray over your message and strengthen your private walk with Christ. Pray for spiritual anointing and protection. Pray over your text and let it sink deeply into your heart. Pray that you might empty yourself to be an honorable vessel, fit for the Master's use.

2. The preacher must seek the fullness of the Spirit.

Earnest preaching comes from a heart moved by the Holy Spirit. Keith Knauss said, "The preacher has more to do with the Spirit of the ages than with the spirit of the age." Before you arrive at church on Sunday morning, be sure that your heart is thoroughly right with God and yielded to His Holy Spirit. For without Him we can do nothing!

3. The preacher must be willing to bear a burden.

Paul wrote, *"For though I preach the gospel, I have nothing to glory of: for necessity is laid upon me; yea, woe is unto me, if I preach not the gospel!"* (1 Corinthians 9:16). Be willing to bear the burden of preparation, the burden of watching for the souls of men, and the burden of standing between the spiritually living and the spiritually dead.

PREPARE THE MESSAGE BIBLICALLY AND METHODICALLY

Prayerfully select your text.

Dr. John Goetsch wrote, "God may bless our homiletical outline, our illustrations, and stories but He does not promise to do so. He only promises to bless His Word." Your text is what God blesses; see it as central to your message, not peripheral.

Build your message upon your text.

The best sermons allow the text to supply its own structure. Spurgeon taught his preacher boys, "Some brethren are done with their text as soon as they have read it. Having paid all due honor to that particular passage by announcing it, they feel no necessity further to refer to it." May we sense a sacred duty and a holy obligation both to God and to His people to stay true to the text of the Word of God.

Consider again what Spurgeon wrote about his text, "I always find I can preach best when I manage to lie and soak in my text, and after I have bathed in it, I delight to lie down in it and let it soak into me."

Study the background of the text.

As you begin to think through your text, research the history and ask questions. From what group of books does it come (poetical, prison epistles, etc.)? What is the historical context of the book? What is the theme of the book? What is the context of the passage? What is the theme of the passage (rebuke, encouragement, etc.)?

It is vital that you commit yourself to understanding the historical and doctrinal context of the passage. You must have a firm commitment to treating God's Word with great caution. Give context a high priority and be sure to interpret and preach God's Word accurately.

Write a declarative introduction.

Your introduction must capture the attention of your listeners with a declaration or a proposition that connects with the heart. A good introduction arouses interest. If a preacher doesn't connect with the listener within the first thirty seconds, he may never connect.

Your listeners should quickly identify with your introduction and want to hear the rest of the message because of it. Remember this simple formula: accusations harden the will, but questions stimulate the conscience. A good introduction will create intrigue and interest in God's truth. It will raise critical questions which the rest of the message will answer. This has been called "creating thirst" in the heart of your listener.

Develop an understandable outline.

As you are studying your text, write out every thought or application that the Holy Spirit places upon your heart. Meditate upon your text and brainstorm the direction that God might lead. From these notes you will begin to see some thoughts flow. When you are compiling your final outline, prayerfully begin to order these critical thoughts by the textual flow or by a logical flow so that the listener can easily connect and follow.

List your main points and then sub-points.

Create a skeletal outline that contains all of your raw thoughts in a logical, flowing order. Cross reference your text and support each of your main points as well as your sub-points with additional Scriptures. Fill your outlines with biblical references and support your message thoroughly. The Bible is its own best commentary, and when your message is delivered, it's the Word of God that will continue to work in hearts long after your oratorical skills and wit are forgotten.

Alliteration is helpful if it is not forced, but it is more important that you wrap profound truth in simple words. Also during the outlining process, ask the Lord to give you the illustrations and practical applications to support your message. Jesus illustrated eternal truth in very practical ways with stories, word pictures, and object lessons. Connect your truth with everyday application and memorable illustrations.

Develop a conclusion that calls for a response.

God's truth always demands a response. As you conclude your message it must come down to this question, "What should I do with this?" Your listener must readily connect what you have taught with a heart decision. On the practical side, make your conclusion brief—review your points, apply the truth, and challenge God's people to respond.

PURGE YOUR MESSAGE BEFORE YOU PREACH IT

Spurgeon wrote, "Brethren, weigh your sermons. Do not retail them by the yard, but deal them out by the pound. Set no store by the quantity of words which you utter, but strive to be esteemed for the quality of your matter."

Before you deliver your sermon, you should spend some time reviewing your message for the express purpose of purging it. A great message should be purged of the following:

Purged of self

Relentlessly rid your message from anything that removes the spotlight from Christ and places it on you. *"Likewise reckon ye also yourselves to be dead indeed unto sin, but alive unto God through Jesus Christ our Lord. Let not sin therefore reign in your mortal body, that ye should obey it in the lusts thereof. Neither yield ye your members as instruments of unrighteousness unto sin: but yield yourselves unto God, as those that are alive from the dead, and your members as instruments of righteousness unto God"* (Romans 6:11–13).

Purged of pettiness and anger

Never preach a message with malice in your heart. Rid your message and your heart of these distractions and let the Word of God do the convicting. Preach from a pure heart. *"Let all bitterness, and wrath, and anger, and clamour, and evil speaking, be put away from you, with all malice"* (Ephesians 4:31).

Purged of preference

Never preach your personal preference as Bible and never preach the Bible as mere preference. Discern between the two and clearly state which is which. *"For this cause also thank we God without ceasing, because, when ye received the word of God which ye heard of us, ye received it not as the word of men, but as it is in truth, the word of God, which effectually worketh also in you that believe"* (1 Thessalonians 2:13).

Purged of insecurity

How often I have heard a message that was based more upon insecurity than upon the Word. The pulpit is not yours; it is God's, and you must steward every preaching opportunity as unto Him. The pulpit is no place for pettiness, insecurity, or manipulation.

Men who are driven to succeed will create issues with other men who threaten them, and in the case of an insecure preacher, those issues are often brought to the pulpit. Don't use your pulpit for personal agenda, political benefit, or personal gain. Use it to preach the pure Word of God to hungry hearts.

Purged of terms without definitions

Read your entire message and ask, "If I were a first-time visitor, what words in this message would need to be defined." I'm not advocating changing Bible words—just be sure to define them and explain them. If you don't, you will certainly ostracize any new Christian or unsaved person quickly. A visitor's emotional response to being ostracized goes something like this: "Everybody here knows what that word means...I don't fit in here...I don't belong here...I'm uncomfortable...I won't be back." Your goal is to connect with the unsaved, and defining words simply helps them feel a connection to what you are teaching and lets them know that they belong in this "new place" called church!

FOCUS ON THREE OBJECTIVES IN PREACHING

I challenge you to focus on three primary objectives every time you stand in the pulpit:

1. *Rightly divide the word of truth.*

"Study to shew thyself approved unto God, a workman that needeth not to be ashamed, rightly dividing the word of truth."
—2 TIMOTHY 2:15

2. Exalt Jesus Christ.

"And he is the head of the body, the church: who is the beginning, the firstborn from the dead; that in all things he might have the preeminence."—COLOSSIANS 1:18

Exalt Him to the saved and unsaved alike. Somehow, preach the Cross of Christ in every message.

3. Equip the saints.

"And he gave some, apostles; and some, prophets; and some, evangelists; and some, pastors and teachers; For the perfecting of the saints, for the work of the ministry, for the edifying of the body of Christ:"—EPHESIANS 4:11–12

KNOW YOUR CONGREGATION AND YOUR CONTEXT

Before you stand to preach, learn about those to whom you will preach and the location in which you will preach. One preacher wrote, "To love to preach is one thing. To love those to whom you preach is another."

Every Sunday morning I preach to a crowd of Southern Californian people, many of whom are unchurched and unsaved. Every Sunday night I preach to our church family— a blended family of many mature Christians as well as new and growing Christians. The messages I prepare for these two contexts are different. The needs differ, the delivery style differs slightly, and the application differs.

Don't misunderstand. The message is in no way compromised; it is merely made understandable to a specific crowd. As you prepare your message, it is vital that you consider to whom you are speaking. Jesus said that we are to be wise as serpents yet harmless as doves (Matthew 10:16). Paul stated, *"Walk in wisdom toward them that are without…"* (Colossians 4:5). Even Jesus and the Apostle Paul spoke differently to different types of people. They were intensely relevant and understandable to the crowd to whom they preached!

PROTECT YOUR VOICE AND USE IT WISELY

Spurgeon wrote, "Never lose the wonder of preaching. Preach with the wonder in your voice."

Spurgeon taught, "We are, in certain sense, our own tools, and therefore must keep ourselves in order. If I want to preach the Gospel, I can only use my own voice; therefore I must train my vocal powers. I can only think with my own brains, and feel with my own heart, and therefore I must educate my intellectual and emotional faculties. I can only weep and agonize for souls in my own renewed nature, therefore must I watchfully maintain the tenderness which was in Christ Jesus."

So much of your message is to be found in the passion of your voice—the dynamics of your heart. When you preach, let your voice be strong. During the week, prepare your voice and protect it so that you can step into the pulpit ready to speak. Learn to protect your throat from weather, from sickness, from overuse, and from misuse. As a preacher, your voice is your primary tool—take care of it.

Be careful not to preach with a "staged voice." Use the voice God gave you—be yourself and don't try to emulate or impress. Let the delivery of your message be authentic and powerful. Let the passion of your heart be felt in the strength and intensity of your voice.

GIVE A CLEAR INVITATION

God still blesses an old fashioned altar call. He is still honored when His people respond in humble obedience to His truth. I urge you not to follow the whims of culture. So many churches no longer give an invitation. Don't be afraid to invite people to respond to Christ and to make decisions based upon the preaching they've heard.

> "And the Spirit and the bride say, Come. And let him that heareth say, Come. And let him that is athirst come. And whosoever will, let him take the water of life freely."—REVELATION 22:17

Let your invitation be clearly understood, spiritual in nature, and patient. Don't prolong it, but don't rush it either. Give the Holy Spirit a moment to work in hearts.

Bill Bennet used this simple formula to describe his preaching: "I read myself full, I think myself clear, I pray myself hot, and then I get up and let it go!"

As we close this chapter, pause for a moment and consider once again, the grave responsibility that God has placed upon your shoulders—to carry the light of His Word into the darkness of this world. Charles Spurgeon said, "The power that is in the gospel does not lie in the eloquence of the preacher; otherwise men would be the converters of souls. Nor does it lie in the preacher's learning; otherwise it would consist in the wisdom of men. We might preach until our tongues rotted, till we would exhaust our lungs and die, but never a soul would be converted unless the Holy Spirit be with the Word of God to give it the power to convert the soul."

May God bless you and use you greatly as a preacher of His Word!

(To grow more in your abilities as an expository preacher, I recommend you read Homiletics from the Heart *by Dr. John Goetsch, available at strivingtogether.com.)*

CHAPTER EIGHTEEN

LEADING A BIBLICAL CHURCH SERVICE

Most churches are horribly ineffective in seeing people's lives truly changed. This is sad, because God still changes lives. His Word is still true; His power is still available; and His Spirit still desires to move in the hearts of men. Too often our sermons are powerless, our church services unprepared, our buildings not cared for, and our people overlooked. Do we wonder why lives are not changed?

Since day one of our ministry at Lancaster Baptist, we have seen God changing lives. Every Sunday morning we see people respond to the invitation to trust Christ as Saviour. Every week I hear testimonies from new Christians and growing disciples—they write me; they email me; they shake my hand in church and tell me what God is doing in their lives. This is the "fruit" of which we read earlier—the fruit that Jesus Christ desires for us to bring forth. Every calendar-quarter we host a new members brunch. This is a wonderful time for meeting new people and hearing their testimonies of life-change. It thrills my heart every time. This is what the ministry of Jesus Christ is all about!

If you desire to see lasting life-change in the hearts of people, it will happen in two primary contexts—one-on-one and in church services, and it will always involve the Word of God.

First, it happens one-on-one through personal soulwinning, discipleship, and follow-up. Lives are changed as mature Christians personally invest time and effort in new Christians.

Second, lasting life-change happens through your church services. Hearts should be touched and changed by the power of God because of what takes place through the worship and the fellowship in Sunday services.

If you're not seeing lives changed, you need to seriously evaluate these two areas of ministry. Ask yourself, "Are we connecting with people personally?" and "Are we seeing the power and presence of God on Sundays?" In these pages I'd like to describe what God blesses in our worship. Let's briefly explore five aspects for effective church services:

INSPIRE PEOPLE TO DEVELOP A HEART FOR GOD

The first purpose of our church and the highest goal of every church service is to inspire people to have a greater heart for God—to grow in their understanding of Him and love for Him. For the unsaved, this means calling them to Christ for salvation. For the saved, this means inspiring a life of worship and love for the Lord. In all of our worship, God is the center of attention. He is the supreme focus for which we gather in any service. Throughout His Word He shows that He desires men to worship Him and to know Him. "O magnify the LORD with me, and let us exalt his name together" (Psalm 34:3).

When the church service is founded upon the worship of God, it instantly takes on a quality of His supernatural character. One pastor stated, "If we can fully explain a church, something is wrong." This is true. When the focus is upon God and when His presence is welcomed rather than quenched, His work will be evident and not fully explainable. You will leave church saying, "God was good today!"

An inspiring worship service begins with an inspired pastor.
By this, I mean that Sunday morning must be the spiritual pinnacle of your week. It must be approached with a heart that is in love with God, aflame with His truth, and compassionate toward His people. You should come into Sunday with adequate rest, with a right spirit, and with a right relationship with God and men. You must ask the Lord for His filling, and you should anticipate what the Lord will do on His day. You must crave the supernatural power of God for every service.

When the worship service begins, participate in it! Enter into His presence and enjoy the music and singing. Be a part of the worship. How often I have seen preachers appear to be disconnected from every part of the service up until the preaching. I believe this sends the wrong message to the congregation. Every church deserves spiritual leaders who love to worship the Lord Jesus Christ.

An inspiring worship service has inspiring music.
We are going to explore the music ministry more in the next chapter, but in the context of the church service, the music should be both biblical and joyful, and it should lift hearts toward the Lord.

The music service is for the Lord, not for the people. It is worship, not entertainment. And yet, music can be very enjoyable. Music is the part of the service where hearts are prepared and a context is set. Everything prior to preaching creates the context for preaching. The greeters, the ushers, the prelude, the music, the offering—all of this creates the emotional and spiritual "backdrop" or environment in which the preaching of God's Word is delivered.

We must pray that the people in attendance will have an awakening of their spirits from the first moments of the service. We want to stir their hearts toward the Lord and develop a connectedness with spiritual things. I do not advocate an "entertainment" type service, but I am also not in favor of a service that is not understood. Lost people need to see our joy in worship and understand our message.

WORSHIP THE LORD FROM PURE AND PREPARED HEARTS

What many modern churches call worship is nothing more than carnality—the marriage of pop-culture and secular music, with a little bit of God thrown in for good measure. Worship in the seeker-sensitive movement has become man-centered and entertainment driven. Many church services have become nothing more than a fifty-minute rock concert with a fifteen-minute "God-talk" at the end. What began many years ago as the Contemporary Christian Music movement has now become a slippery slope in which "anything goes" in church. Today there are churches showing secular movies, projecting the Super Bowl, and performing secular rock music—all in the name of connecting with the lost. Frankly, Christ has little or nothing to do with any of these things. Sadly, these same churches are also failing to produce changed lives. Recent studies show that the "Christians" who attend these types of churches show little to no difference in their lifestyles when compared to the rest of the unchurched world. A carnal church service environment produces carnal Christians. A man-centered worship produces men who worship self and whose Christianity is pervertedly self-centered.

This carnal approach to entertainment is not worship. This is not of God. It has nothing to do with the biblical picture of worship—bowing down before His presence in humility and repentance and giving Him all worth and reverence. It has nothing to do with a lifestyle of worship which would reflect surrender and separation from sin or sanctification in holiness and righteousness. These "worship services" attract a crowd and entertain people, but they do not change lives.

I co-authored with Dr. John Goetsch about these dangerous trends in *A Saviour Sensitive Church*, and I challenge you to lead your church away from this carnal, man-centered type of worship, and to make sure your worship service is biblical. Make it God-centered and inviting to the Holy Spirit.

True worship must be spoken.
This is why we sing, read Scripture out loud, and pray.

True worship must be expressed.

This is why we pray, give, and invite people to respond to the invitation.

True worship must be holy.

"As obedient children, not fashioning yourselves according to the former lusts in your ignorance: But as he which hath called you is holy, so be ye holy in all manner of conversation; Because it is written, Be ye holy; for I am holy" (1 Peter 1:14–16). It must reflect the Lord and His Word, not the world and its passions.

True worship will be convicting.

In Isaiah 6, we see that the result of "seeing the Lord" is immediate conviction and repentance. Conviction is not something you can manufacture, but it *will be* the product of sincere worship in the hearts of believers and unbelievers alike! In today's pop-church, unbelievers are attending church and then leaving with no conviction. In fact, many churches do not want people to experience conviction because it is perceived as a negative emotion. That idea is false! Conviction is a *privilege*—it is the inner working of the Holy Spirit of God. It is a *gift* from God to the hearts of men.

The very nature of our God demands that we avoid the "culture driven" philosophies that abound today. These philosophies focus on growth over God. They are more concerned with drawing a crowd than with changing a life. They would rather tickle the ears than stir the heart. I see five major dangers of a culture-driven ministry.

The dangers of a culture-driven ministry:

1. **No exposition of Scripture**—primarily topical content with little Bible.
2. **No bold preaching**—avoiding a declarative courage that provokes a response.
3. **Shallow teaching on surface topics**—avoiding sound doctrine and biblical content.

4. **Shallow salvation message**—no emphasis on sin or repentance, no call for a decision.

5. **No emphasis on separation from the world**—from the service to the weekly ministry to the lifestyle, there is no emphasis on separation or avoiding sin. The emphasis is usually on a radical teaching of grace in which "anything goes" in the Christian life, contrary to accurate Bible teaching (Titus 2:11–13).

Have the biblical courage to establish a church service that rejects the cultural trends and exalts God. Lift up and participate in pure worship from a holy life.

JOYFULLY FELLOWSHIP WITH GOD'S PEOPLE

Acts 2 so beautifully points out what believers did when they assembled together: *"And they continued stedfastly in the apostles' doctrine and fellowship, and in breaking of bread, and in prayers"* (Acts 2:42). They learned doctrine; they fellowshipped with one another; and they worshipped the Lord through prayer and communion. It's very biblical and very simple. When you see believers assembling to worship, you also see them fellowshipping and encouraging each other.

> *"Not forsaking the assembling of ourselves together, as the manner of some is; but exhorting one another: and so much the more, as ye see the day approaching."*—HEBREWS 10:25

Notice the picture of brotherly love and fellowship that the apostle described to the Philippian Christians, *"If there be therefore any consolation in Christ, if any comfort of love, if any fellowship of the Spirit, if any bowels and mercies, Fulfil ye my joy, that ye be likeminded, having the same love, being of one accord, of one mind"* (Philippians 2:1–2).

Throughout the New Testament church, we see the local church admonished toward encouragement, edification, support, prayer, and fellowship. A church body is designed to be interdependent—a family functioning in harmony, unity, and with loving hearts for one another!

The church service is one of the primary contexts in which this can unfold. What better place for godly fellowship than in the shadow of worship, preaching, prayer, and in the presence of the Holy Spirit.

I love to see the people of our church just "hang around" after the services. They don't want to leave. Our auditorium and virtually our entire campus is a beehive of fellowship and friendship after every service. Occasionally I visit a church on vacation where everyone can't wait until the service is over. Rather than being a *beehive* of fellowship, everybody makes a *beeline* for the parking lot! Something is wrong with this absence of family fellowship in the body of Christ.

Along these lines, I encourage you to spend time greeting God's people personally. Everybody deserves a warm smile, a friendly handshake, and an encouraging word. If you rush out after service, what message does that send? It makes the leader appear disinterested and disconnected, aloof and untouchable.

Every Sunday morning and Sunday night, I stand in our lobby as long as needed, to just be with people.

> *Have the biblical courage to establish a church service that rejects the cultural trends and exalts God.*

This is some of the most effective personal ministry I have every week. I pray with people, rejoice with people, counsel them, smile, and share encouraging words with them. It's one of the highlights of my week just to enjoy the fellowship and encouragement.

During every service, we have a time when our church family stands to shake hands with one another and with visitors. So as not to embarrass the visitors, we simply ask them to remain seated so the ushers can give them a gift and so our church family can greet them.

After services on Sunday evening, my wife and I often open our home to host guests and church members. The fellowship is always sweet and encouraging. Godly fellowship is biblical. We are to be "given to hospitality," and a church service that is surrounded with godly fellowship is pleasing to the Lord.

One of the greatest compliments visitors give to our church is to say that we are the most friendly place they have ever visited! That's a wonderful reflection of the Spirit of Christ at work in the hearts of our church family.

How is this friendly spirit developed? I believe it is the product of the leadership example as well as the preaching and teaching. We have labored diligently to have a joyful church environment with an excellent spirit. Frankly, those with critical spirits or bad attitudes usually do not feel at home for very long at our church, unless they desire to get their hearts right. God has blessed this joyful spirit and our church family has caught the vision of biblical fellowship!

POWERFULLY PROCLAIM THE TRUTH OF GOD

No church service can be effective without the preaching of the Word of God. The preaching of Christ should be preeminent in every service. Everything should lead up to preaching—it should be the centerpiece of worship. Paul admonished Titus in his pastorate, *"Holding fast the faithful word as he hath been taught, that he may be able by sound doctrine both to exhort and to convince the gainsayers"* (Titus 1:9).

Pastors are given to the church for the purpose of preaching and teaching God's Word: *"And he gave some, apostles; and some, prophets; and some, evangelists; and some, pastors and teachers; For the perfecting of the saints, for the work of the ministry, for the edifying of the body of Christ"* (Ephesians 4:11–12).

It should be your goal in every church service to powerfully proclaim the truth of God. God's Word will build up and strengthen His people. God's Word is the life-changing instrument of God. One preacher said, "The Bible is not the Sword of the preacher, it is the Sword of the Spirit."

Your preaching must reach believers and unbelievers alike. It must be relevant to man's needs and offer spiritual and biblical solutions to life's problems.

The psalmist wrote that his despair and backsliding did not stop until he entered into God's house, *"When I thought to know this, it was too painful for me; Until I went into the sanctuary of God; then understood I their end"* (Psalm 73:16–17).

It is not wrong to prepare messages with the needs of people in mind. For instance, when you preach on the family, think of the many broken families that are present. But be careful not to alienate people unintentionally. When you preach on Father's Day and Mother's Day, think of those with no father or mother, or of those who have lost loved ones. Think of those with wayward children and broken hearts. When preaching about marriage think of those who have been divorced and who are hurting. Ask the Lord for wisdom to touch your whole congregation with His Word.

The Apostle Paul was careful to deliver God's truth with power and with compassion: *"For our gospel came not unto you in word only, but also in power, and in the Holy Ghost, and in much assurance; as ye know what manner of men we were among you for your sake"* (1 Thessalonians 1:5).

APPLY THE TRUTH AND INVITE OBEDIENCE

A church service will either be a masquerade or a metamorphosis of people's lives. Every service should include the practical application of truth.

James admonishes us to be "doers of the Word": *"But be ye doers of the word, and not hearers only, deceiving your own selves. For if any be a hearer of the word, and not a doer, he is like unto a man beholding his natural face in a glass: For he beholdeth himself, and goeth his way, and straightway forgetteth what manner of man he was. But whoso looketh into the perfect law of liberty, and continueth therein, he being not a forgetful hearer, but a doer of the work, this man shall be blessed in his deed"* (James 1:22–25).

No church service is complete without a quiet time of invitation when we urge people to respond in obedience to the truth. One preacher said it this way, "Too many people are coming just as they are and leaving just as they came."

The primary goal of a church service is that people experience God because when they experience Him, they will be convicted; they will respond to Him; and their lives will never be the same.

Are your church services in a rut? Are you seeing true worship and lasting life-change? Are you hearing testimonies of what the music, the preaching, and the fellowship are accomplishing in hearts? If not, ask the Lord to help you develop a Sunday service format that invites His work and welcomes His presence.

CHAPTER NINETEEN

THE SPIRITUAL LEADER'S MUSIC MINISTRY

The music ministry of your church will create a spirit—an attitude. It will either be reflective of the Spirit of Christ or a spirit of carnality. Once that spirit is created, you will minister with it, preach to it, and serve with it. Music always develops an accompanying lifestyle. Just consider culture—every genre of music has an accompanying lifestyle seen in those who immerse themselves in that style of music. In the same way, the music of your church will also largely contribute to the "lifestyle" or culture of your church.

As the pastor, the responsibility for this culture, this spirit, will rest upon you. Musical style and choices are not your music director's choices—they are your choices. You will give account to the Lord Jesus for the culture that exists in your church, caused partially as a result of the music.

With these thoughts in mind, I am amazed at how experimental the contemporary church has become with pop-music and entertainment. Pastors of these churches are seemingly more concerned with impressing people than with pleasing the Lord. Even more alarming, they have given little thought to the long-term generational impact of bringing the world's music and lifestyles into the church. They are redefining and lowering the next generation's view of God and their understanding of His holiness. Young people who have grown up in these churches, see the Christian life as a very self-centered universe that feels warm and fuzzy about God, but that doesn't actively practice a distinctive lifestyle.

Many spiritual leaders are afraid of being perceived as "different," when our world is crying out for something different! *"Thus saith the* Lord, *Learn not the way of the heathen, and be not dismayed at the signs of heaven; for the heathen are dismayed at them"* (Jeremiah 10:2). We do not have to use the world's music to reach people!

In these pages, I want to challenge you to have a truly *sacred* music ministry. Sacred music is "set apart" for God's glory. Truly sacred music inspires men to develop a heart for God and helps produce a godly, Christ-centered lifestyle. Sacred music heightens our awareness of the presence of God both in church and in our daily lives.

You may not be required to answer for what your church family listens to in their cars or homes, but you will absolutely answer for the musical diet you give them through the ministry. For this reason, I urge you to approach your music ministry philosophy very biblically and with the Judgment Seat of Christ in view. Let's examine three values of a sacred music ministry.

MUSIC SHOULD SUPPORT THE PREACHING

Music should never replace or usurp the presence and the value of the preached Word of God. God has chosen preaching to transform lives, and He uses music in the process.

Music ministry should be structured with the pulpit ministry in view. Music is to the preacher what John the Baptist was to Jesus—the forerunner preparing the way. The pastor will stand and preach to hearts that have either been distracted or prepared. If the music ministry is carnal, prideful, unprepared, and full of self, it will certainly divert the hearts of men away from God.

I believe an unprepared song or a proud singer quenches the Spirit of God as much as a rock band does. Music ministry must be focused upon God and should lead the people toward the hearing of His Word.

MUSIC SHOULD ALIGN WITH BIBLICAL PURPOSES

God gives clear instructions in His Word for the purpose of music. Consider these purposes as you develop your local church music ministry:

1. **The Purpose of Worship**—*"And all the congregation worshipped, and the singers sang, and the trumpeters sounded: and all this continued until the burnt offering was finished"* (2 Chronicles 29:28).

2. **The Purpose of Thanks**—*"Sing unto the LORD with thanksgiving; sing praise upon the harp unto our God"* (Psalm 147:7).

3. **The Purpose of Rejoicing**—*"Make a joyful noise unto the LORD, all the earth: make a loud noise, and rejoice, and sing praise. Sing unto the LORD with the harp; with the harp, and the voice of a psalm"* (Psalm 98:4–5).

4. **The Purpose of Consecration**—*"Search me, O God, and know my heart: try me, and know my thoughts"* (Psalm 139:23). (Spoken in song!) *"Praise ye the LORD. I will praise the LORD with my whole heart, in the assembly of the upright, and in the congregation"* (Psalm 111:1).

5. **The Purpose of Edification**—*"Let the word of Christ dwell in you richly in all wisdom; teaching and admonishing one another in psalms and hymns and spiritual songs, singing with grace in your hearts to the Lord"* (Colossians 3:16).

6. **The Purpose of Evangelism**—*"And he hath put a new song in my mouth, even praise unto our God: many shall see it, and fear, and shall trust in the LORD"* (Psalm 40:3).

7. **The Purpose of Preservation of Faith**—*"One generation shall praise thy works to another, and shall declare thy mighty acts. I will speak of the glorious honour of thy majesty, and of thy wondrous works"* (Psalm 145:4–5).

In addition to these principles, the Lord gives clarity as to what kinds of songs He desires to hear from His people—psalms, hymns, and spiritual songs. *"Speaking to yourselves in psalms and hymns and spiritual songs, singing and making melody in your heart to the Lord"* (Ephesians 5:19).

Psalms are simply songs based upon the Scripture. *Hymns* are songs of celebration that exalt Jesus Christ. *Spiritual songs* are simply songs of the spirit—they reflect the new nature rather than a carnal one. In three simple phrases God teaches us to sing songs that are based upon His Word, that joyfully exalt Christ, and that reflect the Spirit of God.

> *Music should never replace or usurp the presence and the value of the preached Word of God.*

From this passage we can see that there was obviously music in the first-century culture that did not reflect the new nature of Christ—and so it is today. Many churches have fallen for the contemporary worship movement and have forsaken the proven hymns of Christianity.

I realize that not every hymn is doctrinally sound and not every new song is wicked, but as a general rule, God has blessed our church's commitment to be biblical and balanced. We still sing predominantly the proven hymns of the Christian faith along with a balance of biblically and structurally solid newer songs.

By far, the great hymns of the faith are more doctrinally sound than most newer songs. They have solidified and propagated the faith through many generations, and they do not in any way reflect the world's carnal music.

Church growth experts tell you that you must give people the kind of music they like. I wholly disagree. That's like telling a doctor he must prescribe a medication that tastes good. I challenge you to give your church family the music they need, rather than capitulate to the carnal tastes of men. Ask God to renew the heart and to create new tastes for godly music. I've learned that the musical appetite of your church family should be shaped by the Spirit of God, not the preference of culture or of the "worship leader." Our church growth has been healthy because it hasn't been driven by the appetites of men or the whims of culture.

> *"As obedient children, not fashioning yourselves according to the former lusts in your ignorance: But as he which hath called you is holy, so be ye holy in all manner of conversation; Because it is written, Be ye holy; for I am holy."*—1 PETER 1:14–16

MUSIC MINISTRY SHOULD FOLLOW GOD'S PREFERENCE

I challenge you to take the high road in choosing conservative, Christ-honoring music that is obviously spiritual and not connected to the pop-culture. At the same time, choose music that is energetic and evangelistic. Choose hymns that uplift Christ with strength and expression. Make it God-centered, not entertainment-driven; but also make it enjoyable and celebratory.

Choose music that is structured with a dominant melody, supporting harmonies that create spiritual emotions, and natural rhythms that are not carnal or overemphasized. Rock music emphasizes unnatural rhythms that are dominant in the music, while new-age music emphasizes a non-melodic type of music mostly made up of harmonies. Many genres of music, when taken to the extreme, aid in producing a wrong spirit and lifestyle. May the music in your church produce a Christ-like lifestyle.

In closing this chapter, let me say that this is a sensitive subject among conservative Christians. I stand strongly opposed to the modern Contemporary Christian Music movement. I believe it has done great harm to the cause of Christ and to future generations. At the same time, I know many God-loving Christians who disagree with me on this.

To the opposite extreme, there are many conservative Christians who elevate musical preference to the point of unnecessary contention. While there may be legitimate preferences from one church to another, minor musical differences should not become major divisions between very similar ministries.

These divisions are not only unbiblical, they are often driven by pride and pettiness. In an effort to lift ourselves up, it seems that we must put others down, and sometimes the only difference between two ministries might be a minor musical preference in song selection or delivery style.

Within the bounds of biblical, conservative music, God has given much room for spiritual expression and creativity—much like He has with preaching. Do not expect every pastor with whom you associate to do everything exactly as you do—especially in music ministry, where there are so many variables upon which you could pass a petty judgment. Be patient and gracious toward those who believe what you believe doctrinally and yet have a musical preference different from yours.

Pastor, you don't have to be a musical expert to discern spiritual music. Simply ask: Is it spiritual? Is it beneficial? Does it edify? The music of your church should be Christ-centered in every way—in style, in preparation, and in delivery. Every link in the chain—from the choosing of a song to its presentation in church—should lift the eyes and hearts of men toward Christ.

Your church music will create an attitude. What kind of attitude do you desire for your church family?

(I recommend the Striving Together book, Music Matters *for helping people understand the true purpose and power of music. It is a tremendous tool in leading your church the right direction.)*

CHAPTER TWENTY

THE SPIRITUAL LEADER'S TECHNOLOGY

The information age has brought with it a world of possibilities as well as a host of potential problems to the ministry. On the positive side, information is faster and easier to access than ever. There is a multitude of new technological possibilities for ministry. Personal organization and effectiveness can be greatly enhanced. Study time can be maximized with the use of computers and internet capabilities. And creative communication techniques are easier than ever to employ.

On the negative side, the perversion and filth of the internet has caused many to fall away from the ministry into moral failure. Media and technology have become more prevalent than God's Word in many churches. And ready access to sermon outlines and church service helps have caused many spiritual leaders to become complacent in their study habits.

The spiritual leader's response to and use of technology both personally and publicly should be carefully guarded and predetermined. To the extent that we can use these tools for God's glory, we should. To the extent that we can become drawn away and distracted by the information age, we must guard our hearts, our homes, and our churches.

Let's examine a leader's personal and public use of technology.

THE LEADER'S PERSONAL USE OF TECHNOLOGY

Every week I hear of a man of God who was led astray by his use of the internet. My heart breaks for families who must endure the pain and rejection of a man who ran off with someone he met online. I've counseled many families with a father addicted to pornography or other online activities. The stories are painful and numerous—and you and I do not have to become one of them.

Technology is a tool. In itself, technology is not evil, and for the record, technology is not going away! We can bury our heads in the sand and pretend that the challenges of technology will go away, or we can engage our culture and train Christians toward a biblical response to technology.

If the spiritual leader does not learn to guard and discipline his use of these tools, what hope does the next generation of Christians have? Who will train up the next generation? If we fail to discipline ourselves and fail to train others, we are condemning future generations to failure.

Determine to use technology for God's glory. Allow the information age to enhance your study time. Allow the digital flow of information to bring quality materials to your heart—music, books, audio resources, etc. Save time by banking online, studying with Bible software, and managing your schedule with portable devices. Use email, instant messaging, and text messaging to stay in touch with those you lead. Use these forms of communication to encourage, edify, equip, and publish God's Word, just as you would use any other method. Use blogs, websites, and online media to publish the Gospel, reach the lost, and touch people around the world with God's truth.

But, we must do all of these things with great discernment and careful structure. May I suggest a few basic guidelines that will protect you and keep you in the ministry?

Expect no personal digital privacy.

Whether it's your cell phone, iPod, computer, or some other means of communication, be an open book; be accountable and accessible. Allow your wife to have complete access to all digital communication at any moment. Set up open lines of accountability with friends and your spouse so they may review any of your digital world. If you have any online or digital privacy, you are setting yourself up for temptation and a snare!

Set up filtering and accountability for your whole family.

Find and use a reliable filtering software for yourself and your family. Give your wife the access code. Have your web surfing and that of your family's logged and emailed to your wife or to a godly friend. Remember this phrase: "Elevated accountability eliminates doubt!" Be above reproach in this area.

Avoid web surfing, channel surfing, or excessive technological time-wasting.

Structure every moment that you use the internet, watch TV, or use some communication technology. The bulk of the personal failures in these areas happen because men give idle time to "surfing" TV channels or internet sites. Many men give countless hours to second lives online, social sites, games, and mindless internet browsing. Use technology to help you make better use of your time, not to waste it. Use a cell phone to communicate in godly ways. Use a portable digital music player to bring good music to your home. Use the internet to publish and access helpful information. Grow stronger in these personal disciplines so you can pass them on as examples to the flock.

Teach and train your family on the dangers and disciplines of the information age.

Pastor your family and then your church family through these dangers. First, equip your own children to use technology wisely and biblically and *then* the families of your church. Think of your children and their children twenty and thirty years from now. The seeds of biblical training that you sow will have a generational impact.

> *"Finally, brethren, whatsoever things are true, whatsoever things are honest, whatsoever things are just, whatsoever things are pure, whatsoever things are lovely, whatsoever things are of good report; if there be any virtue, and if there be any praise, think on these things."*—PHILIPPIANS 4:8

THE PASTOR'S PUBLIC USE OF TECHNOLOGY

Publicly, technology can be used very effectively and within the bounds of Scripture to enhance a worship and preaching service. As with any tool of communication, these technologies can be used improperly and ineffectively.

First, let me challenge you not to make the use of a tool in worship a standard for measuring another's doctrinal position or purity. Whether a church uses a sound system, a screen, a spotlight, or a wireless microphone, should not be considered a theological issue. These are environmental and communication preferences—nothing more. They reveal more about a church's electrical system than they do about its doctrinal soundness. Do not judge or criticize someone for using technology that you prefer not to use.

I've read and heard of good churches that were criticized for such ridiculous things as "having a sloped floor," "using projection equipment," "having an auditorium that doubled as a fellowship hall," or "employing a type of architecture that was more affordable to construct." It is a shame that sometimes we are loudest where the Scriptures are silent!

Having a metal building, a sloped floor, or a screen has nothing to do with the heart and health of a church. It is unwise to engage in such criticisms. Thank God for Bible-believing churches and pastors, regardless of the technology or the architecture that they use. I have made it a personal policy and a ministry policy that we will not criticize another pastor or ministry over some area of personal preference.

How these unbiblical discussions even enter into our pastors' fellowships while the world around us is in need of a Saviour is, frankly, *embarrassing*. Let us endeavor to keep our focus on Jesus Christ and our own hearts encouraging like-minded leaders and believers. Let us be so consumed with winning the lost around us that we have little time left for such pettiness.

Second, do not believe that the presence or use of technology in your own ministry is an indication of success. The "cutting edge" of ministry is not about the use of technology; it is about rightly dividing the Word

> *The "cutting edge" of ministry is not about the use of technology; it is about rightly dividing the Word of truth.*

of truth. I'm for doing our very best to create quality print, video, and audio resources. I believe that the Lord's church should set the highest standard. But good layout or quality video does not equal "cutting edge" success in ministry. The Holy Spirit's presence, the glory of God, and rightly dividing the Word of truth are where the "cutting edge" of ministry should be measured. Do not allow the medium to speak louder than the message.

Appreciate the blessings of technology.

Modern technology has provided some amazing blessings to the local church. We should capitalize on them and use them for the Gospel's sake. Technology allows us to cool and heat our buildings for greater comfort, amplify our voices to better be heard, use visual illustrations while preaching, and have instant communication around the globe very affordably.

Use computers and visual aids with your preaching. Jesus was our greatest example of using visuals and word pictures. These things can greatly enhance your congregation's ability to follow your outline, understand God's truth, and remember your message long after the service.

Use computer technology in your church office for keeping membership records and soulwinning databases and for financial accountability. Use media ministry to publish every good thing you can about the Lord and His church. Never before has publishing the Gospel been so easy, so cost-effective, and so world-wide in nature as it is today. Let us seize the moment and do everything we can with these blessings!

Protect from the dangers of technology.

While benefiting from the blessings, let us guard ourselves from the following dangers.

1. **Attempting to imitate the entertainment industry or corporate America**—While the entertainment industry uses technology to entertain, and the corporate world uses technology to make money, let the church use technology to minister God's Word and God's grace. Don't get caught up in an entertainment or secular mentality.

2. **Changing the style of the music**—Some churches, in their move away from hymns and biblical music, and in their thirst for technology, have turned toward rock bands and pop music. Again, let the Word of God be your standard and then use technology to promote it, not to change it.

3. **Malfunctioning of technology**—Whether it's a power-outage, a failed battery, a person who doesn't know how to pull the screen down, or a blown speaker—technology will malfunction. Frequent system checks and thorough maintenance will help, but don't allow your service to become "do or die" dependent upon technology. Lighting, sound, screens, and microphones should be subservient to the all important focus of preaching.

Technology is not intrinsically sinful. It is the use of technology that determines what is sinful and what is righteous. There are many benefits that leaders and churches can gain from modern technology, yet they must be gained with great accountability and discernment. Use technology for God's glory, and let us together raise up a generation of twenty-first-century spiritual leaders who will do the same!

_4_

PART FOUR

THE SPIRITUAL LEADER'S TEAM

The call to spiritual leadership is a call to healthy relationships. It is the call to lead a strong family, to nurture a godly team, and to lead a loving, Spirit-filled church family. A spiritual leader must be deliberate about building and leading strong teams.

> _"Only let your conversation be as it becometh the gospel of Christ: that whether I come and see you, or else be absent, I may hear of your affairs, that ye stand fast in one spirit, with one mind striving together for the faith of the gospel;"_—PHILIPPIANS 1:27

CHAPTER TWENTY-ONE

THE SPIRITUAL LEADER AND HIS WIFE

Marriage and ministry should work together in a beautiful, complimentary, completing fashion. *Because* of my marriage, my ministry should be more abundant and fruitful; and *because* of my ministry, my marriage should be stronger and healthier. I believe this is God's plan. The various relationships and responsibilities He brings into our lives should add wonderful value to each other. They should each significantly impact the other in positive ways. They should *complete* not *compete.*

Dr. Bob Jones Sr. said, "Duties never conflict." When the pastor thinks biblically and makes courageous choices to stay balanced, this is a true statement. Yet, if we do not approach our duties from a biblical paradigm, duties will often conflict. The devil is a master at creating that conflict.

A completing relationship between marriage and ministry is often elusive. How often do marriages seemingly suffer "because of ministry" and vice-versa. Our enemy is insightful and subtle. He is crafty to take these roles and turn them against each other. He is very savvy at creating conflict between two very good relationships or two life commitments. It's what he does—he sows discord and disharmony. He hates unity and truth. He hates lifetime commitment. Let's face it, he hates both marriage and ministry!

There is much good that has been written on marriage, and I cannot pretend to summarize all of God's marriage principles into one short chapter. But I can challenge your perspective of how marriage and ministry should work together. I can try to shift your heart and your paradigm. I would like to share some principles that I believe will strengthen your whole life—your ministry, your marriage, and your family.

H.B. London shared the following statistics in his book *Pastors at Greater Risk*: Ninety percent of pastors worked more than forty-six hours per week. Eighty-one percent of pastors said that they had insufficient time with their wives and families. Eighty percent believed their families were adversely affected by ministry. Seventy-five percent reported significant stress-related illnesses. Seventy percent had no close friend. And seventy percent had financial problems. Considering the drop-out rate for ministry and marriage, there's no doubt that the enemy is winning some victories in this area. It would be a mistake to "blame the ministry" for these struggles. Though they are perhaps *unique* to ministry in some respect, they are not the *fault* of ministry. God does not call us to lose our marriages and families.

> *Fulfilling your life call in ministry should be beneficial to your life commitment in marriage.*

I'm not saying that your marriage will not face challenges in the ministry. Rather, I'm saying these challenges should not be blamed on ministry; they should be blamed on the enemy who is exploiting them! The simple truth is, your marriage would face challenges no matter what vocation you fulfilled. And if it's God's will for you to serve in the ministry, then being out of the ministry might only serve to deepen the marriage struggles. When we point the finger of blame at ministry, we point it at

God and question His sovereignty. These ideas are wrong, and it's time for a shift in perspective.

Fulfilling your life call in ministry should be *beneficial* to your life commitment in marriage. These two should not only co-exist, they should be synergistic. Your marital life should be *better* because of your ministry life—and vice versa.

Let's briefly explore three aspects of marriage and ministry. First, we'll see the challenges that ministry brings to marriage, then the synergy that happens when we invest our marriages into ministry, and finally the strategy for maintaining spiritual intimacy.

THE CHALLENGES THAT MINISTRY BRINGS INTO MARRIAGE

I love being married! I love my wife. She's truly my best friend. I thank God for the wonderful marriage, family, and ministry that He has given us.

God instituted marriage for several basic purposes: to raise up children (Genesis 1:28), to provide companionship (Genesis 2:18), and to provide sexual fulfillment (1 Corinthians 7:4–5, Hebrews 13:4). When you entered ministry, you basically made the statement that you would have a model marriage—that you would be an ensample to the flock. It was about that time when your enemy began plotting the destruction of your marriage. No doubt since that time you have experienced a relentless spiritual attack against your home and ministry.

Every marriage bears the stress of children, finances, relational challenges, unresolved conflict, past pain, unmet expectations, and family turmoil. But the ministry adds a layer of unique challenges. Making your marriage strong and healthy while serving in the ministry requires that you honestly evaluate what you're up against. Consider these specific marital challenges related to ministry:

- The unpredictable ministry schedule
- The unrealistic expectations of church family
- The requirement to always be available

- The responsibility of being a public example
- The stress of criticism and gossip
- The pressure of financial stability
- The struggle for family time
- The burden of the spiritual problems of others
- The struggle for pastoral support for family
- The loneliness of ministry life
- The weight of public scrutiny
- The threat of hurtful people
- The constant presence of spiritual resistance

These challenges are real! They are difficult and they threaten the strongest of marriages. Perhaps you scanned that list and thought, "I didn't realize what I was signing up for!" Perhaps you should take a moment with your wife and talk through this list. Maybe you've never considered all that is coming against you as a couple. In the light of this list, perspective changes. Pastoral couples who think their marriages are alone in some of these struggles can begin to see that they are more normal than the devil would have them believe! Couples who are ready to quit might look at that list and think twice. If God called you into the ministry, He called you *into* these struggles—and He intends for you to *win* against them! He will equip you, empower you, and give you the wisdom you need to guide your marriage to a position of strength and passion.

Don't let this list discourage you. Let it expose the misconceptions. Let it be a reality check that stirs within you a fiery, fighting spirit—a spirit that refuses to accept anything but victory for your marriage and your ministry! Let it renew your full dependence as a couple upon Almighty God, for truly He desires to see you through.

> *"There hath no temptation taken you but such as is common to man: but God is faithful, who will not suffer you to be tempted above that ye are able; but will with the temptation also make a way to escape, that ye may be able to bear it."*—1 Corinthians 10:13

EXPERIENCE THE SYNERGY OF TOGETHER-MINISTRY

The first step I urge you to take in order to resist these challenges and overcome them together is to immerse your marriage into ministry. This is not an individual proposition—it is a *together* proposition. The husband is not the only one called—you are called together. You are one flesh, and one flesh cannot be called in two different directions. If you expect to have intimacy in marriage and if you desire to overcome the challenges that threaten that intimacy, then you must, as one flesh, embrace your call. You must, as one, fully engage together in service to the Lord.

Synergy is a word that simply implies "the product is greater than the sum of the parts." It means that serving God together brings a multiplied blessing to both your home and your church! You cannot overestimate the importance of serving together as a team. It involves a surrender of heart that resists the enemy in a monumental way! You see, his desire is to divide you, and if you bind together with one purpose to serve God, you have claimed a major battle front in this war. Satan has lost significant ground with this one decision. And when you serve together, your impact for Christ doesn't merely double, it multiplies with God's blessing—this is *synergy*.

First, decide that you will minister to one another.

> *"Put on therefore, as the elect of God, holy and beloved, bowels of mercies, kindness, humbleness of mind, meekness, long-suffering; Forbearing one another, and forgiving one another, if any man have a quarrel against any: even as Christ forgave you, so also do ye. And above all these things put on charity, which is the bond of perfectness. And let the peace of God rule in your hearts, to the which also ye are called in one body; and be ye thankful."*
> —COLOSSIANS 3:12–15

Make your spouse your first ministry. Choose to lavish upon each other affection, emotional support, tenderness, care, respect, and kindness. Recognizing that you are each the object of direct spiritual assault from a vicious enemy, determine to stand in the gap for your spouse—to fill the heart with a protective kind of love and nurture. *"…by love serve one another"* (Galatians 5:13).

Second, decide that you will serve others together.

Look at your schedule and plan when you will go soulwinning together or how you will together share hospitality with your church family. Look for opportunities to attend preaching meetings, to be a part of missions trips, or even to serve as a couple in a Sunday school class. Loving and serving God together connects your heart to your call and your call to your marriage in deep, intangible, spiritual ways!

We see a pattern of serving together in Romans 16:3, *"Greet Priscilla and Aquila my helpers in Christ Jesus."* Terrie and I have enjoyed countless hours of ministry together over the years. I love serving the Lord with her and our service together has united our hearts in a very special way. I've thanked the Lord that she hasn't tried to build a wall of division between marriage and ministry. She doesn't limit our ministry by being protective and self-centered. Our marriage and ministry are both stronger because they are connected intimately.

Are you up to the task of overcoming the ministry challenges? Are you fully embracing your call? What about your wife? Is she struggling with a heart surrender to God's call on her life? Don't let the devil have another victory. Quickly come to a point of sweet surrender, and then lock arms and begin serving your Saviour as one flesh. Your marriage and your ministry will never be the same!

DEVELOP AND PROTECT SPIRITUAL INTIMACY

The second step to experiencing victory over ministry challenges is to become spiritually intimate—to develop a "together" walk with Christ that unites your hearts and places a spiritual wall of protection about your relationship. Pastors and their wives *must* walk with God together, or they will be exceedingly vulnerable to spiritual opposition. You must align your lives together under the protecting presence of God and the blood of Christ. You must have a real and tangible spiritual oneness that runs deeply between you.

Protect spiritual intimacy through godly communication.

"Wherefore putting away lying, speak every man truth with his neighbor: for we are members one of another" (Ephesians 4:25). Consider these four different approaches to marital communication, especially during conflict:

Retaliation—destroys positive communication. The direction is against each other and leads to confrontation.

Domination—destroys open communication and squelches the other person's ability to communicate. The direction is over each other and involves intimidation.

Isolation—destroys the hope of communication through withdrawal. The direction is away from each other and leads to frustration.

Cooperation—restores the hope of communication through a desire to listen and understand. The direction is in tandem with each other and is always encouraging.

> *"Behold, we put bits in the horses' mouths, that they may obey us; and we turn about their whole body. Behold also the ships, which though they be so great, and are driven of fierce winds, yet are they turned about with a very small helm, whithersoever the governor listeth. Even so the tongue is a little member, and boasteth great things. Behold, how great a matter a little fire kindleth!"*—JAMES 3:3–5

The central theme of these three verses is simply this: if we want to give the right direction to our lives, we must start with our tongues! If we can direct the tongue (like the rudder of a ship or a bit in a horse's mouth) we can direct our entire lives. The same is true in marriage. If you focus on your words and establish godly communication, you will take great strides in directing and protecting your whole marriage!

Protect spiritual intimacy through vigilance against Satan.

This protection involves setting a spiritual guard over your wife as the weaker vessel. Realize that she is more susceptible to spiritual attack and satanic oppression, and then take every precaution to protect her and your home from Satan's influence.

Maintain a devotional life together—This will give your marriage a spiritual strength that nothing else can!

Maintain prayer time together—How many pastors will pray with church members, yet never pray with their wives? Nothing will protect your marriage like earnest prayer together.

Listen to your wife—Often a spiritual leader's wife feels that she has nowhere to take her struggles and her emotions. She needs a listening ear and a patient heart upon which to lean. Beyond that, listen to and accept her insight. Let your wife be one of your most treasured counselors.

Protect your home from sinful influences—Many times we open the door of satanic opposition because of the entertainment we allow. Guard your home from wrong movies, TV or music.

Protect your wife from unnecessary ministry pressure—There are some things that take place in ministry that a husband should bear privately with the Lord. As the stronger spouse, bear that pressure and protect your wife's sensitive spirit.

Maintain a positive attitude about ministry—More than anything, the devil wants your spirit. Refuse to blame the ministry and keep the finger pointed squarely at the enemy. Keep a positive spirit even through trials. Remember, *"Ye are of God, little children, and have overcome them: because greater is he that is in you, than he that is in the world"* (1 John 4:4).

Protect spiritual intimacy through a commitment to romance.

God has given you a special place in your heart for each other. He's given you the ability to romance each other and minister to each other in ways that no one else can! One of the most common ways the devil fights a marriage is to kill the romance—the emotional, relational, and physical oneness between husband and wife. Among all of your commitments, be committed to protecting the romance between you. When it's absent or at a low ebb, come together again quickly and reignite the fire! Romance is not an event; it's an environment. It's a way of living.

SEVEN GUIDELINES FOR CHRISTIAN ROMANCE

1. Keep a clean slate through forgiveness.
2. Maintain commitment—no flirting, no fantasies.
3. Serve your spouse.
4. Think about your spouse.
5. Pamper your spouse.
6. Affirm your spouse.
7. Surprise your spouse.

Don't even do a romantic thing if you're going to keep score. When you come to the point in marriage that you truly expect nothing, you have caught the heart of a romantic lover.

Protect spiritual intimacy by avoiding common lies and myths about marriage.

Sometimes our hearts are disappointed in marriage simply because we buy into a myth—the enemy has fed us an impossible, unrealistic expectation. Here are a few common myths from which you must guard your heart:

My spouse is responsible for my happiness—Nobody ever *made* you happy. You choose whether or not you are happy in life.

My spouse can/will provide all of my needs—If you believe this, you create a controlled dependency. You become an emotional cripple. The quality of your life is not determined by others. It is determined by your relationship with the Lord. Ultimately, only Christ can meet your deepest needs.

My spouse will give me security (who you are) and significance (why you matter)—Only God can provide a sure foundation for these needs. Your mate can damage them both, but can never take them away.

Pastor, let your ministry begin with your wife! Accept the command of God to love her as Christ loved the church. As we close this chapter, let me share some practical applications—some habits you can begin forming today to protect and nurture your marriage in a growing ministry.

1. *Express appreciation and affirmation regularly*—Establish a personal habit of filling her heart with positive and encouraging communications.

2. *Encourage her individual interests*—Applaud her giftedness and find ways for her to develop them and use them for God.

3. *Encourage her potential for God*—The enemy condemns constantly. Find ways to remind your wife that she has great potential for ministry and for making a difference.

4. *Don't ignore mood changes*—Often these are the warning signs of a deeper physical problem or spiritual attack. Go to these needs and lead her through them.

5. *Take time outs*—Regularly schedule time away together. Often, for a pastoral couple, quality time must be claimed "out of town." Take your wife away several times a year for a get-away, a family vacation, or just a long evening out.

In conclusion, the ministry brings its own unique blend of marital challenges, but God desires to lead you through them by His wisdom. The two most important responses to marital challenges in ministry are to embrace ministry together, as one flesh, serving God together; and establish a spiritual intimacy that protects your marriage from spiritual opposition—through prayer, through the Word, and through spiritual vigilance.

If you desire for God to supernaturally bless your ministry, then make your wife the priority that He commands. Don't expect supernatural blessings if you are dishonoring God by neglecting the wife He gave you. When she takes her rightful place in your heart, God will begin to do wonderful things in your church!

CHAPTER TWENTY-TWO

THE SPIRITUAL LEADER AND HIS CHILDREN

With God's calling comes God's enabling. God has called me to raise my family for His glory, and He has called me to minister to my church family. As with marriage, I believe that ministry and family should not conflict, but rather complement. Statistics indicate that the number of spiritual leaders who lose their children is staggering. How many leaders' children grow up to resent the ministry, resent the Lord, and reject the faith of their fathers.

It seems that many ministry families feel it's normal for ministry and family to conflict—as though it's an either-or proposition. My friend, it's BOTH! Some leaders seem to excuse a sluggish ministry on the fact that they are more focused on family priorities. Others seem to teach by word and example that God expects ministry to be our first priority to the willful neglect of family, and they claim that "God will make up the difference to the family." Oddly, there is not a Scripture with which to back up this claim. Nowhere in His Word does God promise to make up for your lack in family matters as long as you are expending yourself in much overtime in His church. Beyond that, the record says otherwise.

Leaders who neglect their children lose their children, and ultimately hurt their ministries as well.

While you cannot control the choices your children make once they are out of your home, you *can* choose to be the father that God wants you to be. Every spiritual leader must be a family man. The Word of God commands us to rule our houses well (1 Timothy 3:4). This is a command to have a morally honest and righteous home environment where we preside with compassionate, biblical authority. It's difficult to preside in a home where you are never present! It's impossible to establish a morally honest and right foundation in hearts with whom you never spend time.

Every spiritual leader faces the daily challenge to fully embrace ministry and fully embrace family simultaneously. Both are eternally important; both are the gift of God; and both require great amounts of time and energy. It is possible to make wise daily decisions so that neither suffers for the other. It is possible to have a thriving ministry *and* a healthy family. God desires for you to have both!

Let me encourage you to use four principles that I believe will equip you to properly balance the time and energy you expend in both family and ministry.

BLEND GOD'S DIVINE INSTITUTIONS

How easily and subtly the enemy tries to turn family and ministry against each other, as if one threatens the other. If you accept this thinking, you are believing a lie. Ministry does not threaten family; poor leadership, bad character, and fatherly neglect threaten family. Whether a man neglects his family for his favorite sport or for his ministry, the problem is still neglect resulting from individual choice.

The church is God's and the home is God's, and they should work together. Do not think for a second that your ministry is a problem for your family or vice-versa. Though I realize that problems can arise because of poor decisions and external pressures that relate to the ministry/family connection, it is vital that you not resort to blaming either one of God's institutions, as if God's plan is fundamentally flawed. It is not. It is our choices and humanity that are fundamentally flawed; God's plan works beautifully when orchestrated in His wisdom and by His Word.

I challenge you to accept God's plan and begin asking Him to help you properly blend your ministry with your family.

Start by worshipping together as a family.

"The churches of Asia salute you. Aquila and Priscilla salute you much in the Lord, with the church that is in their house" (1 Corinthians 16:19). I love the fact that the church was in the house of Aquila and Priscilla. This family understood the intimate connection between family and church. We doom ourselves to struggle when we allow a natural division between our ministry life and family life. Your relationship with the Lord should be a personal thing, a family thing, and a public ministry thing. There must be no barriers that make family less spiritual than ministry.

Do you worship together as a family? Do you lead your children in prayer? Do you lead them through devotional times? Do you bring your personal walk with the Lord into view in your family environment? Do not allow worship to be strictly a "church thing." Let worship be the continual environment in which your children are raised, both at home and at church.

Children who grow up in ministry often struggle because of the inconsistency they see between their parents' ministry persona and the people they are at home. This is not to say that you must be "perfect," simply real. Practice privately what you preach publicly. Make your public worship consistent with your family worship. Make your lifestyle and your home an ongoing environment of pure-hearted worship to the Lord.

In addition, worship the Lord together by serving Him together. Take your children with you and let them be involved in ministry. Teach them to serve. Teach them to win souls. Allow them to visit mission fields with you, to host guests with you, and to enjoy doing the work of the Lord together.

The Lord has blessed us with four children who love the Lord and want to serve Him. I believe this is in part because we've been sincere and real before our children. We have not put on a facade for the church family. We have walked with the Lord in private, in public, and in our home. We've served Him together as a family and have enjoyed many precious memories as a result.

One of our most memorable family vacations was a trip to Hawaii. Our favorite story from that vacation flows from an incident one evening when we went into a small Thomas Kincaid gallery where we enjoyed looking at the paintings. While we were there, we met the manager of the gallery (the owner's nephew), a young college student named Todd. He was spending the summer working and saving for his next semester of school.

That evening, the Lord allowed our family to share the Gospel with Todd, and he trusted Christ as his Saviour. It was a wonderful experience. Then for several days, we contacted him daily. We spent time discipling him, fellowshipping with him, and teaching him from God's Word—all while we were together on family vacation. It is one of our most precious memories as a family. I thank God for the opportunity that the Lord gave us in that moment to teach our children that ministry is not something we do as a *job*. It is who we are as a family belonging to God!

Behave passionately toward both family and ministry.

"*I beseech you, brethren, (ye know the house of Stephanas, that it is the firstfruits of Achaia, and that they have addicted themselves to the ministry of the saints,)*" (1 Corinthians 16:15). It is possible to be a passionate husband and father and a passionate minister at the same time! You *can* have a fiery family commitment and a burning ministry passion simultaneously. A passionate father fights for family time, makes it a priority, and makes up for it when it is lost to some urgent crisis or need. Yet, a passionate spiritual leader fights for study time and soulwinning time. You do not have to rob family for ministry or vice-versa. In fact, when you give your family quality and quantity time, you are helping your ministry! You are living a godly example and contributing in powerful ways to your influence. And when you pour your heart passionately into ministry time, you are helping your family.

I cannot begin to count the ways that my family and our staff families have benefited from our hard labor at Lancaster Baptist Church. Yes, we work long hours. Yes, we are intense. And yes, these hours have benefited our families greatly! The ministry that exists today—the campus, the teaching ministries, the schools, the sports programs—are the products of many hours of sacrificial labor from God's servants, and all of it has blessed the families of these servants!

Do all these activities and programs mean we are imbalanced? It doesn't have to. Certainly imbalance is a possibility, but I believe that imbalance is a struggle for everyone who is passionate about anything! I would rather fight my whole life to stay in balance because I have much to do in both family and ministry, than live such a purposeless life that imbalance never poses even the slightest threat! This would be imbalance of the worst sort—a life so out of balance that it does not even remotely align with God's purposeful direction.

BEWARE OF IMBALANCES AND RESPOND QUICKLY

Imbalance is a very real struggle for the leader who desires to be passionate about both family and ministry. Quite honestly, perfect balance is a myth. It does not exist in this life. A tightrope walker has excellent balance but never has perfect balance. He simply has acute sensitivity to imbalance and an instantaneous reflexive action to correct it. If you watch a tightrope walker, he is constantly sensitive to his position, and constantly correcting it. Hence, he achieves balance by responding quickly to even the slightest imbalance.

Such quick response is what is needed in the hearts of today's spiritual leaders in balancing family and ministry. You must develop a sensitive heart that quickly recognizes imbalance, and then instinctively, reflexively obeys the Holy Spirit in correcting imbalance.

As stated in the last chapter, ministry schedules cannot always be predicted or controlled. For the spiritual leader's family this presents a unique challenge. How do you remain available for ministry causes and still give your family adequate time? First, there is no choice—*you must*. There cannot be any other alternative. You absolutely must give both your family and your ministry adequate time and attention. Failure is not an option.

I believe the answer to the unique scheduling challenges that ministries bring to our homes is found in one simple word—*flexibility*. If you, your family, or your church family expect you to work by the clock, take a predictable day off, and live by a routine schedule, they are unrealistic in their expectations of your position in ministry. A minister's schedule doesn't fit a time clock, and his family is constantly required to make concessions for ministry. Every week, your family will likely be required to make multiple adjustments so that you can make a visit, be in a counseling session, take a phone call, or do a multitude of other spontaneous tasks related to serving.

> *You must develop a sensitive heart that quickly recognizes imbalance, and then instinctively, reflexively obey the Holy Spirit in correcting imbalance.*

If the same degree of flexibility does not exist in bending back toward your family, you will be extremely out of balance in family time. Your family time will need to be flexible and the ministry will need to flex back toward your family. For instance, when you miss a day off, schedule it for another day. When you work late one day, don't feel badly about leaving early on another. When you come through a special season that required additional sacrifice, take an extra day or two off and bring your family time back into balance.

This is what I mean by acute sensitivity to imbalance and quick corrective action. To even be able to establish this habit, you, your family, and your church must have a great spirit of flexibility. It is unreasonable for the church to expect the pastor to work a straight work day, and then to be available at all other hours—on call for urgent needs. It is equally unreasonable for your wife and children to expect that your family life will never be interrupted by pastoral responsibilities. When urgent needs arise, go to them, but establish a balanced life that balances both ministry and family needs with flexibility.

If your children grow up always giving in to ministry demands and are expected to do so with a good spirit, but they never sense the same flexibility bending back toward them, I guarantee you that they will one day resent your ministry!

Fight passionately for balance. Give your whole heart to ministry and your whole heart to family. Make the most of ministry time; make the most of family time. And expect seasons of imbalance. Expect that building programs, outreach events, and other such major projects will call you into a season of planned imbalance. Just make sure that your family consents to these imbalances and that the imbalances have a definitive *end*. Afterwards, make up the difference to family and return to a healthy balance.

Author Ed Cole said, "You don't drown by falling in the water, you drown by staying there."

BLESS THE MINISTRY IN FRONT OF YOUR CHILDREN

The Apostle Paul wrote, *"Giving no offence in any thing, that the ministry be not blamed"* (2 Corinthians 6:3). It is a great privilege to serve the Lord in ministry, but many are the young hearts that have been turned away from ministry because of the negative spirit of their parents. Frankly, some kids walk away from God because they've grown up hearing their pastor-father and mother do nothing but complain, murmur, and criticize the "hard life of trials" that they have in the Lord's service. The logical conclusion of such an upbringing in the mind of a young adult would be, "Why should I desire that life?"

The offence of the parent becomes the stumblingblock of the child. *"But take heed lest by any means this liberty of yours become a stumblingblock to them that are weak"* (1 Corinthians 8:9). I fear that many ministry couples have unwittingly turned their children away from the service of the Lord simply because of their unwise expressions of frustration, burdens, and turmoil.

Parent, your attitude is your choice. No matter what you are going through in ministry, you have a God who delights to bless you with joy and a right spirit. Ministry and home have no place for a parent with a bad spirit, and it's time that children growing up in ministry environments see a renewed love, joy, and passion in their parents. How long will we expose our children only to the negatives?

Ministry is a delight! It is a privilege. Our children must sense it in us and hear it frequently from us. For every sacrifice you have made to be in ministry, there are a hundred blessings. Have you considered them? Have you rehearsed them in the ears of your children? Perhaps they could repeat your complaints, but could they recall your blessings?

Complaining parents raise indifferent children. If your children see that you despise the ministry, they will eventually despise the God who called you to such a "miserable life." A bad spirit is a cancer in the heart of your home. Confess it, forsake it, and develop a great attitude and a grateful heart for all the blessings that God has extended to you.

I thank God for a wife who has consistently and joyfully blessed the ministry to our children. Terrie's exceptional spirit is contagious to everyone who knows her. Her book *It's a Wonderful Life* has helped many ladies have a joyful perspective of ministry.

Let your children see and experience regularly your overjoyed satisfaction in serving Christ. Magnify the blessings in their minds and minimize the sacrifices. Herald even the sacrifices as a privilege to give and serve. Let them see the joy to be found in serving Jesus Christ. Let them grow up sensing that ministry is the best way to live. Who wouldn't want that life?!

BALANCE YOUR WEEKLY SCHEDULE

The best and most practical way I've learned to stay in balance regarding family and ministry is to establish a weekly time to balance the next seven days. This concept was taught by Stephen Covey in *First Things*

First. The Bible, however, has the best anecdote for balancing time, found in Ephesians 5:15–18, *"See then that ye walk circumspectly, not as fools, but as wise, Redeeming the time, because the days are evil. Wherefore be ye not unwise, but understanding what the will of the Lord is. And be not drunk with wine, wherein is excess; but be filled with the Spirit."*

Every week, take twenty minutes to sit down and look at your time commitments for the coming week. Think through the roles that we discussed earlier. Place every important role of your life into your calendar in some way. Ask yourself when you will spend time alone with the Lord, spend time with your wife, nurture your children, prepare your messages, reach out to the lost, conduct staff meetings, and lead your church. Every role should show up in your time commitment in some way.

> *As you serve in your public role of spiritual leader, do not neglect your private role of father.*

And in the rare week when a role is lost in the fray, you will give it extra attention the following week. With this simple habit, you will never be more than seven days out of balance without deliberately deciding to be.

During this process, it would be wise to listen to your wife. Ask for honest and kind feedback. Do you give her enough time? Do you give the kids enough time? Our wives are often much better at reading the emotional gauges of our children's hearts. Generally *she* knows they need you before *you* know. Accept her godly counsel on balance.

Over time, this routine becomes a way of thinking. Your heart and mind literally become conditioned to balance, and making these weekly decisions becomes much easier to see and do.

John Adams, the second president of the United States, was a truly great patriot who was divinely instrumental in the founding of our country. Yet through the carrying out of his civic duties, he greatly neglected his children, and paid dearly for it later in life. Although his oldest son, John Quincy excelled in life and leadership, his two youngest sons Charles and Thomas lived failed lives of alcoholism.

The difference in Adams' approach to his fathering role was clear. John Quincy spent much time in his young life with his father who was involved in serving his country both at home and overseas. The other two sons were all but ignored and never really had a connection with their father.

David McCullough quotes Adams as recognizing his neglectfulness. The elderly Adams, not long before his death, wrote this solemn word of regret and advice to his eldest son, John Quincy: "Children must not be wholly forgotten in the midst of public duties."

In closing this chapter, I echo Adams' regret to you. As you serve in your public role of *spiritual leader*, do not neglect your private role of *father*. Let it never be said about you that you spent your life serving God and His people to the neglect of your own family. May God give you the daily sensitivity to nurture your family and lead your church family at the same time with great wisdom, great passion, and great balance.

CHAPTER TWENTY-THREE

DEVELOPING NEW LEADERS

A leader wisely said, "Take the high road—but take someone with you!" One leader by himself can only take the ministry so far. It takes teamwork to make the dream work. One of a spiritual leader's most serious and important responsibilities is that of equipping and developing other spiritual leaders for the work. John Maxwell wrote, "It is only as we develop others around us that we permanently succeed." This statement summarizes much of our ministry mandate from the Scripture.

Throughout the New Testament we see the work of the local church being done by teams—by godly people who served together. This is God's heart for His church. We are commanded to perfect the saints for the work of the ministry in Ephesians 4:12. In Acts 6:3–5 we see the process by which the New Testament Church identified, selected, and involved spiritual leaders:

> "Wherefore, brethren, look ye out among you seven men of honest report, full of the Holy Ghost and wisdom, whom we may appoint over this business. But we will give ourselves continually to prayer, and to the ministry of the word. And the saying pleased the whole

multitude: and they chose Stephen, a man full of faith and of the Holy Ghost, and Philip, and Prochorus, and Nicanor, and Timon, and Parmenas, and Nicolas a proselyte of Antioch:"

If you will become an equipping leader, you must have an equipping mindset. Your heart and ministry must become focused on the development and mentoring of others.

Pastors often ask me about the early years of Lancaster Baptist Church. One defining trait of those early years was leadership development—in myself and in young Christian men. For the better part of a decade, I rarely spoke away from our church. I rarely attended a conference or pastors' meeting (not that I shouldn't have). And, with the exception of the first few months, I rarely did anything alone. Every chance I could, I personally involved new Christians in the work of God. Every spare moment was focused on the development of a strong core of leaders, most of whom are still the strong core of leaders in the ministry to this day.

Before we explore leadership development, one word of caution: there is a vast difference between spiritual and secular leaders. Secular leaders "do things right," but spiritual leaders "do the right thing." In an age of corporate politics, we cannot completely transfer secular management principles into the spiritual environment of the church. We must be biblical and intentional in our approach to developing servant leaders.

Your vision will *motivate* people, but your plan will *mobilize* them. In these pages I would like to share the biblical strategy for finding raw leadership potential in your church family and developing it—a *plan* for mobilizing people for God's glory. Dr. Larry McKain once said, "A dream without a plan is a wish."

These thoughts are applicable for both staff and lay leadership, and through them I pray that God will help you develop the equipping mentality that every spiritual leader should have. Let's study a five-step process for leadership development in the local church.

STEP ONE: SELECT AND CHOOSE THE RIGHT PEOPLE

From the earliest days of your leadership in ministry, you must seek out people with leadership potential. This requires discernment and the development of relationships. It requires prayer and the leading of the Holy Spirit. In Acts 6 we see six principles that qualify a person for spiritual leadership:

> **The principle of proving**—men who have a proven testimony in the church.
>
> **The principle of credibility**—men of honest report and integrity.
>
> **The principle of spirituality**—men "full of the Holy Ghost." J. Oswald Sanders wrote in *Spiritual Leadership*, "Spiritual leadership requires Spirit-filled people. Other qualities are important, to be Spirit-filled is indispensable."
>
> **The principle of wisdom**—men full of wisdom.
>
> **The principle of humble service**—men willing to assume a servant's role in the church.
>
> **The principle of active faith**—men faithfully involved in the church body.

Godly leadership is made up of distinct qualities not found in secular management books or seminars.

A GODLY LEADER—

Finds strength by realizing his weakness,
Finds authority by being under authority,
Finds direction by laying down his own plans,
Finds vision by seeing the needs of others,
Finds credibility by being an example,
Finds loyalty by expressing compassion,
Finds honor by being faithful,
Finds greatness by being a servant.

—ROY LESSIN

Help your prospective leaders understand the unique character qualities of a servant of Christ.

It is important to note that leadership development is not about finding prominent people or about appointing leaders to be prominent. It is about discerning spiritual qualities and developing those qualities for the service of Christ. One author wrote, "Never confuse prominence with significance. If you think because you are not prominent that your ministry is not significant, you are wrong."

STEP TWO: IDENTIFY WITH AND MENTOR LEADERS

Many leaders struggle with *identifying* with people. They are either insecure or full of themselves. Both attitudes will kill your ability to truly develop leaders. Potential leaders are drawn to someone who will be real and transparent. They want to be developed by someone who is willing to identify and engage with them.

I often challenge pastors to avoid the "mystique mistake." Jesus identified with people. He walked among them, touched them, and spent time with them. Interaction is the very foundation of leadership development—personally identifying with and mentoring people.

At our church we've chosen some special events and meetings for the express purpose of identifying with and mentoring spiritual leadership. You may choose different environments, but I would encourage you to fill your calendar with mentoring times like these:

Quality men's leadership training meetings—These are usually on Friday nights. All the men of the church are invited and are given a book when they attend. This meeting involves a meal, prayer, good fellowship, and a spiritual leadership lesson or message.

Quality ladies' fellowships—These are also on Friday nights and they involve all the ladies of the church. It's a time of laughter, fellowship, food, and spiritual growth.

Saturday night men's prayer meetings—Each Saturday evening I meet with our men to pray for requests and to pray for Sunday's services. This is a tremendous time of mentoring.

Men's leadership retreat—Annually we take a small group of growing men away for two days (by invitation only) to focus on developing them spiritually.

Men and boys campout—Annually the men and boys of our church meet together for a two-day campout. This has proven to be a valuable time of leadership development and personal identification.

Focused discipleship program—Every Wednesday evening, new Christians and new members of Lancaster Baptist are personally discipled in doctrine and matters of the Christian life in a one-on-one setting.

Annual deacons orientation retreat—Each year we meet with our deacons off campus for two days of encouragement and development.

Annual staff orientation retreat—Each year our staff retreats for two days to grow in ministry training.

Frequent home fellowships—The home fellowships I have previously mentioned are a foundational part of the mentoring process.

Why do we mentor and disciple people? I believe there are five worthy purposes in developing Christians to be spiritual leaders.

THE FIVE PURPOSES OF MENTORING

1. To know the joy of a committed life to Jesus
2. To see that real Christianity is distinct from pagan culture
3. To realize that integrity must begin in their personal lives with God
4. To know that fellow Christians are praying for them and are available to them
5. To believe that God is able to do great things through surrendered people

STEP THREE: IMPART TRAINING TO POTENTIAL LEADERS

Once you have chosen spiritual people and scheduled time to train and mentor them, the question of "what you will teach" arises. Leadership development isn't merely about spending time together in ministry environments. Leadership development uses that time intentionally. Every mentoring moment is a teaching moment; and as the mentor, you must predetermine how you will use each moment. What must you teach these future leaders? Here are the basics:

Mentor in soulwinning—The church family will never rise above the leadership; therefore, it is vital that every church leader have a heart for souls and be involved in telling others about Christ.

Mentor in prayer—Church leaders must be men and women of prayer. They must understand that spiritual battles are won on our knees, and they must uphold the pastor and church in prayer.

Mentor in sound doctrine—Second Timothy 3:15–16 teaches that the doctrine of the Word of God is profitable. Your leaders must be able to rightly handle the Word of God.

Mentor in methods—Methods involve the practical "how-to" of ministry. Equipping is not merely dumping responsibility on the next available body. It is training a leader how to do the work.

Every time you are with a developing leader, impart something in the way of practical, doctrinal, or spiritual understanding. Use your mentoring times deliberately and wisely.

STEP FOUR: DELEGATE AND SHARE THE WORK

Author Ed Cole said, "Maturity does not come with age, it comes with the acceptance of responsibility." I would like to rewrite the "leadership" version of that quote. It would go something like this, "A spiritual leader's spiritual maturity has nothing to with his age, but rather with his sharing of responsibility with other mature leaders."

Delegation frightens us. The process of finding, mentoring, and empowering others is something with which many leaders struggle. Why do we hesitate to delegate? I believe there are two basic reasons— *insecurity* and *disorganization*. Either we are immature in letting others have responsibility, or we are not structured in our strategy of how to delegate.

Insecurity—Leaders who are grasping for influence feel threatened when another leader or ministry is blessed. Leaders who desire to please God feel grateful when another is blessed. These differing attitudes frequently occur within as well as without the local church. If you struggle with letting others handle responsibility, search your heart. If you envy or resent the blessings or recognition of others, or if you cling to responsibility for reasons of personal insecurity, you are greatly limiting your influence and ministry. Get over your insecurity and start helping others succeed. Find your success in the success of *others* around you.

Disorganization—Perhaps the process of leadership development just seems like nothing but work. It is, but it is biblical. Leadership development is the work of the ministry, and it is well worth it. Please do not allow your personal disorder to stand in the way of the health of your church. Don't allow disorganization to prevent others from experiencing the joy of spiritual leadership and ministry involvement. Clean up your processes and start helping others to reach their potential.

Keys to successful delegation

1. Mentor and teach before you delegate.
2. Give clearly identifiable duties.
3. Verbalize confidence in the person.
4. Give them authority to get the job done.
5. Establish budget limits if applicable.
6. Allow them room to fail and learn from mistakes.
7. Set predetermined checkpoints for evaluation.
8. Praise them and give credit for a job well done.

STEP FIVE: REGULATE AND REVIEW WHAT YOU DELEGATE

After you have chosen, trained, and involved others in the work of Christ, you must establish a process of regularly reviewing and overseeing what you have delegated. I encourage you to do this through four primary ways:

1. Written reports
2. Staff evaluations
3. Monthly meetings
4. Individual meetings

People will not *respect* what you do not *inspect*. If you do not oversee that which you have given away, then you are not fulfilling your leadership role.

After step five, you have three serious responsibilities. The first is to expand your vision; the second is to pray for and encourage your team; the third is to continue the process of delegation yourself and to teach your team to apply the same process as well.

Leadership development is not about making your life easier; it's about making ministry more effective and making people stronger in God's work. It's about removing something from your workload so God can do something greater through you.

> *To add to your church, raise up followers, but to multiply, raise up spiritual leaders.*

As soon as you give something away, your load will be lighter for the moment, but very soon God will bring a greater vision to your heart. Your ministry life will quickly be just as full as it was before you delegated, and even fuller. God uses the multiplication of ministry leaders as a means to bless your ministry greatly!

Developing leaders to help in the work is essential if your church will grow and move forward. This chapter has been about having "breakthrough ministry" by developing other leaders. Dale Burke writes in *Less is More Leadership* about "breakthrough ministry"—ministry that breaks through barriers to new growth and new levels of effectiveness. He shares three times that leaders will have "breakthrough ministry":

1. When we hurt enough that we have to
2. When we learn enough that we want to
3. When we receive enough that we are able to

Leadership development is about breaking through to another level of ministry. It has been said, "To add to your church, raise up followers, but to multiply, raise up spiritual leaders." May God grant you His wisdom as you raise up new leaders!

CHAPTER TWENTY-FOUR

THE SPIRITUAL LEADER'S STANDARDS OF CONDUCT

E very church has standards and every pastor will give account to God for the standards established in the church he leads. While every church draws the lines of biblical standards differently, every church still has lines. What we *believe* should determine how we *behave*, and every pastor must define the standard of corporate "behavior" related to ministry and outreach that the church will uphold.

By *standards,* I'm referring to the practical aspects of dress, lifestyle, and leadership behavior that the pastor will teach to the staff and church leaders. Organizational standards are not new. They are everywhere—in churches, in businesses, at golf courses, at restaurants, and throughout corporate America. People generally expect them and accept them everywhere—except within the local church. In recent years there has been an uprising against any kind of lifestyle guidelines in Christendom. The root of this uprising is often rebellion against God by self-willed Christians—people who want God and Christianity their *own way.* Just as a pastor must not capitulate to culture, neither should he capitulate to carnal Christians. The same man who would argue that he can wear "whatever he wants" to church, would not debate a golf-course standard of collared shirts. Strange. The same Christian who would argue for his biblical liberty to have long hair would not argue with an employer who required a clean hair cut. It seems that the paycheck makes the difference.

In much of Christendom, a spiritual leader's attempt to establish an organizational standard for the church (I'm referring to church leadership and within the ministry context) is deemed legalistic. Establishing standards is not legalism unless the keeping of those standards is somehow equated with earning or keeping salvation or acceptance from God. Most Bible-believing churches I'm familiar with make no such application. We know that our outward works do nothing to gain God's acceptance. We are accepted because of Jesus Christ and our salvation is sure because of His finished work. Furthermore, we are accepted in God's family regardless of our behavior—God's love for us never changes.

However, it is possible to be accepted by God and yet still displease Him in our daily walk (2 Timothy 2:1–2). It is impossible to separate the outward appearance from the inward man of the heart—the former should flow from the latter. The Bible clearly teaches us that our liberty in Christ must not be used as license to sin. *"For, brethren, ye have been called unto liberty; only use not liberty for an occasion to the flesh, but by love serve one another"* (Galatians 5:13). We should not abuse grace, but rather allow grace to teach us to deny ungodliness. In other words, God's grace does not allow us *to* sin, it allows us *not* to! *"For the grace of God that bringeth salvation hath appeared to all men, Teaching us that, denying ungodliness and worldly lusts, we should live soberly, righteously, and godly, in this present world"* (Titus 2:11–12).

It is your biblical responsibility to teach your church to deny ungodliness and to live separated, distinct lives in a sinful world. The church should once again be a standard of holiness in a dark society. Christians should live differently from the lost. It is this distinctiveness that makes us "salt" and "light." Spurgeon said it this way, "We must cultivate the highest degree of godliness because our work imperatively requires it. Our work is only well done, when it is well with ourselves. As is the workman so will the work be."

A godly leader will lovingly institute godly standards within the church and will enlist leadership to help him uphold those standards as a model of godliness to all. At the same time, this leader will love those who do not immediately adopt, agree with, or live up to the standards. And that leader will biblically teach and preach God's standards for a distinct outward lifestyle that flows from a pure heart.

Again, these are not standards for acceptance from God; they are a model of godliness that the church family must first see to be able to emulate. For instance, although we have an established dress standard for our staff and leadership on Sundays, we do not have a dress standard for our church family or guests. Everyone is welcome at our church whether they come in jeans and a tank-top, or a suit and tie. Yet those who lead, teach, sing, and serve publicly must follow the standard that we have established.

> *God's grace does not allow us to sin, it allows us not to!*

Years ago, we began to call these standards *leadership requirements*. This was a critical decision, for we did not want to mislead the church by using the word *standard*. We did not want new Christians, visitors, and guests to believe they were in any way unwelcome or out of place if they did not conform to a "standard." The goal of our ministry is not to conform people to our standard; it is to see them transformed by God's Spirit and conformed to the image of Christ! Additionally, we wanted our church workers and leaders to understand that living according to a higher standard was the privilege of leadership and influence.

Although I preach specifically against sin and powerfully for separation from the world, our primary way of teaching our standards is not the preaching. For many years we have chosen two primary methods of communicating standards.

WE MODEL STANDARDS THROUGH A DISTINCT BUT COMPASSIONATE LIFESTYLE

Outward guidelines for Christian living are first seen and experienced through godly examples in our church family. When visitors walk into our church, they immediately sense the loving, friendly spirit and they immediately see the difference in lifestyle. The church family is warmly inviting. Guests are drawn to a right spirit, not repelled by it. It is appealing and intriguing. I see this on a weekly basis—the distinctiveness of our church family truly is "salt and light" to newcomers. I do not believe that unsaved people come to church looking for an atmosphere somewhere between a beach party and *The Tonight Show*; they come looking for something to fill their empty lives.

In addition, Christians and families are constantly seeing a biblical model of appropriate dress, music, appearance, and lifestyle through our staff, deacons, and lay leaders who have agreed to support the leadership requirements. These people desire to be a godly influence within the church.

WE TEACH AND MENTOR NEW CHRISTIANS AND POTENTIAL LEADERS

This is done personally and in specific settings. For instance, although I preach about modesty in biblical terms, we focus more specifically on standards of modesty in personal discipleship and mentoring settings. A lady might take a new Christian to lunch and talk with her. A lady youth worker might take a newly saved teen girl out to the store and help her buy some modest clothes. In this way the principles are preached and taught, and the specifics are lovingly put into place through personal discipleship and leadership training.

In short, we *lead* people to the point of standards, we don't *drive* them there. We accept them as they are, where they are, just as the Lord does, but we don't want them to *stay* that way. So, we uplift the right life-model in many ways. We teach them that a Christian life is a distinct lifestyle, and we love them into spiritual growth (Romans 12:1–2).

Many churches stifle their ability to reach and disciple new Christians because they have forgotten what it is like to enter a church with standards for the first time. We have no concept of how alienated unsaved people can feel and how ostracized they can be by sermons that are preference or issue oriented rather than biblically oriented. We cut people off and seemingly reject them before they ever get planted. We give the appearance that we expect them to adhere to our standard before they've had a chance to meet our Saviour or walk with Him for very long.

While I urge you to establish leadership requirements, I also encourage you to do it biblically. Most people will appreciate the lines you draw, if they are communicated with compassion and patience. Often it is not our *position* that turns people off, so much as our *disposition*. And somewhere along the way, many churches and spiritual leaders became so proud of their standards that they lost sight of what it takes to get people to accept those standards. To the lost or newly saved, these churches seem to be intolerant of anything less than their standard. This was not the practice or the spirit of the Lord Jesus as He ministered on this earth. He met people where they were, accepted and loved them, and discipled them to become His followers.

R.B. Ouellette shares a biblical view of how to establish standards. We have used this view with our church family for many years:

1. Begin with a biblical principle—a Bible truth that I must live by.

2. A biblical principle should lead to a conviction—a personal belief based upon a principle.

3. A conviction should lead to a standard—a guideline that helps me live by my convictions.

An example of this would be the biblical *principle* that we are commanded to witness for Christ. This *principle* leads to the *conviction* that telling lost souls about Christ is my responsibility. This *conviction* leads to the *standard* that I will go soulwinning personally. Every one of your church leadership requirements must flow directly from convictions based upon biblical principles.

In closing, let me share a few practical thoughts about establishing your own leadership requirements:

1. Recognize that doctrine is the glue that holds the church together. Teach people what you *believe* before you teach them how to *behave.* Our behavior should always flow from our belief.

2. Establish your core values and leadership requirements. Place a high value on holiness and remember that these are requirements for leaders, not for members or visitors. This does not imply that you tolerate immoral behavior in your membership. It does mean you will expect a higher level of faithfulness from leaders.

3. Make sure every requirement flows from a biblical principle. Standards must be the product of specific Scriptures or clear principles. Teach the principle and not just the standard.

4. Emphasize a right heart with God. Establish your ministry upon principles of the heart, not on mere surface standards of appearance. Teach your church that godliness is *first* a condition of the heart, *then* a reflection in the life.

5. Don't push people into standards or leadership. Most mature Christians will accept God's biblical principles for a Christlike lifestyle. Focus on bringing someone to biblical maturity before you lead them to adopt a standard or accept a position of leadership.

6. Don't expect the whole church to agree with the leadership requirements. Not everyone in your church will adopt your standards. This does not mean you cannot have meaningful ministry in their lives. Don't lower the standard, just love people who don't agree with them.

7. Develop a godly atmosphere through modeling. Model a holy life rather than just demanding it.

8. Meet with potential leaders and discuss the level of commitment. Generally, these should be people whom you see maturing in grace and godliness already. Extend grace even if they choose not to accept the responsibilities of leadership.

9. Allow lay leaders to freely resign. When someone chooses to step out of a position of leadership, do not shame or manipulate him. Do not make him feel guilty. Nurture him. Disciple him. Help him stay faithful after he stops serving. Try to help him eventually into another ministry, but don't be afraid to allow people to take a break.

10. Make sure your staff upholds the standard you have raised. In general, the church family will only grow to the lowest example of the staff.

11. Establish a discipleship program. In these one-on-one settings, new Christians can be personally mentored, and they can ask tough questions about "why" we live the way we do.

12. Stay true to your convictions. No matter how hard you try to be patient and compassionate without lowering the standards, you will have people who leave the church because they do not wish to live holy lives. Some of them will one day return and thank you for taking a strong and loving stand. These people usually say to me, "Please don't ever change!"

The leader must set the standard. It must be biblical; it must be modeled; and it should be upheld by leadership. Yet, a new Christian must be given grace, patience, and nurture. People who adopt standards on a social level, in order to fit in or be accepted, will one day resent them. Those who embrace them biblically with maturity will be thankful for them and will pass them on to future generations.

THE SPIRITUAL LEADER'S STAFF

A s our church grew to approximately six hundred people in the early years, I had a conversation with Dr. Jack Hyles. At the time, he was the pastor of one of America's largest churches. He said to me, "After the church reaches about seven hundred, the future will depend upon the staff that you hire. The church has come as far as one man can take it."

The Lord used that statement to cause me to think very prayerfully and seriously about the development and future of the church staff. God has given us a wonderful team of co-laborers. It is a great privilege when God gives helpers in the ministry, and in these few pages, I'd like to encourage you regarding the hiring, development, and leading of your church staff.

The Apostle Paul worked at training like-minded men with whom he could do the work of God. He said, *"But I trust in the Lord Jesus to send Timotheus shortly unto you, that I also may be of good comfort, when I know your state. For I have no man likeminded, who will naturally care for your state. For all seek their own, not the things which are Jesus Christ's"* (Philippians 2:19–21).

One of the greatest responsibilities of the senior pastor is to identify, recruit, and challenge a leadership team and a staff around him. In his book *Execution*, Larry Bossidy describes his efforts in the amazing turn of the Honeywell corporation. He says, "I had devoted what some people considered an inordinate amount of attention to hiring, providing right experiences for, and developing leaders." He went on to say he spent thirty to forty percent of his day on this process. He also said, he did not merely have the human resources department do the hiring, he did it himself.

Dr. W.A. Criswell shared this story in his book, *Criswell's Guidebook for Pastors*:

> My predecessor in the First Baptist Church in Dallas was the famed prince of preachers, Dr. George W. Truett. He had been the pastor of the congregation for forty-seven years. When the pulpit committee talked with me about becoming pastor of this great church, I frankly and boldly told them I could not build the church as Dr. Truett had done. He built this church by the powers of his personal magnetism, his magnetic presence, and preaching. He had a small staff, maybe a half dozen or less. I truthfully said to the pulpit committee that I could not build the church on the power of preaching alone; I am no Truett. I asked the men and one woman on the committee if they would look with favor upon my selecting a staff to help me, one chosen by me and responsible to me alone. They readily acquiesced. Then we began and thus we continue after these thirty-six full years. Even the great Truett could reach just so many. The staff we have built reaches and holds many thousands more.

WHEN DOES A PASTOR NEED A STAFF?

The following principles apply whether your staff is volunteer or paid. I believe there are two basic moments when a spiritual leader should hire help:

1. When church growth demands it

One man can only do so much. A church is like a tree trunk. It grows from the inside. On the inside are the staff and deacons assisting the pastor.

2. When there is a need for balanced leadership

All leaders have strengths and weaknesses, and a wise spiritual leader will hire with these qualities in mind. There seem to be three types of pastors: the preaching pastor, the administrating pastor, and the shepherding pastor. In other words, some are stronger in public speaking, others in leadership or oversight, and yet others in mercy or care-giving.

One of the greatest responsibilities of the senior pastor is to identify, recruit, and challenge a leadership team and a staff around him.

F.B. Meyer wrote in *John the Baptist*, "Here is the secret to making the best of your life. Discover what you can do best. The one thing which you are called to do for others…Set yourself to do it." God qualifies or "gifts" us all differently and we are wise to hire to compensate for our weaknesses—in areas where we are not gifted. This requires sincere humility and honesty. John Adams provided a great example of this truth when he persuaded Thomas Jefferson to write the Declaration of Independence, saying that Jefferson was a better man and more qualified.

> "Now there are diversities of gifts, but the same Spirit. And there are differences of administrations, but the same Lord. And there are diversities of operations, but it is the same God which worketh all in all."—1 CORINTHIANS 12:4–6

HOW SHOULD A PASTOR BUILD A STAFF?

There are right and wrong ways—ethical and unethical ways—to hire a staff. As you develop your team seek to follow these principles:

Pray for laborers.

Ask God for wisdom regarding who the church needs. Pray for laborers with gifts to match the needs of the church. Pray for laborers who desire to serve.

It is easier to hire the right person than relieve the wrong person. Be patient to wait upon the Lord and have a perfect peace from God.

Recruit and hire fellow servants.

Remember that your staff are men of God, but they are not your buddies. My staff are my closest friends, but I guard my testimony in order to retain their respect, and they must give me deference as their spiritual leader.

Your staff members are worthy of honor, but they are not your accountability structure. We honor them as men of God and there is a certain level of accountability and friendship that happens naturally, but only within the bounds of the biblical authority structure of the relationship.

Be willing to receive their input, but understand their input is not the reason for their hiring. A good chemistry exists when the leader *desires* input from his staff, and when the staff *accepts* the fact that their input will not *always* be implemented.

Your staff must be examples in the local church and not independent contractors with other agendas on the side. In most churches and Christian organizations the staff is considered as employees of the church hired to implement and support the vision of the pastor or leader. Make sure your staff members don't see themselves as independent contractors with a variety of side jobs and ministry involvements which compete with or hinder the primary vision of the leader.

Consider some of these thoughts as you recruit and hire new staff:

Recruit constantly. Always be seeking men who will know your heart and believe it, know your hope and promote it, and know your hurt and protect it. Hire those with a like spirit and those who can complement your weaknesses. (You must first admit that you have them!)

Recruit and hire ethically. Speak to another senior pastor before offering a job to one of his staff. For younger people, counsel with their home pastors before talking to them.

Recruit and hire prayerfully. I often tell spiritual leaders that when I'm hiring I'm looking for God to give me a peace about three aspects of a prospective staff member's life:

+ Character—Is there a passionate, godly life?
+ Competency—Is there intelligence and teachability?
+ Chemistry—Is there a strong, pleasant personality?

Recruit and hire strategically. Usually a church and pastor first need a secretary, then a music and education combination—typically a pastoral staff member to help with music, youth ministry, and other needs.

Recruit and hire servant leaders. Look for people who can be productive, but who are also willing to serve in a less than glamorous situation. John Maxwell wrote in *The Seventeen Indisputable Laws of Teamwork*, "The goal is more important than the role."

Recruit and hire carefully. Give a thorough interview, check references, and learn as much as you can about a person. There are three primary considerations I have in hiring a pastoral leader:

+ Can he add people to the ministry?
+ Can he administrate effectively?
+ Can he teach for life change?

Most new pastoral staff members will have a strength in one of these areas and they will need your training in the others. Some new staff may not have done any of these well and you must discern if they have an aptitude for any one or all three. I would rather train a man with godly character and a right spirit than risk giving influence to an unproven man with "expertise."

DEVELOP LIVES SYSTEMATICALLY

It has been said, "Leaders *know* the way, *go* the way, and *show* the way to go." A wise spiritual leader will intentionally develop his staff on a regular basis. I think of my responsibility to develop the staff in these five basic words:

1. Model—*"Those things, which ye have both learned, and received, and heard, and seen in me, do: and the God of peace shall be with you"* (Philippians 4:9). Everything the senior pastor does becomes a model to the entire leadership team. Endeavor to personally model your ministry philosophy to your staff.

2. Mold—Establish formal training times such as weekly staff meetings, annual reviews and retreats, and personal one-on-one times.

3. Move—This is the greatest challenge I face in staff development—being able to transfer responsibilities among a growing staff without hurting people. I challenge the staff to own a ministry, and then I ask them to give it back when I feel their responsibilities have grown or that someone else should handle it. The smoothness of the transition greatly depends on the spirituality of the staff member. You are somewhat at their mercy, but a mature staff member will be understanding and godly during times of transitions. Again, a growing church—and a growing staff—are *always* in transition.

4. Mend—Do not be so naive as to think that you will never have conflict, misunderstandings, or relational struggles with your staff. But godly men who serve together will always pursue spiritual reconciliation and forgiveness.

5. Motivate—Paying them, caring for their families, and building them with positive words of encouragement and affirmation are necessary to motivation. *"Masters, give unto your servants that which is just and equal; knowing that ye also have a Master in heaven"* (Colossians 4:1). Someone wisely said, "Help people reach their full potential, catch them doing something right."

(There are excellent studies on compensation published by *The National Association of Church Business Administrators* or *The Church Law and Tax Report*.)

TRAIN NEW LEADERS CONTINUALLY

No matter the age of your church, I encourage you to develop an ongoing process of developing new leaders. Why? Here are four reasons:

Because it is our calling—We are to pass our faith on to future generations and prepare the church for the next era of leadership.

Because of life-stages in church—An aging staff will relate better to older members, newer younger staff will better relate to the next generation, etc.

Because of the growth of the church—As your church grows and transitions, you will be constantly needing new staff.

Because of attrition—Not everyone who starts the journey with you will finish it.

LEAD THE STAFF LOVINGLY

Your staff is a part of your church family. You are *first* their pastor and *second* their employer. They need a shepherd. With that in mind I encourage you to remember this:

Pray for your staff.

Have them on your regular morning prayer list and lift them up to the Lord. They are waging spiritual warfare alongside you and need your spiritual support.

Love the staff families.

Help the spouses and children of your team to enjoy the ministry. Remember them at Christmas, host fellowships for them, and reward them when they are deserving.

Forgive the staff.

When they fail and they repent, biblically forgive them and move forward. In the case of moral failure, a staff member should be removed, but many other failures can be worked through and can lead to greater grace and victory.

Be sensitive to their needs.

Help the staff have days off, balanced lives, and extra time when the season or family needs call for it. I am not responsible *for* my staff men to have the right amount of family time—that is their choice and responsibility. Yet, I am responsible *to* them to make sure family time is possible and within the bounds of their work-load and required schedule.

Be kind when they leave.

You *will* lose staff. I have a dream of living my life with the same team in ministry and doing great things for God together. I dream for the longevity of every member. Yet, in reality, some will follow the leading of God into other opportunities.

In the case of dismissal—I like the humorous quote of Dr. David Gibbs that he has shared in teaching our staff on several occasions: "If you're not fired with enthusiasm, you should be fired with enthusiasm!" On a more serious note, you should dismiss a staff member for immorality, disloyalty, or a variety of indiscretions; but be scriptural, be gracious, and be restorative. Help them transition in life.

In the case of transfer— There will be times when staff members will choose to move on for a variety of reasons. Be gracious, be quick to replace their responsibilities, and be careful to maintain a right heart and relationship after they leave.

When staff members leave, your church family will wonder why and some will be hurt. Some will sympathize with those who leave and try to drive a wedge between you. With limited information, they will sometimes assume the worst. Communicate with the church and be loving toward people.

A staff is a wonderful gift to the pastor and the church. A great staff is the product of much love, investment, and care on the part of the pastor. The spirit of the staff will be contagious to the church family—so pour your best heart and love into your team!

If God blesses you with co-laborers, thank Him for them and build them into a team of true yoke-fellows for God's glory! *"And I intreat thee also, true yokefellow, help those women which laboured with me in the gospel, with Clement also, and with other my fellowlabourers, whose names are in the book of life. Rejoice in the Lord alway: and again I say, Rejoice"* (Philippians 4:3–4).

THE SPIRITUAL LEADER AND GOD'S VISION

One of the most often quoted verses in the Bible regarding vision is Proverbs 29:18, *"Where there is no vision, the people perish…."* The word *vision* here is in reference to the Word of God. To the extent that your vision is free of personal ambition and driven purely by Scripture, it will be pleasing to the Saviour.

The word *perish* means "to cast off restraint." In other words, where biblical truth and direction is not dominant, people cast off restraint and self destruct. The same could be said about a church. Where God's truth is not blazing a forward course of faith, God's people descend into complacency, and the church stops bearing fruit.

Spiritual vision is viewing my life and ministry through the lens of God's Word. The implementation of vision is primarily an act of obedience to the Word of God. When you truly delve into the Word of God, seeking His heart for your church, the result will be revival and faith. It will be a compelling study that moves you to action in ministry. God's Word challenges us to an obedient, building, growing, forward-moving life of faith. He always calls His people forward. He commands us to occupy until He comes (Luke 19:13). He tells us to press toward the mark (Philippians 3:14) and to fight the good fight of faith (1 Timothy 6:12).

At this very moment, Jesus is building His church, and you are a part of that mission (Matthew 16:18). One of the great needs of this day is for men of faith to gain a fresh glimpse of God's vision for their churches and then to passionately lead their church families forward to accomplish the vision. God still blesses people who follow Him in faith and claim His promises.

Pastor, at what point did you decide that God had taken you as far as you could go? At what point did you conclude that ministry growth was complete? Have you accepted the status quo for too long? I pray this book enlarges your vision for ministry and jump-starts you into a new era of faith with your church family.

> *The implementation of vision is primarily an act of obedience to the Word of God.*

Peter Drucker said, "The test of an organization is not genius. It is its capacity to make common people achieve uncommon performance." In this chapter I want to call your attention to your role as the visionary leader of your ministry. Let us briefly study several aspects of God's vision for your church:

BIBLICAL VISION MUST FLOW FROM GOD'S WORD

The only way to truly capture God's vision for your church is to get alone with God and to immerse yourself in His Word. You must allow His Holy Spirit to remind you of His call and His commands. You must capture a fresh glimpse of God's purposes for your church. Spurgeon said, "The secret of all ministerial success lies in prevalence at the Mercy Seat."

From your time with God, the Lord will revive your purpose in ministry and will place specific projects or steps of faith on your heart. He will connect His purposes with *practical steps* He wants you to take in ministry—whether it's building a new building, starting a new ministry, hiring a person for a new position, or starting a new service time. God always blesses a vision that flows from His heart. Beware, for your enemy will constantly prevent your vision from growing. As one pastor said, "Monday rips vision right off the wall!"

I encourage you to nurture this vision by scheduling an extended time with the Lord. For me, this has usually been in the early to mid-summer. I try to schedule a couple of weeks exclusively for prayer, study, personal growth, and seeking God's vision. The church family understands it; the deacons support it; and I have come to rely heavily upon it. This is an essential time when the Lord directs my heart as a leader. Make this time a priority.

BIBLICAL VISION MUST FOLLOW GOD'S PURPOSES

To what purpose do we seek and follow God's vision? Are we merely building our own kingdoms? Not if we see ourselves as shepherds. Shepherds don't have kingdoms; they have flocks. Are we merely trying to mobilize people for the sake of activity and organizational energy? Not if we understand that the fields are white unto harvest. Are we trying to become notable or recognized as "successful" by others? Not if we understand that He must increase and we must decrease (John 3:30)!

Seeking and following God's vision is biblical. It is right, healthy, and faith-oriented. You may be accused of impure motives. Some may say you are "building a kingdom." Some will unjustly criticize or attack your vision. Let none of these things sway you when you truly have God's vision. The simple three-fold purpose of biblical vision is this:

1. To obey the Word of God
2. To fulfill the Great Commission
3. To lead from a heart of faith

Faith invents the future; faith invites the future; faith invests in the future. Align your heart with God's purpose. Have a clear conscience that you are acting in faith-filled obedience to fulfill the Great Commission.

When these are your motives and purpose, you can have a clear conscience with God and men.

Anything less than following and fulfilling God's vision by faith is direct disobedience to God. *"...we ought to obey God rather than men"* (Acts 5:29).

BIBLICAL VISION MUST HAVE A CLEAR PICTURE

One definition of *vision* is "a mental image of a preferable future." As you study God's Word and understand the needs of people and the needs of your church, His vision for your particular ministry will begin to come clearly into focus. Every church is different and deserves a spiritual leader who will seek God's heart in specifically applying and developing God's vision.

God's future plan for your church will undoubtedly look considerably different than God's future plan for another church. This is where broad biblical principles (such as "go reach the world") come into specific focus for each individual church.

Author David Allen in *Getting Things Done,* shares the multiple perspectives one should have of time and life management. He uses the word picture of an airplane when viewing life. The runway view looks at the immediate. The 30,000 foot view looks at a bigger picture. Still the 50,000 foot view sees a more long-term vision. He challenges his readers to look at all the views on a regular basis.

The same principle can be applied to God's vision for your church. The broad biblical principles could be compared to the 50,000 foot view—this could be the Great Commission. The 30,000 foot view might be compared to the purpose of your church relating to specific ministries and practices. The runway view would be the next specific step of faith that God has led you to take in fulfilling the bigger picture.

As you lay out and articulate the biblical vision that God develops in your heart, test it and purify it through these questions:

+ Is it consistent with God's heart?
+ Is it compelling to the hearts of God's people?

- Can it be clearly defined/developed by leadership?
- Does it reflect faith in God?
- Does it fulfill the specific purpose of our church?
- Does it meet a need?

Take the specific vision that God places on your heart and put it on paper. Define it, describe it, develop it. Turn it into a plan of action with concrete, measurable timelines and goals. Explain the "what." The "how" may still have some question marks—that's where faith comes in. But don't leave the vision intangible or vague; otherwise it's merely a fantasy. If spiritual vision will survive it must be accompanied by a strategy of faith.

Another author writes, "Process is vital. You can have the right vision or idea. You can even have the right result. But if your process is wrong you will have disaster." Develop a complete picture of your vision—one that you and others can understand, embrace, and act upon. If you don't, the vision will remain *conceptual* instead of *concrete*—and concepts are like good intentions, they're useless without action. Peter Drucker said, "Plans are only good intentions unless they immediately degenerate into hard work."

BIBLICAL VISION MUST BE PRESENTED TO GOD'S PEOPLE

Once you have dreamed the dream, you must share the dream. Vision must spread from the visionary to the visionless. This is called "vision-casting."

Once each year we have a special night at our church called "Vision Night." This is usually New Year's Eve or the first Sunday of a new year, and it's one of my favorite church services of the year. It's the time when we cast fresh vision to the church family. We share goals, express plans, and hand out materials to energize and rally our church family around a new twelve months of ministry. We hand out ministry goals, share PowerPoint presentations and visuals, and preach God's Word. There are other times each year when I share vision with the church family as well.

When God lays a vision upon your heart, you must define it, picture it, and then stand before people and inspire them to love and trust God enough to realize it. There are few moments so exciting in a church life than when God brings to reality what was once embraced by a spiritual leader and church family only by faith. These moments are simply awesome! They exalt God. They turn faith into sight. They energize a church to press forward. They literally catapult a church into a new era of ministry.

The casting of your biblical vision should be something you do prayerfully and strategically. Here are some thoughts:

Explain again the church's purpose and connect the new vision to that purpose. The church should already understand your purpose, so any new vision should relate in some way to fulfilling that purpose on a new level.

Prepare quality visual materials. In the early days of our church I used charts and signs. When we were buying our original twenty acres of land, we had a map of the acres, and we colored in each acre as we paid for it. This sign was displayed before the church family for many months.

When you communicate vision, choose and use every tool within your power to help people visualize and understand the vision. Over the years we have used thermometer charts, large signs, banners, videos, projection, PowerPoint, maps, printed brochures, budget plans, models, artist renderings, lapel pins, sticky-note pads, and a host of other gifts and memorabilia to communicate and cast vision.

Emphasize biblical purpose over budget. When you cast a vision by faith, you may not always know how the vision will be paid for. Be sure to follow your vision and trust God with the budget. If you are 100% sure of His vision, He will provide in time.

BIBLICAL VISION MUST BE PROVED

When thinking of vision, we don't often think of this part of the process, but I share it to give you fair warning. God often places a vision on the heart of a leader long before it will ever be realized. Often between the conceiving of the vision and its realization, there is a long journey involving both mountain-tops and valleys. God usually has much molding and preparation work to do upon His man and in His church before the vision is complete.

Entering into the process of realizing God's vision will bring you through stretching, trials, and testing. It will push you to your limits in every way—what we often call "reaching our potential." It will cast you utterly and irreversibly out of your comfort zone and place you uncomfortably out on a limb where you will feel absolutely vulnerable—and yet at peace—knowing this is God's limb!

One author wrote about pursuing new vision with these insightful terms: *pace* yourself, *brace* yourself, and *grace* yourself!

Every vision goes through a season of proving. Like a clay vessel in a kiln, this time solidifies and strengthens both the heart of the visionary and the vision itself. There are three qualities upon which you must rely during the proving process:

Prove vision through prayer—Test your heart, your motives, your vision, and your reliance through your time with God.

Prove vision through patience—Allow God to give you the peace and provision that you might move forward. Remember that He works on His timetable, not ours. What God originates, He also orchestrates.

Prove vision through persistence—It has been said, "Any time you step out to kill a giant there will be criticism." Every vision attracts criticism, and your persistence must lead the vision forward in spite of it. Another man wrote, "Change is the chief price of vision, and with change comes resistance."

Every man who ever set out to do anything for God encountered resistance. It would be wonderful to think that everyone would encourage you in obeying God's vision, but that's not reality. Your vision will experience criticism from three types of people: the fearful, the complacent, and the short-term thinkers. Don't let small-minded people keep you from obeying God's leading. Author Ed Cole said, "Don't let others create your world for you, they will always create it too small!"

BIBLICAL VISION HAS A POWERFUL PRODUCT

God is pleased with faith—Hebrews 11:6 states, *"But without faith it is impossible to please him: for he that cometh to God must believe that he is, and that he is a rewarder of them that diligently seek him."* Every time you capture and follow a biblical vision, you are acting in faith, and the product will be powerful and wonderful.

Over twenty-two years, we have experienced the product of fulfilled vision many times together as a church family. Every time, the product was worth the price—though often, in the midst of the process, I was tempted to wonder! Here are a few of the results we've enjoyed—I believe your church family, too, will be blessed by the realization of biblical vision.

God's people are inspired to be a part of something great. Everybody desires to be a part of something bigger than himself.

The church furthers its mission. Every time we have launched out in faith, the purpose of the church multiplied and grew. One preacher said, "Today's churches are either risk-taking, care-taking, or under-taking."

The people grow in faith. Nothing has stretched and grown our faith more than these seasons of forward momentum and excitement.

The pastor grows in leadership. The leader is always stronger, wiser, and more equipped to lead through the growing process. This truly is the "working out" of our faith (Philippians 2:12).

The Lord is glorified. People stand in awe at God's blessings and power when His vision becomes real.

The first time Dr. Lee Roberson preached at our church, I was about twenty-eight years old. We were still meeting in our small, downtown building. On Tuesday morning of his visit, I drove him to the site of our future campus, four miles east of Lancaster. As we came to a stoplight, he put his hand on my arm and said, "Brother Chappell, you need to pastor this city."

I asked him what he meant. He began to challenge me to enlarge my vision for my role of spiritual leadership. He told me of soulwinning opportunities, neighborhood surveys, special days to honor public servants, and other ideas to reach out to our whole city. His challenge helped me broaden my vision for the work of the Lord.

I have no desire to be known as the pastor of our city for vain reasons, but I do desire that everyone in our city know there is a place where they can be loved and where they can meet Jesus Christ as their personal Saviour. Since that challenge by Dr. Roberson, very few people have ever lived in our city without multiple opportunities to know Christ, and thousands have accepted Him through the years. To this day, I thank God for the moment that Dr. Roberson challenged me to have a greater vision.

Following a spiritual vision will lead you in finding God's destiny for your life. It will broaden your understanding of God's call. Are you ready to experience God's destiny for your life and your ministry? Has this chapter ignited a flame in your heart to capture and realize God's best? I pray it has.

Godly vision must be biblically based, personally inspiring, change oriented, customized to your ministry, detail oriented, people oriented, and Christ centered. He still does great things! He's looking for leaders who will seek Him, listen to Him, and then obey Him by leading others to obey Him also.

Helen Keller said, "The most pathetic person in the world is someone who has sight, but has no vision."

Get alone with God; capture His vision in your heart; and then get out on a limb—right into the palm of His hand!

5

PART FIVE

THE SPIRITUAL LEADER'S TRIALS

The life of a spiritual leader inevitably leads through some deep valleys—both personally and with the flock. The winding trail of Christian service leads through personal pain, suffering, loneliness, discouragement, sacrifice, and burdens; but the almighty hand of God is always there to offer grace, strength, and comfort until the journey is done.

> *"Wherein ye greatly rejoice, though now for a season, if need be, ye are in heaviness through manifold temptations: That the trial of your faith, being much more precious than of gold that perisheth, though it be tried with fire, might be found unto praise and honour and glory at the appearing of Jesus Christ:"*—1 PETER 1:6–7

CHAPTER TWENTY-SEVEN

THE SPIRITUAL LEADER'S MOTIVATOR—GRACE

S ome of the enemies of Bible-believing churches are convinced that your faithful church members are duped by demagoguery or control tactics. They say it's all about your ego. They are not content to let (what they believe is) wood, hay, and stubble burn at the Judgment Seat of Christ; they are going to burn it for Him now, and some are hoping you get burned in the process.

No matter how biblically correct your life or ministry, no matter how blameless your morals or doctrine, you will face criticisms in the ministry. These difficult times often revolve around the burdens or trials of ministry. Other times they involve the painful attacks of critics and hurting people.

The ministry is a call to expend your life in loving people. That love expresses itself in tenderness, rebuke, encouragement, and reproof. Paul instructed Timothy to *"reprove, rebuke, and exhort with all longsuffering and doctrine"* (2 Timothy 4:2). But not everybody will appreciate or respond positively to your love. In 2 Corinthians 12:15 Paul wrote, *"And I will very gladly spend and be spent for you; though the more abundantly I love you, the less I be loved."*

The apostle wrote often of the trials he experienced in ministry. In 2 Corinthians 11 he shares of the "trials from without" which included perils, physical suffering, hunger, and a variety of persecutions. He spoke of the burden from within of "the care of all the churches." He wrote in chapter 12 of a thorn in the flesh—a messenger of Satan—referring to spiritual warfare. Paul called his ministry a *course* to be run, a *fight* to be fought, and a *faith* to be kept. He wrote of being vigilant, being aware, and being "not weary."

> *Grace is the spiritual leader's great motivator.*

The writer of Hebrews wrote in Hebrews 10:32, *"But call to remembrance the former days, in which, after ye were illuminated, ye endured a great fight of afflictions."*

It's difficult to read a page of the New Testament without seeing in some way the trials of the Christian life and of ministry. We could spend the next few chapters having "group therapy," recalling all of our hurts and pains. But I'd rather call your attention to a higher principle.

Every trial, every critic, every hurt that you experience in ministry has a divine purpose. God wants to do something in you through these trials. He wants to establish your ministry in His grace. He desires to do a cleansing, purifying, and distilling work in your heart and motives. He desires to strengthen you for greater ministry and bigger blessings. He plans to broaden your shoulders so that you will be able to shoulder larger opportunities.

Through trials He desires to purify your motivations and strip away all but one of them. After you endure your own "great fight of afflictions" you will discover:

- A paycheck won't keep you in ministry.
- Approval of man won't keep you in ministry.
- A dynamic growth spurt won't keep you in ministry.
- A perk or benefit won't keep you in ministry.
- An invitation to preach won't keep you in ministry.
- An ego or selfish agenda won't keep you in ministry.
- Were it not for God's *grace*, no minister would finish his race.

Grace is the spiritual leader's great motivator. It is your endless supply and your only eternal motive. It is the source of both your strength and your passion, and it is the only tool you have by which to deeply and spiritually motivate God's people.

What was the great lesson Paul gave after he rehearsed all of his trials and spiritual battles? *"And he said unto me, My grace is sufficient for thee: for my strength is made perfect in weakness. Most gladly therefore will I rather glory in my infirmities, that the power of Christ may rest upon me"* (2 Corinthians 12:9).

In the next few pages, I desire to help you glory in your infirmities and rejoice that the power of Christ rests upon you. I pray that these words will lift your eyes from the pain of your burden to the grace of your Saviour. Truly His grace is sufficient for whatever He asks you to endure. In this chapter we will explore the primary source of motivation in all spiritual leadership—grace. The surest way to make your ministry foolproof and to leave your critics' words empty and baseless is to have a thoroughly biblical, grace-led ministry.

ESTABLISHING A GRACE-LED MINISTRY

You will never bulletproof your ministry from all attack or all criticism. You will never make everyone happy. The Word of God has enemies, and sometimes they come from within (1 Corinthians 11:18). The only biblical response to trials, attacks, and criticisms is the response of grace. The surest way to make your ministry "blameless" is to have a grace-based ministry philosophy. You might call this chapter the biblical way to preemptively defend yourself from carnal critics. Your best answer, before critics ever speak, is to establish a biblical and gracious testimony.

God has commanded us to confront wickedness with boldness. *"Awake to righteousness, and sin not; for some have not the knowledge of God: I speak this to your shame"* (1 Corinthians 15:34). Yet, He also desires that our spirit be bathed in the grace of God. *"Be not carried about with divers and strange doctrines. For it is a good thing that the heart be established with grace; not with meats, which have not profited them that have been occupied therein"* (Hebrews 13:9). *"But grow in grace, and in the knowledge of our Lord and Saviour Jesus Christ. To him be glory both now and for ever. Amen"* (2 Peter 3:18). In 1754 President John Adams wrote, "It is the duty of the clergy to accommodate their discourses to the times, to preach against such sins as are most prevalent and to recommend such virtues as are most wanted." Spiritual leadership involves leading people in the path of God's grace—a grace that inspires, encourages, bears burdens, and confronts ungodliness. Spiritual leaders lead from a platform of grace, but fleshly leaders push their own agenda.

First, let's examine several wrong ways to motivate ourselves and God's people.

MOTIVATION THAT HURTS CHRISTIAN GROWTH

This list represents a few unbiblical motivational techniques. These things not only hurt people, but also give credence to critics. These things flow from our own flesh and our impure hearts. As you read, allow the Holy Spirit to search your heart and purify your leadership style. Ask the Lord to rid your pulpit or ministry life of any trace of these harmful habits.

Guilt or Shame

Are you trying to create conviction in your own power? There is a difference between guilt and conviction. Guilt brings condemnation and shame. Conviction leads to repentance and growth. Don't ever confuse the two, and don't allow someone to label conviction as guilt. Guilt is often the result of a leader trying to manufacture conviction. Some people respond to this tactic for a season, but eventually they resent it. I have been to preaching conferences where the speakers have tried to intimidate listeners to take a particular position. Sometimes this type of preaching is entertaining, but it is not life-changing!

Anger

Do you have a "short fuse"? The ministry and the pulpit have no room for unrighteous anger. Too often leaders hurt the credibility of ministry and of Christ because of their own unresolved anger. A temper tantrum is not biblical preaching. Shepherds don't beat sheep, they lead them.

Manipulation

Don't try to manufacture emotion. This is manipulative and it preempts and bypasses the work of the Holy Spirit. For instance, make sure your own message or the testimonies others share are authentic and reverent. Be careful of creating a "performance-based acceptance" environment in your church. Don't motivate people to serve the Lord just so they will feel more accepted or have a higher place of recognition or leadership.

Furthermore, try not to be known as the pastor who is always in a health or financial crisis. You may have these types of challenges, but it's not wise to lead from the "poor me" platform.

Fighting

Who can ever forget Winston Churchill's immortal words: "We shall fight on the beaches, we shall fight on the landing grounds, we shall fight in the fields and in the streets, we shall fight in the hills." It sounds exactly like some of our Christian leaders!

Are you drawn toward carnal disputes and discord? Some leaders are. I've known many Christians who seemingly have a bent toward division. It's like they love picking scabs. They don't want resolution or healing because then their purpose for living would be gone, and they would have nothing at which to pick! Pastor, this is a carnal way to live life and a carnal way to lead. Get over your need to "pick a fight" with the pastor across town or across the state and get back to fighting "the good fight of faith." *"And the servant of the Lord must not strive; but be gentle unto all men, apt to teach, patient"* (2 Timothy 2:24).

Intimidation

Do you use your position of authority to "lord over" people and to get them to do what you want them to do? Do you hurt people with your raised voice, your demanding tone, your unapproachable spirit, or your caustic vocabulary?

"Feed the flock of God which is among you, taking the oversight thereof, not by constraint, but willingly; not for filthy lucre, but of a ready mind; Neither as being lords over God's heritage, but being ensamples to the flock."—1 PETER 5:2–3

As a leader, your position will naturally intimidate people. Your shepherding spirit should work to balance out this natural factor. God's people should not be intimidated by their spiritual leader.

MOTIVATION THAT HELPS CHRISTIAN GROWTH

How do we stay motivated when we don't feel like going on? How do we biblically motivate God's people? How can we know that the service taking place in our church is truly the result of "growing in grace"? God has given us some motivational tools in His Word that are pure, right, and effective. We saw them briefly in the chapter about stewardship. When you stand before Christ and give account for your ministry, let it be these tools that you used to motivate God's people:

The love of God

When you get a fresh glimpse of God's love, a heart-level desire to live for Him wells up in your life. His love for you and your love for Him are the purest of all motivations! *"For the love of Christ constraineth us; because we thus judge, that if one died for all, then were all dead"* (2 Corinthians 5:14).

The grace of God

God's grace creates a joyful, sweet, willing-hearted disposition. When people serve God out of guilt, they ultimately resent the leader and possibly even the Christian life! When they serve Him out of grace, they willingly, joyfully, and selflessly continue in faithfulness. *"Thou therefore, my son, be strong in the grace that is in Christ Jesus"* (2 Timothy 2:1).

The Word of God

You will never go wrong using Scripture to motivate. God's Word is powerful and it effectually works in the hearts of men. *"All scripture is given by inspiration of God, and is profitable for doctrine, for reproof, for correction, for instruction in righteousness: That the man of God may be perfect, throughly furnished unto all good works"* (2 Timothy 3:16–17).

The people of God

God commands us to provoke each other to good works: *"And let us consider one another to provoke unto love and to good works: Not forsaking the assembling of ourselves together, as the manner of some is; but exhorting one another: and so much the more, as ye see the day approaching"* (Hebrews 10:24–25). One of the greatest motivators in a church family is the godly example and encouragement of other Christian friends.

Frankly, I've seen both biblical and unbiblical models of motivation in Bible-believing churches. Every spiritual leader is human, and we all have our fleshly tendencies. The filling of the Spirit will evoke these biblical motivations. These motivations will guard you and protect God's people. You will still be criticized; you will still be attacked. But the undeniable record of your grace-based ministry will easily silence those critics. As President John Adams stated, "Facts are stubborn things...."

FIVE WAYS TO DEVELOP A SPIRIT OF GRACE:

1. Seek the filling of the Holy Spirit.
2. Avoid crudeness in the pulpit.
3. Don't retaliate when you are attacked.
4. Forgive when you are mistreated.
5. Don't bring ministerial battles to your pulpit.

MOTIVATION THAT PRODUCES GODLINESS

Grace is a disposition—a lifestyle created by the Holy Spirit. *"This I say then, Walk in the Spirit, and ye shall not fulfill the lust of the flesh"* (Galatians 5:16). *"If we live in the Spirit, let us also walk in the Spirit"* (Galatians 5:25).

"And God is able to make all grace abound toward you; that ye, always having all sufficiency in all things, may abound to every good work:"—2 CORINTHIANS 9:8

When you have a grace-based ministry, great things happen, and they are singularly attributable to God's work in the hearts of men. This is the desire of God—His glory! If men serve God in your church, let it be because they were motivated by His grace and not by your good charm. For then is God glorified and Christ exalted.

What are the results of a grace-based approach to ministry? There are four I would share:

We live separated lives by grace.

"For the grace of God that bringeth salvation hath appeared to all men, Teaching us that, denying ungodliness and worldly lusts, we should live soberly, righteously, and godly, in this present world."—TITUS 2:11–12

The greatest way to establish a separated church family is through God's grace.

We serve God by grace.

"As every man hath received the gift, even so minister the same one to another, as good stewards of the manifold grace of God."
—1 PETER 4:10

"And the multitude of them that believed were of one heart and of one soul: neither said any of them that ought of the things which he possessed was his own; but they had all things common. And with great power gave the apostles witness of the resurrection of the Lord Jesus: and great grace was upon them all."
—ACTS 4:32–33

God's grace draws out sincere-hearted service. No church is ever more active or more abundant in service than when God's grace is at work.

We sacrifice to God by grace.

"Therefore, as ye abound in every thing, in faith, and utterance, and knowledge, and in all diligence, and in your love to us, see that ye abound in this grace also."—2 Corinthians 8:7

Nothing motivates more cheerful, willing surrender and faithful stewardship like God's grace.

"But this I say, He which soweth sparingly shall reap also sparingly; and he which soweth bountifully shall reap also bountifully. Every man according as he purposeth in his heart, so let him give; not grudgingly, or of necessity: for God loveth a cheerful giver." —2 Corinthians 9:6–7

We continue in trials by God's grace.

"And he said unto me, My grace is sufficient for thee: for my strength is made perfect in weakness. Most gladly therefore will I rather glory in my infirmities, that the power of Christ may rest upon me."—2 Corinthians 12:9

"Let us therefore come boldly unto the throne of grace, that we may obtain mercy, and find grace to help in time of need." —Hebrews 4:16

The greatest sustaining factor in trials is not our own strength or determination, it is God's grace.

Pastor, do you see the path of leadership? It is *grace!* Your heart desires to see God's people do all the things we just listed. How you lead them to *do* those things will either be *biblical* or *carnal*. It is possible to lead a church family to do the *right things* the *wrong way!* God gives the right way—*grace!*

May we be models of the grace of God. May we call upon His grace to motivate His people. May we reflect His grace from the pulpit and in our daily lives. Grace is the great motivator. *"And all bare him witness, and wondered at the gracious words which proceeded out of his mouth"*

(Luke 4:22). *"Let your speech be alway with grace, seasoned with salt, that ye may know how ye ought to answer every man"* (Colossians 4:6).

John Adams' quote "Facts are stubborn things…" continues this way, "and whatever may be our wishes, our inclinations, or the dictates of our passion, they cannot alter the state of facts and evidence." Your critics' inclinations cannot alter the foundation of grace in your ministry.

Occasionally, if you are pressing forward in faith, you will have scornful critics rise up against you. They will scrutinize every detail of your life. They will nitpick at little nothings. They will distort reality. They will scrape and scavenge for any scrap of negativity or impurity in your heart and life. They will be inclined toward and passionate about hurting you.

If, for all their wasted time and frivolous personal turmoil, all they scrape up is *grace*, then their charges will be left as an empty echo and your ministry will be stronger for their unwitting contribution!

CHAPTER TWENTY-EIGHT

THE SPIRITUAL LEADER'S CRITICS

One pastor wrote, "The qualifications of a pastor are to have the mind of a scholar, the heart of a child, and the hide of a rhinoceros." It has also been said, "Treat both criticism and praise like bubble-gum—chew on it a bit, but don't swallow it!"

The ministry certainly hasn't become any easier in the past fifty years. Studies show that leaders are leaving the ministry at greater rates, and Americans have a less favorable view than ever of fundamental Christianity. In fact, much of the world hates our beliefs. Recently *USA Today* reported that fifty-seven percent of Catholics had a favorable view of Muslims, while only forty-six percent had a favorable view of fundamental Christians!

Abraham Lincoln wrote, "If I were to try to read, much less answer, all the attacks made on me, this shop might as well be closed for any other business. I do the very best I know how—the very best I can, and I mean to keep doing so until the end. If the end brings me out all right, what is said against me won't amount to anything. If the end brings me out wrong, ten angels swearing I was right would make no difference."

In this chapter I'd like to take a closer look at the criticism and hostility that is mounting more and more against Bible-believing Christians and churches. While we cannot control it, we can respond biblically to it, and by walking in wisdom, we can do much to prevent it.

WHY HOSTILITY TOWARD CHRISTIAN LEADERS IS GROWING

We are attempting to lead people in a very unusual day. More than ever, pastors are suspect. Gone is the day when you were trusted and respected merely because you were a minister. More and more, this title automatically brings you under closer inspection and greater suspicion. Harold Myra wrote, "The furnace that forges leadership burns steadily, and this is particularly true among those charged with very large responsibility."

Warren Wiersbe shares in *The Integrity Crisis*, "The church has grown accustomed to hearing people question the message of the Gospel, because to them the message is foolish. But today, the situation is embarrassingly reversed, for now the *messenger* is suspect."

Why is this? What factors influenced such a decline in respect toward spiritual leaders? I believe there are seven:

Media portrayals of ministry

Rarely does a news program or entertainment venue represent spiritual leadership in a positive light. From ministry scandals to cultic abuse cases to outrageous caricatures, pastors and spiritual leaders are almost always positioned negatively on TV and other media.

Proliferation of cults

More and more books are being written and documentaries produced about the growth and bizarre behaviors of cultic groups. In recent years we have seen mass suicides, polygamy, child abuse, and money-laundering. Many of these cults (such as the Mormon Church) have co-opted Christian terminology and tried to identify themselves as mainstream

Christianity. Their duplicity greatly increases our need to clearly define ourselves and walk wisely.

Secular humanism/New Age cults

With the rise of eastern mysticism and spiritualism, there is a growing outright hatred of Jesus Christ, His Cross, and His Gospel.

Failure of Christian leaders

It seems annually that there is another nationally recognized leader in Christendom who falls publicly to either moral failure or to financial improprieties. To the average unchurched person (whom we are trying to reach) this has a growing negative impact.

Unbelievers owning Christian publishing houses

Christian literature has progressively become less and less doctrinal and distinctive and more profit-driven by a broad market. The more vague and obscure the spiritual thirst of the nation has become, the more vague the Gospel has become from mainstream publishers.

Jealousy/envy

This kind of hostility is usually from within Christendom and from those who share our faith. We experienced much more of this when our church became larger. I will never understand why we do not rejoice in God's blessings for another ministry, and I cannot comprehend why we have to actively undermine what God is doing, even if we choose not to rejoice!

Imbalanced ministries

Frankly, some criticisms spiritual leaders face are brought on by themselves, usually when employing the unbiblical motivations that we studied in the last chapter. A lack of discernment in the pulpit, an inability to control the tongue, and a prideful attempt to "take a stand" have often exposed a carnal side of an otherwise good man. These actions prove a man to be full of the flesh and not the Spirit (at least in those moments).

A critic is someone who points out how imperfectly other people do what the critic does not do at all!

HOW HOSTILITY IS REVEALED

In short, you're going to have painful things coming at you from four different directions—a secular work place, a hateful world, carnal Christians, and jealous leaders. It probably helps just to know you are not alone! Every leader who ever tried to do anything for God faced this kind of opposition. Let's look more closely at the sources of hostility:

From the public at large

A world that hates Christ will not appreciate your knocking on their doors or making a difference in their communities. First John 3:13 says, *"Marvel not, my brethren, if the world hate you."*

From some government/industry personnel

We live in a secular environment that is tolerant of everything and everyone but a Bible-believing Christian. Acts 5:18 says, *"And laid their hands on the apostles, and put them in the common prison."*

From antagonistic church attendees

There are those who are pathologically drawn to controversy, to the point of instigating it when it cannot be found. Every church has these kinds of members. They like to fester around conflict. Where conflict doesn't exist, they imagine it and then fester around their imaginations. One evidence of a pathological antagonist is the fact that he has been a member of numerous churches in the same community throughout his lifetime. They have great difficulty planting anywhere and serving God graciously.

Titus 3:9–11 warns of this type of person, *"But avoid foolish questions, and genealogies, and contentions, and strivings about the law; for they are unprofitable and vain. A man that is an heretick after the first and second* admonition reject; Knowing that he that is such is subverted, and sinneth, being condemned of himself."

When you compassionately confront them to resolve the conflict, you are deemed legalistic and "a gestapo agent." If you do not confront them you are labeled as "unapproachable" and a "dictator." You cannot please them unless you respond in kind and step into the "ring." They are disturbed and hurting, and they are often envious of you. The only way they feel better is if you hurt as well.

From religious leaders

These are leaders who must demean you in order to lift themselves up in the eyes of others. In a grasp for influence or out of internal envy, they respond with carnality to injure a brother. Bob Smith wrote, "All you have to do to make some Christian people angry with you is to become a failure or a success. When you know more, do more, or have more, people hate you. The Christian world is looking for leaders who are brilliantly mediocre!"

Third John 1:9–10 teaches, "*I wrote unto the church: but Diotrephes, who loveth to have the preeminence among them, receiveth us not. Wherefore, if I come, I will remember his deeds which he doeth, prating against us with malicious words: and not content therewith, neither doth he himself receive the brethren, and forbiddeth them that would, and casteth them out of the church.*"

Another author states, "When you're small they'll dismiss you. When you're growing they'll criticize you, and when you are large they will resent you. So ignore them and go on with what God has you to do."

Being attacked hurts—especially when you know the attacks are untrue, distorted, and unfair. When you know your record is clean—you have been faithful to your wife, true to strong doctrine, sincere in your ministry, and pure in your motives—it's painful to discover that others are still unhappy with you. After all, you didn't envision attacks when you were in Bible college. You never dreamed that spiritual leaders could generate enemies simply because of their ministry position. You longed to serve God and love people, and for it, you've been slandered—sometimes by the very ones you tried the hardest to love!

In these moments, everything within you wants to rise up and defend yourself and protect the Lord's sheep. You want to engage and win. And if you have a true servant's heart, your greatest concern is the younger Christians and weaker members of your flock. You know the wolves will be looking for the weaker, struggling, and more vulnerable sheep. They always do. They find them at the grocery store or the mall and they typically invite them to a "Bible study." The essential question is, how should a godly leader respond? What would God have us to do in the face of such growing hostility?

Rarely have my critics gone to the stronger Christians in our church with their issues. Normally a person who has recently trusted Christ is chosen, and the wolf is usually very subtle and deceitful. Doubtful comments and crafty words can easily lead a naive new Christian astray. This danger is a shepherd's first thought when wolves are near the fold.

HOW BIBLICAL LEADERS RESPOND

Allow me to share with you a twelve step course of action when you are under assault. (And, no, I'm not assuming your trials have led you to start drinking!)

Go to God in prayer.

First, take your burden to the Lord. This is His flock, and you are His man. In His presence you will gain strength, wisdom, and perspective. You will be reminded of your dependence upon Him.

Rest in the sovereignty of God.

Early in the process there must be a yielding of your will to God's. You must accept that He has allowed the attack, and you must rely on His timetable and His process to respond to it. God has not forgotten you. He is working in you and He is preparing you for a greater work—even through the efforts of the critics. Remember, anything out of your control is in His plan. There is not a season of criticism in our ministry that has not been immediately followed by a far greater season of growth and blessing—and the harder the trial the greater the blessings! Though the criticism and attacks were hurtful for the moment, months later and in retrospect, I have often felt that the trials moved me forward in God's grace.

Receive difficulty as a friend to develop you.

Ask the Lord to help you, by faith, to see the blessings that will result from the burden. Accept the trial that you might win the crown. The psalmist wrote, *"It is good for me that I have been afflicted; that I might learn thy statutes"* (Psalm 119:71). Looking back, spiritual burdens and trials have always helped us to go forward in ministry—every time.

Don't retaliate.

Mark Twain said, "Few slanderers can stand the wear of silence." In moments of attack, you want to react. He who throws mud always loses ground. Hold your tongue, hold your pen, hold your internet postings; grab hold of your words and submit them to the approval of the Holy Spirit of God. Don't abuse your authority or use your pulpit as a battering ram.

> *A critic is someone who points out how imperfectly other people do what the critic does not do at all!*

Every time our ministry has been attacked, I have called on the counsel of godly leaders and friends. Without fail, they have urged me not to retaliate. A few times I found myself in a position where retaliation would have been very easily accomplished. Thankfully, the Holy Spirit guided me in those moments to protect the testimony of the ministry.

Many years ago, one of the most painful and slanderous attacks against our church was delivered by some individuals who served in positions of civic public service. Their actions were not only wrong; they were an abuse of their positions. Several years later, I had an appointment in my office with a very prominent public figure who happened to be the head of the organization where these individuals served. The appointment was requested by this man for the purpose of hearing the Gospel. It was a tremendous open door, and I labored for two hours to share Christ with him, very nearly seeing him trust the Lord.

Early in our conversation, he asked me the names of those who had slandered me from within his organization. He said he would "take care of it." Without hesitation, I refused. I'm still praying that the Lord will reconcile those relationships and restore those brothers to my heart. I could not dishonor the Lord and injure those critics in that moment. I pray you won't either.

Grow in grace.

"And God is able to make all grace abound toward you; that ye, always having all sufficiency in all things, may abound to every good work" (2 Corinthians 9:8). Allow God to use this time to call you more deeply to prayer and Bible study. Soften your heart and grow. If you don't make this conscious decision, your heart will likely harden and your spirit will become calloused toward people. Keep your heart soft and your spirit right during these times of difficult growth.

Humble yourself before God.

John Adams, toward the end of his life, wrote to his grandson, "The longer I live, the more patiently I think, and the more anxiously I enquire, the less I seem to know. Walk humbly. That is enough." Let these trials cause you to decrease so Christ can increase.

Love your family.

In moments of pain and discouragement you start to feel like the whole world is against you. Isn't it amazing how Satan can do this? You might have a whole church family praying for you and loving you, but two critics can rob your joy in the Lord. In these deceptive moments, God has always encouraged me with thoughts like this: "Well, I can love my wife and love my kids. As long as they are for me, we're still in this together!" Somehow these trials have always drawn our family closer. No one knows your integrity and sincerity more than your family. Let the trial renew your commitment to loving them passionately.

Make important assessments.

Henry Blackaby wrote in *Spiritual Leadership*, "Past leaders had certain times in their day when they were inaccessible to people. During such times they could reflect on their situation and make decisions about their next course of action." He continues, "Leaders realize they must occasionally step back from the day to day operations in order to gain perspective on the broader issues such as the nature and the future of an organization." Often it is a moment of criticism that will cause you to pause and evaluate. Don't ignore criticism. Step back; lay it before the Lord; and ask Him to reveal the truth to you.

During every season of criticism, we have identified areas where we could have communicated better or could have taken preventative measures to help people understand our position or our polity. We have grown greatly from the information given to us from critics. Many of the principles in this chapter flowed from teaching moments during trials. As with Joseph, what they meant for bad, God used for good. My only regret is that I would have liked to redeem the relationship and not merely benefited from the criticism.

One pastor said, "When criticism is a threat, a leader becomes defensive, but when it is viewed as a natural occurrence and a challenge, it can become a source of constructive energy."

Don't react.

All leaders get criticized. It's their response to criticism that sets them apart. John Adams wrote to a friend in Massachusetts after he had been hurt by a rival, "When a man is hurt he loves to talk of his wounds." This might mean you need a wise listening ear. It also means you could say the wrong thing in a moment of reaction! Some battles are not worth fighting. An old Chinese proverb states, "A bulldog could whip a skunk at any time, but it's not worth the fight."

Hurting people hurt people. When you are hurting, don't react; respond. Prayerfully seek God's direction, obtain godly counsel, and follow a very predetermined course of action that pleases the Lord.

Increase your accountability and accessibility.

The more your ministry grows, the more important it is that you protect yourself with accountability and accessibility. With broader influence comes broader accountability—embrace this as a preserving agent, not a restraining one.

When we have been attacked, the Lord has always led us to strengthen the structure of accountability and to more effectively communicate transparently. Increased accountability has always positioned the ministry for bigger influence and greater responsibility. It's a paradox that God would use a trial this way, but the results are wonderful.

Develop leaders around you.

One man said, "Courage is contagious. When a brave man takes a stand, the spines of others are often stiffened." When the leader is attacked, people usually look to the surrounding leadership for a response. In other words, the church family will watch your pastoral staff, your deacons, and other leaders around you. It is no doubt then that these leaders will often come under attack as well. Satan will do everything he can to undermine the respect and trust of those in leadership. You can be sure that you are not his only target and neither are your leaders. He's going after the sheep. In distracting the undershepherd, he's hoping to steal a few lambs!

This is one of the great benefits of developing strong leadership around you. There is safety and strength in a team of leaders. Even the Lone Ranger had Tonto!

Furthermore, instead of creating a dependency mentality in your congregation, teach the Bible and help your members to grow in discernment and to follow the Spirit's leading in their lives. Develop leadership within the church body. The stronger your church, the more easily they will see through and withstand the deception of the wolves. *"And the things that thou hast heard of me among many witnesses, the same commit thou to faithful men, who shall be able to teach others also"* (2 Timothy 2:2).

Don't quit.

Let the trial strengthen your resolve. Often trials are the greatest indicator that we are on the right path doing the right things. Everything that is moving forward encounters resistance—so thank God you are apparently moving forward. One man said, "Defeat may serve as well as victory to shake the soul and let the glory out!"

If you quit, your critics win, and much is lost for the cause of Christ. Don't let petty people determine your destiny. God planned even your enemies and they are serving His purposes in your life.

It has been said, "For every action there is an equal and opposite criticism." As we close this chapter, I want to remind you that not all critics are your enemies! Not all critics have the intention of being hurtful or scornful, and if you lump them all into the same category, you will often be wrong. Proverbs 27:6 reminds us, *"Faithful are the wounds of a friend…."* Some critics are truly seeking to understand. They genuinely have a concern. Even if their spirit is wrong in the way they raise it, their heart may be in the right place. You sometimes have to presume a genuine heart when it is hard to see one.

The critic may be a friend seeking to help you. He may have the insight to see one of your blind-spots. He may be genuinely seeking to protect you and grow the ministry. It would be a mistake of gigantic proportions to stop your ears to all criticism.

Generally we find it easier to take criticism from someone we know and trust, but I challenge you to receive it even from those you do not know. If God brings someone into your life with a negative insight, receive it with a soft heart, pray about it, and communicate with that person openly and transparently. Most importantly, be willing to change! Positive, growth-oriented change is good for you and the whole church.

There are many times when I have benefited from such negativity and have gained a friend in the difficult, but worthwhile process.

Pastor, a smooth sea never made a skillful sailor. Suffering truly qualifies and equips you for the ministry.

CHAPTER TWENTY-NINE

THE SPIRITUAL LEADER'S RESPONSE

In the last chapter we addressed the fact that not all critics are scornful. Some are sincerely seeking truth and reason. They *want* to understand. Your love and grace can lead them to a point of peaceful resolution. We have seen this many times at Lancaster Baptist. Over the years a few have left our church with hurtful criticisms and a wrong spirit. We do not hurt back. We love and forgive. As a result, many of these people have returned to our church.

I believe one reason God has given His favor in these situations is that we have remained approachable. We have welcomed questions and responded kindly and truthfully to even a wrong-spirited inquiry. We have established a habit of going to a brother and seeking resolution. This practice is biblical and it has helped me many times to gain a brother. *"Moreover if thy brother shall trespass against thee, go and tell him his fault between thee and him alone: if he shall hear thee, thou hast gained thy brother"* (Matthew 18:15).

In this chapter we will examine how to address some of the more common questions faced by Bible-believing churches. This is a bit more lengthy than the other chapters, out of necessity. Yet I believe that this response will equip you to handle questions and criticisms biblically and compassionately.

A SPIRITUAL LEADER'S RESPONSE

New Testament churches and leaders have faced challenging issues and questions since the first century. None of us can predict or control when a challenge will arise, but by the grace of God, and the inner working of His Spirit, we can respond in meekness and wisdom to difficulty.

The Apostle Paul continuously faced challenges to his ministry and personal integrity. I believe that is why the Holy Spirit led him to write 1 Thessalonians 2:1–8:

> "For yourselves, brethren, know our entrance in unto you, that it was not in vain: But even after that we had suffered before, and were shamefully entreated, as ye know, at Philippi, we were bold in our God to speak unto you the gospel of God with much contention. For our exhortation was not of deceit, nor of uncleanness, nor in guile: But as we were allowed of God to be put in trust with the gospel, even so we speak; not as pleasing men, but God, which trieth our hearts. For neither at any time used we flattering words, as ye know, nor a cloke of covetousness; God is witness: Nor of men sought we glory, neither of you, nor yet of others, when we might have been burdensome, as the apostles of Christ. But we were gentle among you, even as a nurse cherisheth her children: So being affectionately desirous of you, we were willing to have imparted unto you, not the gospel of God only, but also our own souls, because ye were dear unto us."

As the apostle was led to define his motives and manner in the ministry, similarly, in today's ministry environment I have found it helpful and necessary to respond to questions along the way. I do not believe spiritual leaders should be aloof or unapproachable. I also realize we will never please everyone. Frankly, pleasing everyone should not be the goal of a spiritual leader. In 2 Timothy 2:3–4, Paul said this: *"Thou therefore endure hardness, as a good soldier of Jesus Christ. No man that warreth entangleth himself with the affairs of this life; that he may please him who hath chosen him to be a soldier."* Paul's ultimate goal was to please the Lord as he served Him.

Dr. Monroe Parker once said, "Your friends don't need an explanation, and your enemies won't believe you anyway." Thankfully, when it comes to the final analysis, we can be comforted in the Scriptures:

> *"Let a man so account of us, as of the ministers of Christ, and stewards of the mysteries of God. Moreover it is required in stewards, that a man be found faithful. But with me it is a very small thing that I should be judged of you, or of man's judgment: yea, I judge not mine own self. For I know nothing by myself; yet am I not hereby justified: but he that judgeth me is the Lord. Therefore judge nothing before the time, until the Lord come, who both will bring to light the hidden things of darkness, and will make manifest the counsels of the hearts: and then shall every man have praise of God."*—1 CORINTHIANS 4:1–5

In the coming pages, I hope you will consider some wise responses to common criticisms and questions that biblical ministries have faced throughout all ages.

Spiritual leadership has always required growth in grace, and a quick glimpse through the book of Acts reminds us that the message and manner of early church leaders was not always appreciated.

Our desire must be to *"please him"* who has chosen us (2 Timothy 2:4). To re-focus us on that goal, God allows seasons of trials or criticisms from leaders and church members. Whether or not they are *fair* is not the issue. God always has a purpose for them. The trials and difficulties experienced by twenty-first century leaders and churches are, in some ways, peculiar to our day and age; but in other ways, traceable back to the early church.

From time to time, in the life and history of a church, questions and challenges arise. With the changing trends of our culture, the complexity of the questions seem to be on the rise. Sometimes the questions and statements are legitimate and can help the church. For example, in Acts 6 the early church was urged to better care for the widows. The need was real, and the response was both effective and useful.

Sometimes, issues that are raised in church life are preference oriented—the color of carpet, the décor of buildings, or the location of classrooms.

At other times issues are raised with a desire to wound. Sometimes these issues can be like an aching sore (2 Timothy 2:16–17) and sometimes, even worse than this, they can become like a fire. Churches in every denomination across the country have experienced critics who call through membership lists, email members, or simply share their negative feelings in various settings throughout the community. Unfortunately, even people without a relationship with Christ have been affected by such wrong spirits and hurtful words.

James 3:5–6 says, *"Even so the tongue is a little member, and boasteth great things. Behold, how great a matter a little fire kindleth! And the tongue is a fire, a world of iniquity: so is the tongue among our members, that it defileth the whole body, and setteth on fire the course of nature; and it is set on fire of hell."*

ADDRESSING CRITICISMS OF MINISTRY PHILOSOPHY

The first area of questioning these days is often that of leadership philosophy. Over the past decades, there has been much study and evaluation of the leadership philosophies of Bible-believing churches. Some of this discussion has been led by men who were involved in a very strict upbringing and have reacted against their past church upbringing by categorizing it as being *abusive* or *hurtful.* To counteract their negative experiences in previous churches, some of these church leaders began to develop and teach a concept called "radical grace." The teaching generally says that a ministry philosophy emphasizing faithfulness in areas such as tithing, church attendance or witnessing is a church that is abusing people.

While these men may have identified some potential imbalances in ministry, the "radical-grace" approach to solving the problem has allowed many people to classify good and godly environments of spiritual growth as abusive, harsh, or harmful—simply because they disagree with the way these churches choose to worship and serve the Lord.

I dealt, at great length, with some of these questions in a book I wrote entitled *Guided by Grace*. After *Guided by Grace* was published, I was actually criticized by some conservative, Christian leaders for emphasizing the necessity of growing in grace, and modeling a servant style of leadership. In reality, we have at times in our ministry experienced comments from those who feel we are too conservative or "harsh" in our approach to leadership, and from others who feel that we are too soft and do not have strong enough "standards."

In an effort to equip us better to biblically respond to criticism and to properly grow in spiritual leadership, let me admonish you to live by the following principles:

Remember, the church is the Lord's.

Acts 20:28 says, *"Take heed therefore unto yourselves, and to all the flock, over the which the Holy Ghost hath made you overseers, to feed the church of God, which he hath purchased with his own blood."*

The Lord has placed you in the church to be an overseer, but never forget that you are the undershepherd and Jesus Christ is the Chief Shepherd. He owns the church and will call each of us into account one day.

Remain teachable.

Do not ignore critical comments. Rather, ask the Holy Spirit to help you consider the criticism and make any needed adjustments. Our church is a more balanced, gentle and loving church today because we have grown in God's grace through criticism. Criticism can be helpful—even that which was from a hurtful spirit.

Remain accountable.

Remain personally accountable as a leader, first and foremost, to the Lord, and second, to godly men. Dr. David Gibbs, Dr. Don Sisk and Dr. R.B. Ouellette are men with whom I regularly meet for the purpose of spiritual growth, fellowship, and assessment. Several other men of God have been kind and helpful to me in this way. We discuss my spirit toward the Lord, my family, my ministry, and the ministry in general. When I am going through a season of trial or criticism, I share with them the comments that are made in their entirety. I follow their counsel and value their support.

Work with the deacons.

On a local level, I have endeavored to be very transparent with the deacons of our church. The Scriptures do not command a pastor to "submit" to the deacons in the sense of church government, but it is biblical that we are to be spiritually accountable to one another. Gladly share personal and spiritual requests with godly men in your church. Foster an environment with them that welcomes helpful questions and comments. Make the deacons well aware of church finances as well as of your personal finances and giving.

Be accountable that you are following the Word of God and seeking the filling of the Holy Spirit on a daily basis. Be spiritual enough to change, grow, and remain in balance.

Love people.

Though you will disagree with some of the lifestyle elements and habits of people who attend your church, choose to love them regardless. Be patient and willing to let people grow, and be compassionate as you nurture them in a closer walk with the Saviour.

Develop hearts for God.

Let the emphasis of your whole ministry be on preaching, teaching and encouraging people to cultivate their hearts as they walk with the Lord. How their change of heart is reflected in an outward manifestation is something between God and them. But, be sure to foster an environment that is conducive to grace and growth. Acceptance is the optimal environment for growth; therefore, accept people where they are and allow them to grow at their own pace. But at the same time, do not apologize for having distinctive convictions that are based on the Scriptures.

On the other hand, there are churches that started off in the "radical grace" mode and have had to make some shifts back toward the realm of scriptural obedience in order to maintain balance in their ministries. For example, in 1991 one pastor and author stated that "*obedience* and *submission* are two words that are often used in abusive churches."

Last year *Leadership* magazine interviewed the executive pastor of his church. In the interview he stated this:

> Our senior pastor has confessed openly that in the past we have unintentionally denigrated giving. We gave people permission not to give and we were wrong. That was a hard confession.
>
> The message of "radical grace," which we teach, for years focused on the first half of the epistle. We are freed by grace. But in a way that allowed people to ignore their obligations brought out on the last half. It wasn't said this way, but the message was clear; your behavior, your choices, your attitudes don't matter.
>
> A real turning point for us was when we preached a sermon called, "The Spirit of the Tithe." For the first time our church heard about tithing in a positive way. We heard that obedience is freedom.

I am thankful that this radical-grace teacher grew to teach "obedience is freedom," but saddened to think of the prior harm that was caused to Christians who were taught that they could abuse the grace of God. Obedience *is* freedom. Titus 2:11–13 says, "*For the grace of God that bringeth salvation hath appeared to all men, Teaching us that, denying ungodliness and worldly lusts, we should live soberly, righteously, and godly, in this present world; Looking for that blessed hope, and the glorious appearing of the great God and our Saviour Jesus Christ.*"

The point in this matter of church philosophy is simply this: If someone feels he would rather worship in a different style, with a different level of commitment, time scheduling or other differences, he should simply find the church or ministry that best suits him and lovingly and kindly begin serving there.

In *Grace Gone Wild*, Robert Jeffress wrote, "There is a difference between good grace and bad grace. Good grace recognizes that behavioral boundaries exist for our benefit not our detriment. Bad grace removes all barriers and standards for behavior. Good grace always motivates the child of God to cling as closely to his or her heavenly Father as possible. Bad grace will encourage the child of God to live as close to the edge of disobedience as possible."

Again, every Christian is on a spiritual journey. Ministries that are harsh or judgmental, need to grow in grace to the point that they do not even resemble an abusive ministry. On the other hand, Christians who are so involved in "radical grace" that they begin to engender choices, behavior, and attitudes that are unbecoming of the Scripture, need to come back to the reality that "obedience is freedom."

ADDRESSING QUESTIONS ABOUT FINANCIAL POLICIES

A second commonly questioned area among growing churches in America today is church financial management. The first group of questioning concerns accountability. I urge you to work diligently to maintain financial integrity. I recommend you protect yourself and your ministry in the following ways:

Annual audits and reviews

To maintain proper checks and balances, our church has submitted to financial audits and reviews on an annual basis for many years. These audits have always been available for the members to review upon request. Also, our deacons review the church accounts monthly. This review provides the highest levels of accountability and financial integrity on behalf of our church family. The deacons ask questions and make suggestions at every meeting.

Financial policy to new members
Each new member of Lancaster Baptist Church receives a copy of our financial policy in a new member's packet. Among other things the policy says, "We will provide an annual report to our church members and welcome questions throughout the year." One of the signs of a healthy church is that the leadership remains approachable to these sorts of questions. Invite questions from the earliest moments of one's membership. No matter what you do, some will claim that they feel they can't ask questions, but the ones who do ask will be grateful for your transparency.

Training seminars
Develop a policy manual for the church employees. Many of our policies relate to the handling of finances and reflect the years of training our staff has undergone as well as the seminars our staff has attended hosted by groups such as the Christian Law Association and the National Association of Church Business Administration.

At some point, you may need to add to your staff a financial administrator with the education needed to establish helpful systems to the ministry.

Fair and reasonable compensation
Endeavor to be vigilant in the compensation of the church staff. You should study churches and Christian ministries similar to yours in scope and size. Additionally, the National Association of Church Business Administration annually conducts a national church survey of compensation. This survey provides ranges of compensation for each position within the local church.

On a personal level, Terrie and I are grateful for the care of our church and we have tried to be wise and Christ-honoring stewards. We have tried to invest wisely and have given sacrificially over the years. We have never asked our church family to do what we have not done. Pastors are people who have families and family needs like anyone else. Godly leaders are worthy of their hire.

Also remember, salary and family finances are personal issues. When people raise questions about these issues, they are dealing primarily with their personal preferences. People may disagree with the way a leader dresses, the investments he makes, the home in which he lives, or the salary the deacons select for him. These disagreements are often matters of personal opinion and interpretation.

ADDRESSING QUESTIONS OF CHURCH GOVERNMENT

Another area in which questions arise is the way a church operates. I am a Baptist, and Baptists believe in the autonomy of the local church. Autonomy means that we believe every church has the right to follow the Lord and the Bible as they believe He is leading them.

I encourage you to take the following steps to help your church family understand the basic structure of your church:

Conduct a new members' reception.

At this reception give each new member a copy of the purpose, affiliations, and working order of the church. Also encourage any questions about how decisions are made in the church.

Distribute the church constitution.

Place the constitution into a new members' packet and designate a deacon to deliver it. This is significant because it allows the new member an opportunity to meet one of the men who helps the pastor with the church needs on a monthly basis. Rather than secretly running the church any way we want, we have given every member his own copy of the Constitution and By-laws so they can see how the church operates, biblically and legally.

Preach about "The Operation of the Church."

Finally, consider preaching a message to help the church understand its structure. Every few years I have preached a message entitled "The Operation of the Church." This message breaks down how the church functions with respect to the calling of the pastor, ratification of budgets, nomination of deacons, and so forth.

ADDRESSING QUESTIONS ABOUT PASTORAL LEADERSHIP

Often the questions that arise regarding church government revolve around the leadership of the pastor. The role of the pastor is specifically spelled out in the Scriptures.

While many models exist for church government, it is my conviction that the church should be led by the pastor. This responsibility is outlined in Scripture. Adrian Rogers, in *Kingdom Authority*, states this:

> **1. God appoints leaders.** God gives divinely appointed and anointed pastors to lead His church: *"Take heed therefore unto yourselves, and to all the flock, over the which the Holy Ghost hath made you overseers, to feed the church of God, which he hath purchased with his own blood"* (Acts 20:28).
>
> **2. The pastor is not a hireling.** The hireling flees. A good shepherd lays down his life for the sheep. How foolish to speak of "hiring" a pastor. This conveys the idea that the minister is paid to do spiritual work on behalf of others. The truth of the matter is that he is to lead them and teach them to work.
>
> **3. The pastor is not a dictator.** I am often amused when people talk about dictatorial pastors. I believe there are few, if any, in Baptist churches. I serve at the pleasure of my congregation. The only leadership I have is what they allow me to have. They may dismiss me whenever they choose.

I heard of a pastor who subscribed to the theory of dictatorial leadership—but the congregation cancelled his subscription! Seriously, no man, including a pastor, is free to pursue his own course within a local church. He is under the authority of the Word of God and the Spirit of God.

However, it is not reasonable that a pastor should be given responsibility without corresponding authority. A pastor with authority is not a dictator. A dictator has authority with no accountability. A spiritual leader has responsibility and authority *with* accountability. The Bible makes clear that pastors must one day give an account of their responsibilities: *"Obey them that have the rule over you, and submit yourselves: for they watch for your souls, as they that must give account, that they may do it with joy, and not with grief: for that is unprofitable for you"* (Hebrews 13:17).

4. The pastor is a servant leader. Lastly, the pastor's leadership is servant leadership. The pastor is first a servant and then a leader. Any pastor not under authority has forfeited his right to exercise authority. Jesus is the sovereign Lord of the church, but notice His method of loving leadership.

Quite simply, your church will be blessed as the pastor and people work together in the power of the Holy Spirit of God. I often tell people that I am a leader in my home because my wife allows me to be! Similarly, as the Holy Spirit has given you the privilege of serving at your church, thank God for people who have allowed you to exercise leadership gifts in moving the church forward for the cause of Christ!

Romans 12:8 says, *"Or he that exhorteth, on exhortation: he that giveth, let him do it with simplicity; he that ruleth, with diligence; he that sheweth mercy, with cheerfulness."* And in Ephesians 4:11–12 it says, *"And he gave some, apostles; and some, prophets; and some, evangelists; and some, pastors and teachers; for the perfecting of the saints, for the work of the ministry, for the edifying of the body of Christ."*

ADDRESSING QUESTIONS ABOUT GRACE

Another subject that is continuously questioned and sometimes debated in today's Christian circles, is the doctrine of grace. As we've seen, on one hand there is the "radical grace" movement, which has empowered some believers to approach the Christian life with a "do what you want" approach. On the other hand, the Bible teaches that grace is the inner working of the Holy Spirit which conforms us to the image of Christ. *"For the grace of God that bringeth salvation hath appeared to all men; teaching us that, denying ungodliness and worldy lusts, we should live soberly, righteously, and godly, in this present world"* (Titus 2:11–12).

One thing is certain: real life-change must take place through the inner working of the Holy Spirit. The theme of Lancaster Baptist Church in 2003 was "Streams in the Desert" and the focus was following the leading of the Holy Spirit. More than emphasizing individual commands of Scripture (which we also do), we preached hundreds of times about allowing the Holy Spirit to work in and through our lives . We must allow Him to do the work of grace that will cause us to desire to give, serve, or even live a sanctified and separated life.

Apparently, the interpretation of the book of Romans, and the doctrines of grace have been subjects of varying opinions for some years. Dr. J. Vernon McGee, in his notes on Romans 6, stated this: "This section delivers us from the prevalent idea that you can do as you please. Union with Christ means He is Lord and Master."

Galatians 5:13 teaches: *"For, brethren, ye have been called unto liberty; only use not liberty for an occasion to the flesh, but by love serve one another."* We should, by love, serve even those whose view of grace is different from ours. We should not sow discord toward them or castigate their character in any way.

Jerry Bridges, in *The Discipline of Grace*, wrote about grace as follows: "Turning Christian liberty into a license to sin is an evil that is ingrained in sinful human nature. It is easy to construe liberty as the right to do what one wants to do.

"In my younger years the Christian community attempted to do this watching for us as it came up with its various list of don'ts. This practice resulted in a modern pharisaism.

"More recently there has been a reaction against such legalism, but we need to be watchful that in our assertion of our freedom we do not give the flesh the opportunity to lead us over the precipice unto sin."

Whether or not we agree with Bridges' definition of "legalism," we must agree that the "assertion of freedom" has led many to follow the flesh. It is my conviction that a mature Christian leader is not a person who stresses his rights in this life, but one who stresses his responsibilities to the Lord and the church. I do believe that responsible Christian leaders will have some "do's and don'ts" by which they live. But our goal must never be the list; our goal must be Christ and His glory.

ADDRESSING QUESTIONS ABOUT GIVING

Another area often questioned in this age of church ministry is that of giving. I believe the downfall of prominent televangelists in the 1980s fueled the fire of distrust in many hearts.

Giving reflects the personal commitment in the heart of each believer and the Holy Spirit is the one who must prompt both the amount of giving as well as the proper attitude toward giving.

In Malachi 3:9–10, the Bible says: *"Ye are cursed with a curse: for ye have robbed me, even this whole nation. Bring ye all the tithes into the storehouse, that there may be meat in mine house, and prove me now herewith, saith the Lord of hosts, if I will not open you the windows of heaven, and pour you out a blessing, that there shall not be room enough to receive it."*

We teach grace giving. Beyond the basic principle of the tithe, the Bible teaches a higher principle of love and grace. For example in 2 Corinthians 8:8–9, the Bible says: *"I speak not by commandment, but by occasion of the forwardness of others, and to prove the sincerity of your love. For ye know the grace of our Lord Jesus Christ, that, though he was rich, yet for your sakes he became poor, that ye through his poverty might be rich."* Second Corinthians 9:8–9 says: *"And God is able to make all grace abound toward you; that ye, always having all sufficiency in all things, may abound to every good work: (As it is written, He hath dispersed abroad; he hath given to the poor: his righteousness remaineth for ever…).*"

The predominant theme of all of your teaching or preaching about giving should be "grace giving." Grace giving simply means that the Holy Spirit must produce within us the desire to give and must show us what to give.

While the New Testament shows examples of lavish sacrificial giving, never advocate any type of giving that would go against sound biblical principles of stewardship or create a detrimental situation for anyone's family. The following are some direct quotes from sermons preached here at Lancaster Baptist Church in the recent years:

"We are not to give under pressure. We are not to give because we are being pressured. We are to give because we love the Lord and want our giving to be a reflection of that love."

"Our motive for giving to God is the grace of God which works

> *Mature Christian givers are not motivated by guilt, pressure or sad pictures. They are motivated by the grace of God.*

within us. When God's grace is your motivation, there is no need for pressure." (In spite of these statements some critics will still say that they feel pressured.)

Further statements from our message include the word *offering*. The word *offering* is the Greek word *toruma* which means a "free will gift."

A recent sermon quote from one of my own messages says: "We are dependent upon God to make us willing-hearted. We are not going to try to get some kind of manipulation giving or trick some people into giving. That is not what this is about."

"If you ever feel pressured to give, please don't give."

A quote from a message entitled "Grown Up Givers" states: "Mature Christian givers are not motivated by guilt, pressure or sad pictures. They are motivated by the grace of God."

Our teaching in the area of giving and stewardship is consistent with many churches across many denominations. Our approach has been to challenge our members with the clear teaching of Scriptures, as well as with what we believe to be the godly vision for our church. The vast majority of our members have lovingly and cheerfully given to the Lord. Only God knows the hearts of those who may feel otherwise from time to time.

In this chapter I have shared with you some of the responses I have given critics over the years regarding these topics. Some critics have accepted these answers and allowed them to resolve their questions. Others do not want resolution; they simply seek other things to criticize. I will never be able to help these critics, for the festering problem lies within their own hearts. Undoubtedly, there will be other issues and challenges faced by any church endeavoring to preach the Gospel of Jesus Christ in these last days.

Your church is on a journey and you have not yet arrived at your destination. As Paul the apostle said, *"Brethren, I count not myself to have apprehended: but this one thing I do, forgetting those things which are behind, and reaching forth unto those things which are before"* (Philippians 3:13). Yours is not a perfect church nor will it be until we see Christ.

Pastor, every organization and every church will have former members and employees with less than positive feelings. Love these people and do not criticize them or tolerate gossip about them. One sign of a healthy church is that people who have left feel as though they can come back. Dozens of people over the years have left Lancaster Baptist Church and returned happily.

Finally, let us remember that "the tongue is a fire." With that thought in mind, we must each choose whether we will be an *arsonist* or a *firefighter*. It is my prayer that we will be graceful men of God, especially toward God's people—even when they disagree with us.

LEADING
THROUGH CRISES

W hen God called me to the ministry, I envisioned preaching, leading, serving, and pastoring; but, I had very little pastoral perspective of the kinds of trials God's people and God's churches encounter. One of the roles of a servant leader is to give care and help in times of crisis.

Trials come in seasons. This was true in the life of Job as well as in the life of Jesus. About Jesus' temptation, Luke 4:13 says, *"And when the devil had ended all the temptation, he departed from him for a season."* In addition, 1 Peter 1:6 teaches, *"Wherein ye greatly rejoice, though now for a season, if need be, ye are in heaviness through manifold temptations."* The seasonal nature of hardship shows us God's sovereignty and reminds us that God has a very specific purpose for our trials. Any circumstance *out* of your control is *in* the will of God.

One of the most unusual seasons of hardship that our church ever faced began the first week of 1997 and ended twelve months later. It would be impossible to accurately describe the spiritual oppression that came upon me and the ministry during this time.

In the first few weeks of the year three precious church members went home to be with the Lord. Right after that, in mid-February, while I was returning home from a lunch with Dr. Bobby Roberson, I received a phone call that three of our Bible-college students had been driving off campus and were broadsided by a large utility truck during the school dismissal hour.

This event shook the entire church family and the Antelope Valley. The young lady who was hurt the most critically, Jessica Downey, had grown up in our church (as I mentioned earlier, Terrie and I had led Jessica and her family to Christ). In those first hours after the accident her life hung in the balance. Several times the doctor suggested that she was brain dead and asked her parents to consider organ donation. That evening, kept alive by life-support, she slipped into a deep coma. For the better part of three months we spent whole days and nights in the hospital—praying, caring, serving, and asking God to spare her life. He did, and she serves Him today on our school staff as a vibrant testimony of God's goodness.

> *Any circumstance out of your control is in the will of God.*

In March we held another home-going service and had another dear member injured in a car accident. In April the father of one of our kindergartners passed away. In May, just before the 10:00 AM service, one of our deacons, his wife, and two daughters were in a tragic car accident just a half mile from the church. Once again I found myself at the scene of an accident with a life hanging in the balance and a life-flight helicopter in the distance. I will never forget stepping aside from the scene, standing against a Joshua tree, brushing the tears from my eyes and saying, "Lord, what is this?" I was utterly at a loss.

In June a dear church family lost a child and another member went home to be with the Lord. In July there was another accident. Later in the fall we held two more memorial services—one for a young husband and the father of three. For a young church, nine home-going services and four accidents in the space of a year seemed nearly unbearable.

God taught our church much during this season. He taught us to pray, trust, and cling to Him as a body. He taught me much about compassion and care. The question is, how can God's men serve His people during such times? What does a spiritual leader do during crises?

Allow me to encourage you with ten biblical responses that will help you lead well during times of suffering.

GO TO THE NEED

Trials are times when God rewrites your agenda. What *was* important must now take a backseat to the *immediate need*. No spiritual leader knows exactly what to say or how to act in desperate situations. Yet, just the spiritual presence of a loving undershepherd can speak volumes to a burdened church member.

Over the years I've met leaders who refused to give this kind of care. They viewed themselves as public speakers or visionaries, but they didn't view themselves as servants or caring shepherds. As much as you can, go to these needs. When you can't, appoint someone to go to them in your stead.

Be sure to think of the spiritual *and* the physical needs. We *pray* with someone before a surgery, but we also *provide meals* to the home after the surgery. Sometimes it is a comforting prayer and Scripture that is needed; other times it is someone to watch the children or keep the house.

MAKE PRAYER THE PRIORITY

Establish a church prayer chain. Start a prayer ministry. Put in place a church family network that communicates the need for prayer. As you visit a hospital bed or a waiting room, make prayer your top priority.

I will never forget the dozens and dozens of church members who prayed in the hospital waiting room during Jessica's coma. The *Antelope Valley Press*, a local paper, actually ran an article on the front page that said, "Who is Jessica and Who are All These People?" The reporter had happened through the waiting area when fifty or sixty of us were gathered there to pray.

In every crisis, prayer will make a vast difference!

ADJUST YOUR SCHEDULE ACCORDINGLY

When God leads you into a time of crisis, you must step back and reevaluate the priorities. Sometimes crisis changes the entire life of your church. It may be that God leads you to change your personal schedule. He may lead you to preach a new series, patiently pull back on a program idea, or adjust something in the church calendar.

Crisis moments require listening hearts. Sometimes, for our church, the program, the schedule, and the entire forward momentum seemed to come to a halt simply so we could collectively listen to God in the moment. In time, God allowed the momentum to move forward again, but I would never trade those seasons of pause. We learned in those moments what we could never have learned any other way.

PREACH MESSAGES OF COMFORT

Our God is a God of comfort, *"Blessed be God, even the Father of our Lord Jesus Christ, the Father of mercies, and the God of all comfort"* (2 Corinthians 1:3), and He has given us the presence of His Holy Spirit as a Comforter, *"And I will pray the Father, and he shall give you another Comforter, that he may abide with you for ever"* (John 14:16). He also intends that believers would comfort one another, *"Wherefore comfort one another with these words"* (1 Thessalonians 4:18).

Choose songs and deliver messages that communicate God's comfort and grace to His people. Crises bring a sensitivity to the heart that nothing else brings, and you can be sure that God will use your messages to accomplish something very special in your church family.

WAIT ON THE LORD

Isaiah 40:29–31 teaches, *"He giveth power to the faint; and to them that have no might he increaseth strength. Even the youths shall faint and be weary, and the young men shall utterly fall: But they that wait upon the*

LORD shall renew their strength; they shall mount up with wings as eagles; they shall run, and not be weary; and they shall walk, and not faint."

Personally, you must wait upon the Lord as the leader. You must pull aside, rest upon God, and follow His leading during these times. You must teach your church to do the same. God's vision does not always follow our timetable. When He calls us into a season of waiting, it's for a very specific spiritual need.

Remember, God is at work, even if you aren't at the office.

LISTEN TO THE LORD

Like no other trial our church has ever been through, Jessica's accident brought us to a spiritual moment of listening and waiting upon the Lord. During that time, I tried to journal what God was teaching me. Late one evening on the floor of a hospital waiting room, I sat alone with the Lord and listed these eight things that God was doing in my life:

1. My heart was wide open to God's will and direction more than at any other time in my life.
2. Prayer had become more real than at any other time in my life.
3. Prayer had become more spontaneous than at any other time in my life.
4. Witnessing opportunities had increased through the trial.
5. Refining was underway in my heart and throughout the church.
6. There was a humbling taking place in my heart.
7. God's presence was known more intimately.
8. God was being praised, honored, and glorified more readily.

I shared these truths with the church family, and together we grew spiritually in ways that are indescribable. When the Lord leads you into a crisis, listen very carefully to what He is teaching you.

LET OTHERS BE YOUR MINISTERS

As a growing church and pastor, we had never been in a season like this before—at least not that intense. While we were depending upon the Lord, we were also gleaning much from spiritual leaders who had come through similar times. I'll never forget the phone calls and personal meetings I had seeking counsel and guidance from older men of God.

Also during this time, the Lord allowed some precious people to minister to our church family through music, through teaching and preaching, and through friendship. These wonderful people were literally His grace personified to our church family. They blessed us in ways that we will never forget!

WATCH AS GOD STRENGTHENS THE BODY

Toward the end of 1997, I could trace the spiritual growth of our church family through that year. Since that time, when we've entered crisis moments, I've always seen God's hand strengthening and building His church. It's what He does through trials!

A wise preacher once said, "The road to a miracle is always uphill!" We have experienced valleys of crises as a church, but in every one of them, God was strengthening us for an uphill journey that led to a mighty miracle.

During crises, I've seen God strengthen our church primarily through two avenues—prayer and service. When a church family prays together and serves each other, they grow together, and they grow stronger!

LEARN TO REJOICE AND PRAISE GOD

I'm amazed how God gives laughter and rejoicing, even in the middle of tears. In seasons of crises, be sure to praise God and rejoice in His goodness. Like Paul and Silas who sang in prison, cast your eyes upon the Saviour and thank Him for His wonderful grace. This kind of faith moves God to action.

Leading our church through crises has always involved singing, serving, and rejoicing in the goodness of God. Start by rejoicing personally and privately. Thank God for His comfort and His presence. Then, lead your church publicly to praise God.

During those dark, desperate hours at the hospital with the Downey family, Jessica's father, John, led his own parents to the Lord Jesus Christ. He had prayed for years for their salvation. Only a few days prior to the accident, Jessica had just pleaded with the Lord "Please save my grandparents...even if it means you have to kill me." Even in sorrow, we saw the powerful hand of God, and we rejoiced in answered prayer.

PREPARE FOR THE BLESSINGS AHEAD

G. Campbell Morgan said of a young preacher boy, "He is a very good preacher, and when he has suffered, he will be a great preacher!" God uses suffering to prepare us for greater ministry.

The year 1997 came to a close and Lancaster Baptist Church was stronger and more sensitive to the Lord than ever before. A young church really grew that year. The very next year, the Lord allowed us to construct the largest single building project on our campus up to that point—a new 2,500 seat auditorium. The church opened the new building in March of 1999 to the theme "Let God Arise." The entire ministry was thrust forward into a more dynamic season of growth and effectiveness than ever before. Our greatest season of trials preceded our greatest season of blessings.

Since these particular trials, Lancaster Baptist Church has more than doubled in attendance, missions support, and outreach. In many ways, God was building and preparing us for greater blessings. Perhaps He is doing the same for you now.

If God leads you into a season of trials, you can expect that it is preceding a season of victories. Don't quit. Don't get discouraged. Keep your eyes on the Lord and keep leading forward. Soon enough, the clouds will part, and you will see God's purpose in all of the trials. The reward will be worth the enduring.

A young boy carried the cocoon of a moth into his house to watch the fascinating events that would take place when the moth emerged. When the moth finally started to break out of his cocoon, the boy noticed how very hard the moth had to struggle. The process was very slow. In an effort to help, the boy reached down and widened the opening of the cocoon. Soon the moth was out of his prison. But as the boy watched, the wings remained shriveled. Something was wrong. What the boy had not realized was that the struggle to get out of the cocoon was essential for the moth's muscle system to develop. In a misguided effort to relieve a struggle, the boy had crippled the future of this creature.

Trials are necessary for growth. No spiritual leader plans to experience crises, but crises are a part of ministry. Hardship is a part of the life of every believer. Caring for people through difficult seasons is a part of your call. Lead well through crises and keep following Christ, even when the road leads uphill. Your most powerful message is *you* in the *valley*!

CHAPTER THIRTY-ONE

LEADING
BY INTERVENING

O ne of the greatest aspects to positive and sustained ministry momentum is a spiritual leader's ability to confront those situations which could potentially hurt the work of God or the people of God. Leaders must intervene. They see the need and take the lead. The word *intervene* means "to come between so as to prevent or alter a result or course of events." Intervention is always preventative and restorative. It is rooted in a leader's ability to see where a small problem could eventually take a person, a team, or a ministry—and it is compelled by compassion and others' best interests.

Loving spiritual leaders are willing to go to a problem and compassionately confront it to help resolve it. This is always with a mind to prevent "what might have been." They speak to unfaithful church members. They approach parents about a child's academic struggles. They approach a teacher about a weakness in the classroom. They approach two Christians at odds and try to bring restoration. They seek out the gossiping Christian and attempt to put the issue to rest. There are ten-thousand scenarios that might require intervention. Spiritual leaders don't run from them; they go to them.

The way spiritual leaders respond to problems or failures will largely determine the success of their ministries. Proverbs 24:10 says, "*If thou faint in the day of adversity, thy strength is small.*" This is one area where pastors and leaders often "faint"—one aspect of ministry we would like to neglect. For some, it is the most difficult part of ministry. All too often leaders attempt to run from or ignore a problem rather than solve it. Yet, intervening leadership is a biblical and needful aspect of helping individuals and a ministry grow in God's grace.

Christendom is severely lacking in intervening leadership, that is, leaders who will care enough to step in and provide preventative guidance and growth. This kind of leadership is rare, and takes great discernment. The wrong type of intervention can come across as harsh, controlling, or intrusive. By *intervening*, I'm not referring to micromanaging the church family or being overbearing as a leader. I'm talking about being a problem solver—a leader who brings hearts together and encourages people to live up to their calling and reach their potential. Spiritual leaders are not afraid to step into problem situations, see the spiritual warfare behind the scenes, and with a right spirit, resolve the issues with biblical authority and compassion.

To help someone reach his potential, you sometimes have to tell him where he needs to change. To help a church family grow, you sometimes need to expose what is hindering growth. To develop a future leader, you have to deal honestly and directly with immaturities. Mentoring is not always positive words of affirmation. Sometimes it is a reprimand or a disciplinary action. Not all discipleship is exhorting. Sometimes it involves rebuke and reproof followed by correction.

Confrontation is usually uncomfortable, but it doesn't have to be carnal or hurtful. The simple truth is, if you love people enough, you will tell them what they need to hear, even though it's difficult. Again, Proverbs 27:6 teaches, "*Faithful are the wounds of a friend....*" Mature Christians will eventually be grateful that you spoke the truth in love rather than avoiding the "tough love" that leadership requires.

The Bible is full of examples of intervening leadership. Jesus displayed this often and so did the Apostle Paul. Here is one example: *"Therefore, my brethren dearly beloved and longed for, my joy and crown, so stand fast in the Lord, my dearly beloved. I beseech Euodias, and beseech Syntyche, that they be of the same mind in the Lord. And I intreat thee also, true yokefellow, help those women which laboured with me in the gospel, with Clement also, and with other my fellowlabourers, whose names are in the book of life. Rejoice in the Lord alway: and again I say, Rejoice"* (Philippians 4:1–4).

> **If you love people enough, you will tell them what they need to hear, even though it's difficult.**

Over the years, I've seen many different types of responses to problems in ministry. Unbiblical responses always make the problems worse. Biblical responses are usually more difficult, but they bring about healing and restoration sooner. There are generally three types of responders to problems.

Three types of leaders in dealing with problems:

1.   **The neglectors**—They are afraid to face the truth, so they hide it or hide from it. They try to ignore the problem and hope it will go away, or they simply say there isn't a problem, and eventually they start believing themselves.

2.   **The fighters**—They speak the truth but not in love. They expose the problem, but they enjoy doing so. They relish the intervention and make it as "confrontational" as possible. They act from insecurity or from an overly authoritative approach. Servant leaders don't relish the act of rebuking others, and they don't "bash" critics or those who oppose them.

3.   **The restorers**—They share the truth for the purpose of prevention and restoration. They do not subjugate others or abuse their authority. They simply speak the truth in love for the purpose of healing and moving forward.

What is your tendency? Are you a neglector, a fighter, or a restorer? As a spiritual leader, you *must be* a restorer. This is the heart of the Holy Spirit, and as He fills you, it will be your heart as well. We have plenty of neglectors and fighters in ministry—we truly need more restorers.

There are some right and wrong ways to confront problems and intervene in situations. In God's wisdom, you can go to a problem with a pure heart, right motives, and a biblical solution. Adrian Rogers said there are three kinds of leaders—natural leaders, entrepreneurial leaders, and *anointed-appointed* leaders. The key to biblical intervention is to be an *anointed* leader—one filled with God's power and presence.

In this chapter, I want to encourage you to embrace this uncomfortable but rewarding role of leadership. These truths are applicable both to your staff and to your church family in general, although the approach will differ slightly when working with those you employ. I want to explore a biblical perspective of intervening leadership and challenge you to deliberately develop this skill. Without it, you will limit yourself and others. First let's find the truth about problems:

TRUTHS ABOUT MINISTRY PROBLEMS

Intervention and confrontation are usually needed because of a *problem*. Somewhere along the way, many spiritual leaders seem to get the idea that other churches and pastors don't have the same problems they do. It's like a young married couple thinking that theirs is the only marriage that experiences difficulty. The devil wants to isolate us, distort our thinking, and cause us to feel as if no one else has "our kinds of problems." This is always a lie. Every ministry has problems, and the first step to being an intervening leader is to accept the reality of problems. Consider these truths:

1. Every person and every church has problems.
2. Problems rarely disappear when they are ignored.
3. Problems are solvable by God's grace.
4. Problems are usually temporary if we respond to them.
5. Responding correctly to problems enhances our lives.

6. A right spirit is the most important factor in problem solving.

7. Problem solving often prevents a greater problem.

Paul Harvey said, "In times like these, it is helpful to remember there have *always been* times like these." No problem you will ever face in ministry is new, unusual, or unique to you. The devil fights everybody and he uses the same tactics over and over again. Don't believe the lie. Your church is not unusual—problems are everywhere. Often the only difference between a *thriving* ministry and a *dying* one is not the presence of problems but the way they are handled!

THE PURPOSE OF INTERVENING LEADERSHIP

The first key to handling confrontation correctly is to have a right *purpose*. When your motives and heart are pure, your vision will be clear. A right heart will help you see clearly and respond correctly. Yet if your vision is tainted by personal emotions, harbored hurt, or bias, your purpose will be skewed.

The first major advice I would give regarding confrontation is this: don't do it until you are absolutely sure your heart is pure and that you have the other person's best interest at heart. When you intervene with a selfish agenda or manipulative motive, you will make a bigger mess.

Four essential reasons you should intervene:

1. **To retain the integrity of a leadership position**—These are the times when a failure to intervene leaves others wondering why. When obvious problems are festering and spiritual leaders do nothing, good men are left doubting the integrity of those they follow.

2. **To restore or mature the heart of a Christian brother**—Sometimes growth involves growing pains. God teaches us to provoke each other to love and good works (Hebrews 10:24). He teaches us to restore each other with meekness (Galatians 6:1). Tough love will sometimes confront someone for the purpose of turning him in the right direction.

3. **To preserve the spiritual state of other Christians**—At times confrontation is primarily done to keep others from following the unspiritual influence of another. Protecting the flock is a part of the shepherd's responsibility.

4. **To prevent larger problems from developing**—Again, intervention is preventative as much as it is restorative. You are not only turning someone the right direction, you are preventing greater problems and hurt.

THE KINDS OF LEADERS WHO DON'T INTERVENE

Hirelings don't intervene; they find it inconvenient, requiring too much extra sacrifice. *Comfort-zone* leaders don't intervene; they find it uncomfortable and risky. *Carnal* leaders don't intervene; they're too busy with distracting or competing interests. *Blind-sighted* leaders don't intervene; they don't even see the problems to begin with. *Unloving* leaders don't intervene; they don't really care enough to expend the time or energy. *Selfish* leaders don't intervene; they are only concerned about having friends. Intervention would negatively impact their high approval ratings.

Leaders who are afraid to take a risk by intervening ultimately lose their influence and respect.

THE KINDS OF LEADERS WHO DO INTERVENE

So, what kinds of leaders actually enter into this tough part of spiritual leadership? I believe there are five:

Spiritual leaders intervene—Galatians 6:1–2
Observant leaders intervene—Proverbs 27:23
Caring leaders intervene—Philippians 2:20
Courageous leaders intervene—Joshua 1:7
Selfless leaders intervene—Philippians 4:17

Spiritual leaders want to see others restored and growing. *Observant* leaders want the state of things healthy and strong. *Caring* leaders truly want to see God's best unfold in people's lives. *Courageous* leaders will do what is right regardless of the consequences. *Selfless* leaders truly have the best interest of the other person in mind.

These leaders cannot help but intervene when they see a circumstance where they can make a difference; it's in their blood—it's hard-wired into their ministry call. They *must* help people, even when it means taking a risk!

Ken Blanchard wrote, "Leadership is the capacity to influence others by unleashing the power and potential of people and organizations for the greater good. Leading at a higher level, therefore is a process. It can be defined as the process of achieving worthwhile results while acting with respect, care, and fairness for the well-being of all involved. When that occurs, self-serving leadership is not possible. It's only when you begin to realize it's not about you that you begin to lead at a higher level." When leadership ceases to be about you and is purely for the good of others, you *will* intervene!

THE RIGHT TIME TO INTERVENE

There is a right time and a wrong time to "step in." Much of this depends on the leading of the Lord because no two situations are exactly alike. There *are* times when wise leaders wait. Intervention is not about being a "bull in a china shop." There *are* problems that require patience and wisdom in discerning God's timing before you intervene.

A good spiritual leader will move toward intervention when he sees one of the following six scenarios playing out:

1. When there is a consistent pattern of apathy
2. When there is a flagrant disregard of Scripture
3. When there is open sin in the church
4. When there is a disregard for written policies
5. When there is a schism in the body
6. When there is a rebellious or proud spirit

HOW TO PRACTICE INTERVENING LEADERSHIP

When you know the Lord is leading you and you know your motives are pure, it's time to intervene. How does a loving leader step in to solve a problem and gain a brother? How do you stamp out a fire without stepping on people?

Over the years I've found myself involved in more of these situations than I could possibly count or recall. It seems I spend much of my time in appointments and meetings, practicing the content of this chapter. Daily, I try to bring people together, strengthen relationships, and resolve problems, and our ministry is much healthier and stronger for it. These are the steps that I've seen God bless many times in moments of intervening ministry.

Remember the importance of praise.

It has been said, "One with a sharp tongue often cuts his own throat." Jesus began His rebuke in Revelation 2:2–4 with words of praise. Start every confrontation with loving words of affirmation and tenderness. Throughout the confrontation be kind and carefully choose your words.

Choose the right venue.

Consider when and where you will intervene. Every situation is different and requires discernment. Is there a location that would be more conducive to a biblical response and a gentle spirit? Would a meal together be appropriate? A few problems can be dealt with over the phone; most should be handled face to face. Is this a one-on-one talk, or do others need to be involved? More often than not, you should meet in your office.

Intervene with prayer first.

Before you intervene, bathe the situation, the person, and your own spirit in prayer. Ask for wisdom and insight. Ask the Lord to guide you and to help you see the truth. Ask the Lord to help you communicate a heart of love and a desire to help, not to hurt. Ask for the filling of the Holy Spirit.

Prepare for intervention.

Prepare your own spirit. Sometimes these intervening moments can be emotionally charged. Determine before that you will allow the Holy Spirit to control your heart and emotions.

Also, determine the nature of the problem. Is it a *spiritual* problem or an *administrative* problem? Sometimes you cannot know until you talk with people. Don't spiritualize every problem. You can't solve an *administrative* problem with a sermon and you can't solve a *spiritual* problem with a new administrative process. Sometimes the problem will boil down to a simple misunderstanding—a lack of communication between two sincere hearts.

Finally, prepare through fellowship and encouragement. Sometimes a moment of fellowship or a note of encouragement can pave the way for a rebuke or reprimand to be well-received. Is there something you can do before you intervene that will help your heart to be more readily received?

Go to the Christian one-on-one.

By far, most intervening moments in my ministry happen one-on-one and are resolved at that point. Don't take these things to the pulpit or to a public setting. Deal forthrightly with your co-laborer or Christian brother. If he will not hear you or respond correctly, then follow the Lord's instructions in Matthew 18 and go a second time with a witness if necessary.

THE RESULTS OF INTERVENING LEADERSHIP

Being an intervening leader is difficult, but worth it. If you develop the courage and ability to intervene in sensitive situations—to effectively resolve problems and bring about healing—your leadership will stand out as biblical and highly effective. People will respect you more and will respond on a deeper level to your leadership. Consider these wonderful outcomes of intervening leadership:

1. Other people respect the ministry.
2. A brother is gained.
3. A greater problem is avoided.
4. A worker or staff member grows.
5. A misunderstanding or a wound is healed.
6. Frustrated Christians regain their joy.
7. The ministry is more effective.
8. A right spirit between people glorifies God.

There is one real negative possibility, but in my experience it's not all that common. The person you are confronting may end up resenting you. Your efforts to help may fall on a hard heart that misunderstands your motives and misreads your intentions. However, confrontation between two godly people will always result in the settling of emotions, the resolution of a problem, and the strengthening of a relationship. This biblical approach to intervention pleases the Lord and invites His hand of blessing upon a ministry.

A few years ago, our principal informed me that we would need to expel three students from our Christian school. In order to nurture the families who were going through this trial, I asked a few of our pastoral staff members to take these families out to lunch for the purpose of encouragement. Personally, I chose to take a family I had never met. The Galdamez family, who attended our Spanish department, agreed to have lunch with us rather reluctantly. During lunch we shared with them our love and hope for their daughter. Toward the end of the lunch, Brother Galdamez began to soften in his spirit. In fact a few days later, he requested to have lunch with me once again.

This time he wanted to share with me his testimony of salvation in his home country of El Salvador. He also shared that his uncle had recently passed away and had left him a large school complex near the capitol city of San Salvador, El Salvador. With tears in his eyes, he told me that he would like this facility to be used to establish a church like Lancaster Baptist Church in his home country.

At first, I was rather dismissive of the concept and a little suspicious of its validity. But over the next several weeks Brother Galdamez showed me pictures and met with me again to share his burden for his home country. The Lord began speaking to my heart and a few months later, at Brother Galdamez's invitation, I boarded an airplane at Los Angeles International Airport on a Sunday night at midnight with five young men from West Coast Baptist College and a few pastor friends. We were headed to El Salvador to see how the Lord would lead. Over the next few days God began to open doors like I have never seen Him move in my entire ministry.

The chief of police of San Salvador had provided police escorts from place to place as we preached the Word and toured the facilities. Toward the end of our stay, I had the privilege of leading this same chief of police to Christ. In addition, I had the privilege of leading a businessman to the Lord in the northern most city of El Salvador—Metapan.

As we surveyed the property, it was obvious to me that God was opening a great door to plant a church and re-establish a Christian school. Now, a few years later, God has already placed two godly families in El Salvador, who are currently working to establish churches in this needy country.

The businessman—whom I led to Christ on that first trip—has provided the building for the church in the northern part of the country, and the chief of police is eager to help start the next church. Two more couples are presently preparing at West Coast Baptist College to go to El Salvador and to plant local churches.

Incidentally, the young lady who was expelled from our school came back to the school the next year, accepted Christ as her Saviour, and is now enrolled at West Coast Baptist College and serving faithfully in our Spanish ministry.

Several hundred souls have since been saved, two churches are being planted, a Christian school has been donated, and a young lady has been saved, all because of a choice to intervene. Making the right decision to discipline a young lady in her teenage years and then to nurture a family through the trial has made a profound difference in many lives. Intervening leadership is not always easy, but God blesses a ministry and a man who endeavors to do that which is right.

Remember, caring for people should precede confronting people. Conflict or contention is like a cancer—early detection increases the possibility of a healthy outcome. While intellectually it's simple to resolve conflict, emotionally it can be difficult. It requires honesty, humility, and dedication to the relationship.

Servant leaders truly feel that their role is to help other people to reach their potential. They are willing to take a risk. They want to make a difference in the lives of people, and they want to help others be successful. A huge part of this process is intervention—being willing to address what *isn't right*, and correct it in love.

Seek to be an intervening leader. Few practices will impact the strength and health of your church as much as your ability to go to the problems and resolve them biblically and with grace. Godly leaders are biblical problem-solvers. When we truly love people, we help them solve problems, even when it means risking our own popularity for a while. May God grant you courage and wisdom to intervene in the problem you've been ignoring recently. In so doing, you may save a family or a ministry, and one day someone will thank you for loving him enough to confront him in the Spirit of Christ!

6

PART SIX

THE SPIRITUAL LEADER'S TRIUMPHS

A leader longs for the day when he will fall before his Saviour having expended his life for Christ and for His people. He longs to hear, "well done," and he lives for the day when he will cast his crowns down at the feet of his Great Shepherd, Jesus Christ.

> *"Cast not away therefore your confidence, which hath great recompence of reward. For ye have need of patience, that, after ye have done the will of God, ye might receive the promise. For yet a little while, and he that shall come will come, and will not tarry."*—HEBREWS 10:35–37

CHAPTER THIRTY-TWO

THE SPIRITUAL LEADER'S FINISH LINE

Jesus came to this earth with passion to do His Father's will and to *finish* His work. He said in John 4:34, *"My meat is to do the will of him that sent me, and to finish his work."* As we come to the closing pages of this book, I pray that you have that same passion—to finish the work to which God has called you.

In recent years, we have been handed a torch of faithfulness by great men of God who have gone on to Heaven—men whom I knew personally or whom I heard preach as a young man. These men are now in Heaven, men like Dr. Lester Roloff, Dr. Tom Malone, Dr. Curtis Hutson, Dr. B. Myron Cedarholm, Dr. Lee Roberson, Dr. Bob Kelly, Dr. John R. Rice, and others. Not all of these men saw eye-to-eye on every issue, and no leader reading this book would agree with one-hundred percent of their ministry philosophies, yet these men finished their course. They started in the ministry as young men, and they were faithful to their families and their Lord until they went home to Heaven. They served with joy and integrity for a lifetime!

In 2 Timothy 4:1–8 Paul gives some of the most powerful closing words of his life: *"I charge thee therefore before God, and the Lord Jesus Christ, who shall judge the quick and the dead at his appearing and his kingdom; Preach the word; be instant in season, out of season; reprove, rebuke, exhort with all longsuffering and doctrine. For the time will come when they will not endure sound doctrine; but after their own lusts shall they heap to themselves teachers, having itching ears; And they shall turn away their ears from the truth, and shall be turned unto fables. But watch thou in all things, endure afflictions, do the work of an evangelist, make full proof of thy ministry. For I am now ready to be offered, and the time of my departure is at hand. I have fought a good fight, I have finished my course, I have kept the faith: Henceforth there is laid up for me a crown of righteousness, which the Lord, the righteous judge, shall give me at that day: and not to me only, but unto all them also that love his appearing."*

I remind you that there is a *finish line!* Your race has a final destination. In these pages we've studied spiritual leadership from many different vantage points. We've studied both philosophy and practice. We've talked about the mountaintops and the valleys, but I must remind you, all of it is about *finishing the course!*

> *To finish your course, you must never doubt the call of God.*

God tells us, *"Better is the end of a thing than the beginning thereof: and the patient in spirit is better than the proud in spirit"* (Ecclesiastes 7:8). It's one thing to start in ministry, but it's a better thing to end still in ministry—to cross the finish line into the presence of our Lord Jesus Christ having run a faithful race and having fought a good fight of faith.

One of the dearest friends I have in the ministry is Dr. Don Sisk. He has been a co-laborer, a friend, a mentor, and a godly counselor in my life. Dr. Sisk has faithfully served the Lord for more than fifty-two years, and he has done it with abundant joy. I've known some grumpy Christians, and I've seen spiritual leaders with calloused hearts as the years of ministry drew to a close. One reason I am drawn to Dr. Don Sisk is that his joy in life and ministry is contagious! Throughout his life, he has maintained a child-like wonder about serving Jesus Christ. He has never gotten over the delight of waking up and living for the Lord. His warm smile and delighted heart bless everyone with whom he comes in contact.

That attitude is what I want. I want to finish my course with joy! I don't want to limp across the line, barely clinging to a thread of faithfulness. I want to leap across it delighted to finish the work that God has given me to do. I want to cross the finish line smiling and rejoicing in the abundant goodness of God. As the song writer said, "It will be worth it all when we see Jesus!"

I'd like to close this book by briefly examining the heart of a leader who finishes his course with joy—a *finish-line leader* who loves serving Christ until his very last breath.

A FINISH-LINE LEADER HAS A SETTLED HEART

Second Peter 1:10 states, *"Wherefore the rather, brethren, give diligence to make your calling and election sure: for if ye do these things, ye shall never fall."* Strong spiritual leaders are settled on their call. They never second guess or have a "Plan B."

We live in a day of doubt, a day when no good decision is final. Any good course can be reconsidered. Reject this thinking! To finish your course, you must never doubt the call of God.

A FINISH-LINE LEADER HAS A YIELDED HEART

First Corinthians 9:27 states, *"But I keep under my body, and bring it into subjection: lest that by any means, when I have preached to others, I myself should be a castaway."* Paul saw himself as a yielded vessel. He presented himself as a living sacrifice. He was fully surrendered to the perfect will of God.

To finish your course, you must daily reckon yourself dead—dead to sin, to criticism, to praise, to self, and to your personal agenda. Yield yourself daily as a vessel unto the Lord.

A FINISH-LINE LEADER HAS A GRACE-FILLED HEART

First Peter 5:10 says, *"But the God of all grace, who hath called us unto his eternal glory by Christ Jesus, after that ye have suffered a while, make you perfect, stablish, strengthen, settle you."* We've seen "grace-based" ministry. Leaders who finish their course do so by the grace of God. It is grace that enables them, grace that motivates them, and grace that flows through them to others.

The God of all grace—the God with unsearchable eternal resources—places all of those resources at your disposal. He will sustain you, empower you, and transform you by His grace! And He desires your ministry to be abundantly based in grace.

A FINISH-LINE LEADER HAS A FOCUSED HEART

Philippians 3:13–14 says, *"Brethren, I count not myself to have apprehended: but this one thing I do, forgetting those things which are behind, and reaching forth unto those things which are before, I press toward the mark for the prize of the high calling of God in Christ Jesus."*

With laser-like focus, the Apostle Paul kept his eyes on the Lord and on the future. He pressed forward to the finish line. Lifetime leaders focus their hearts on Christ and never look back.

A FINISH-LINE LEADER HAS A FORGIVING HEART

In Philippians 3:13, Paul said that he was *"forgetting those things which are behind...."* He was good at forgiving others, forgiving himself, and accepting God's forgiveness. As you press forward in ministry, you will make mistakes. You will fail. Finish-line leaders get back up and keep running. I'm reminded of the famous proverb, "If at first you don't succeed, you are running about average!"

Charles Schultz shared the secret to his comic success in this quote, "The success of my cartoon comes from the fact that Charlie Brown was always so unsuccessful!" Finish-line leaders see mistakes as the building blocks of success. They deal appropriately with their own failures and the failures of others—they forgive and move forward.

A FINISH-LINE LEADER HAS A TRUSTING HEART

Psalm 84:12 teaches us, *"O Lord of hosts, blessed is the man that trusteth in thee."* Whether by trials or by realizing big vision, spiritual leaders must lead from a platform of faith. Only faith pleases God and only faith will move Him to work in your church. He is trustworthy; He will never let you down.

First Corinthians 10:13 says, *"There hath no temptation taken you but such as is common to man: but God is faithful, who will not suffer you to be tempted above that ye are able; but will with the temptation also make a way to escape, that ye may be able to bear it."* I recently read a story of a father and a son who were shopping together. As they were leaving the store, the boy was carrying several large packages. A lady passing by stopped and commented, "Oh my, that's a lot for a boy your size to carry!"

With calm assurance the boy looked up and said, "Oh don't worry, my dad knows just how much I can carry!" Finish-line leaders understand that their Heavenly Father knows just how much they can carry!

A FINISH-LINE LEADER HAS A HUMBLE HEART

First Samuel 15:17 says, *"And Samuel said, When thou wast little in thine own sight, wast thou not made the head of the tribes of Israel, and the Lord anointed thee king over Israel?"* Saul's biggest mistake was pride. At one time in his life he was "little" in his own sight. Those were the times when God showed Himself strong in Saul.

Finish-line leaders know "It's not about me! It's all about Him!"

A FINISH-LINE LEADER HAS A RENEWING HEART

Second Corinthians 4:16 says, *"For which cause we faint not; but though our outward man perish, yet the inward man is renewed day by day."*

Weariness, fatigue, and depletion are a regular part of the journey for a spiritual leader.

Many people are not overly familiar with acute thirst because they rarely exert themselves. Olympic runners, on the other hand, are close friends with intense thirst—it is a frequent, recurring sensation. In the same way, exhaustion or depletion is a recurring condition for finish-line leaders. They know it well. They exert themselves often, and they become familiar with the sensation of being exhausted and depleted in every way. They run hard and long, and they push to their limits.

Finish-line leaders respond well to weariness. They replenish. They quench their thirst for God, for grace, for His Word, for rest, and for restoration. They work passionately and rest just as passionately. They serve with all their might and restore with all their hearts.

Never make a major decision when you are weary! When you are weary, you don't think right; you need rest and replenishment. Become good at renewing your heart. Like a long distance runner, between here and your finish line, you will need to renew frequently.

Press forward my friend. In God's grace, keep serving until you cross the finish line to rest in His arms and hear "well done!" *"His lord said unto him, Well done, good and faithful servant; thou hast been faithful over a few things, I will make thee ruler over many things: enter thou into the joy of thy lord"* (Matthew 25:23).

> *"Wherefore seeing we also are compassed about with so great a cloud of witnesses, let us lay aside every weight, and the sin which doth so easily beset us, and let us run with patience the race that is set before us, Looking unto Jesus the author and finisher of our faith; who for the joy that was set before him endured the cross, despising the shame, and is set down at the right hand of the throne of God. For consider him that endured such contradiction of sinners against himself, lest ye be wearied and faint in your minds."*—HEBREWS 12:1–3

CHAPTER THIRTY-THREE

CONCLUSION

D r. Tom Malone said, "When God is going to do something wonderful, He starts with the difficult. When God is going to do something miraculous, He starts with the impossible."

The journey toward becoming a spiritual leader often seems impossible. It is a long, and sometimes embarrassingly slow process of growth! Yet, I can thankfully testify that there is no greater joy than looking back over the years and realizing God, by His grace, has used you for His honor and glory.

For the spiritual leader who will begin each day at the foot of the Cross, reckoning himself dead unto sin and alive unto Jesus Christ, there will be continued victory. Even as the psalmist said in Psalm 139:23: "*Search me, O God, and know my heart: try me, and know my thoughts,*" so the wise spiritual leader opens his heart each day and asks the Lord to purge him of his fleshly desires and personal agenda. Truly the desire of a spiritual leader is that the life of Christ would be evident through him.

Galatians 2:20 sums it up best: "*I am crucified with Christ: nevertheless I live; yet not I, but Christ liveth in me: and the life which I now live in the flesh I live by the faith of the Son of God, who loved me, and gave himself for me."* Our Lord Jesus Christ was the greatest spiritual leader to ever walk on this planet. As the King of kings and Lord of lords, He established the bench mark for every one of us to follow. Each of us, like the Apostle Paul, must pray that the life of Christ would be seen in and through us.

There are many sources available that teach and explain concepts pertinent to Christian leadership. What we have tried to share in the pages of this book, however, has been concepts and principles that are strictly Bible-based—principles that will honor and glorify the Lord Jesus Christ.

A few days ago, I had the privilege of preaching at a leadership training event in Sacramento, California. Prior to the meeting, I had the joy of gathering with about forty graduates of West Coast Baptist College for a meal and time of fellowship. As the graduates rose to their feet and introduced themselves, they told where they were serving as pastors, assistant pastors, and workers in local churches in the northern part of California. My heart was truly blessed to see these young people and realize that they have a strong passion to reach souls for our Saviour and to lead others in the ways of Christ.

As I listened to their questions before and after the meeting, something dawned on me: I realized that the questions they were asking were very similar to the questions I had at that point in ministry. Some had questions about balancing family time and ministry time. Others had questions about dealing with antagonists within the church, and others were asking how to get new converts involved in the discipleship program of the local church. As I challenged and encouraged them in these areas, my mind raced back to the verse God gave me when I began serving as the pastor and spiritual leader of Lancaster Baptist Church. This verse—2 Timothy 2:2—formed the basis of our ministry philosophy and has guided for many years.

> *"Thou therefore, my son, be strong in the grace that is in Christ Jesus. And the things that thou hast heard of me among many witnesses, the same commit thou to faithful men, who shall be able to teach others also."*—2 TIMOTHY 2:1–2

There you have it! A spiritual leader is a man or woman who is growing in the grace and knowledge of our Lord Jesus Christ. As they grow, they are able to commit biblical truth to other faithful men who then will teach others also.

Spiritual leadership, then, is not about climbing the corporate ladder of ambition. Spiritual leadership has very little to do with what position we obtain in life or with what recognition is given us during our sojourn in this world.

The effective spiritual leader will be known by his or her fruit. Were there others who were taught and are now faithful? Were there others who were able to follow our example? It should truly be our desire, as spiritual leaders, that all who come behind us will find us faithful.

> *What Christians need desperately today is not more entrepreneurial leaders in the church, but more spiritual leaders.*

Wherever you are on your spiritual leadership journey, let me encourage you to finish strong for the Lord Jesus. The greatest gift we can give to the next generation is our example of faithfulness and godliness. The devil screams at young ministers and young servant leaders about the failures and short-comings of their mentors and of the so-called "successful and famous" spiritual leaders who have now gone by the way of compromise, moral failure, or discouragement. The teenagers in our churches, the widows, the young couples, and everyone in between, need us. They need our faithfulness and the teaching from the Word of God that comes forth from the pulpit and from our lives.

As we look around at Christianity today, we see an abundance of entrepreneurial leadership. We see men who are able to provide ministry on multiple campuses with high-tech tools and stunningly prepared graphic materials. But if powerful organizational structure and high-tech prowess is all we need to know, we can learn that from the Microsofts, the IBMs, and the other giant corporations of the world. What Christians need desperately today is not more entrepreneurial leaders in the church, but more spiritual leaders. They need to see men and women who love God, who love their families, and who faithfully apply biblical principles to their lives.

May God bless you with His anointing and may you continue forward as an anointed leader, appointed by God to do the work He has called you to do. May you never doubt in the night what God has given you in His light, and may you be the spiritual leader He has called you to be in this generation!

Allen, David. *Getting Things Done*. New York: Viking, 2001

Barna, George. *A Fish Out of Water*. Brentwood, TN: Integrity Publishers, 2002

Bennet, Bill. *Thirty Minutes to Raise the Dead*. Cambridge, Ontario: Thomas Nelson Publishers, 1991

Blackaby, Henry. *Spiritual Leadership*. Nashville, TN: Broadman & Holman Publishers, 2001

Blanchard, Ken. *The Heart of a Leader*. Colorado Springs, CO: Honor Books, 1999

Bossidy, Larry. *Execution*. New York: Crown Business, 2002

Bridges, Jerry. *The Discipline of Grace*. Colorado Springs, CO: NavPress, 1994

Burke, H. Dale. *Less Is More Leadership*. Eugene, OR: Harvest House Publishers, 2004

Collins, Jim. *Good to Great*. New York: HarperCollins Publishers, 2001

Covey, Stephen R. *First Things First*. New York: Free Press, 1994

Criswell, W.A. *Criswell's Guidebook for Pastors*. Nashville, TN: Broadman Press, 1980

Drucker, Peter F. *The Effective Executive*. New York: HarperCollins Publishers, 2006

Goetsch, John. *Homiletics from the Heart*. Lancaster, CA: Striving Together Publications, 2003

Jeffress, Robert. *Grace Gone Wild*. Colorado Springs, CO: WaterBrook Press, 2005

Johnson, Spencer. *The Present*. New York: Doubleday, 2003

Kent, Homer. *The Pastoral Epistles*. Chicago: Moody Press, 1986

Leadership Journal: "God, Money, and the Pastor". October 1, 2002

Lincoln, Abraham. *Life and Works of Abraham Lincoln*. New York: The Current Literature Publishing Co., 1907

London, H.B., Jr. *Pastors at Greater Risk*. Ventura, CA: Regal Books, 2003

Maxwell, John C. *Developing the Leaders Around You*. Nashville, TN: Thomas Nelson Publishers, 1995

Maxwell, John C. *The Seventeen Indisputable Laws of Teamwork*. Nashville, TN: Thomas Nelson Publishers, 2001

McCullough, John. *John Adams*. New York: Simon & Schuster, 2001

Meyer, F.B. *John the Baptist*. Fort Washington, PA: Christian Literature Crusade, 2002

Rogers, Adrian. *Kingdom Authority*. Nashville, TN: Broadman & Holman Publishers, 2002

Sanders, J. Oswald. *Spiritual Leadership*. Chicago: Moody Press, 1994

Spurgeon, Charles. *Lectures to My Students*. Grand Rapids, MI: Baker Book House, 1981

Wiersbe, Warren W. *The Integrity Crisis*. Nashville, TN: Oliver Nelson Books, 1988

SCRIPTURE INDEX

Visit us online

strivingtogether.com

dailyintheword.org

wcbc.edu

lancasterbaptist.org

paulchappell.com

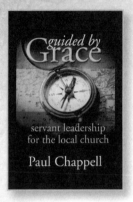

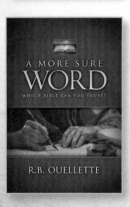